LEADERSHIP SKILLS FOR MANAGING TECHNICAL PROFESSIONALS

LEADERSHIP SKILLS FOR MANAGING TECHNICAL PROFESSIONALS

A Self-Study Program

IRV GAMAL, M.A.

Copyright © 2019 by Irv Gamal, M.A.

Library of Congress Control Number: 2019913472
ISBN: Hardcover 978-1-7960-5750-8
Softcover 978-1-7960-5749-2
eBook 978-1-7960-5748-5

All rights reserved. No part of this book may be reproduced or transmitted in any form or by any means, electronic or mechanical, including photocopying, recording, or by any information storage and retrieval system, without permission in writing from the copyright owner.

The views expressed in this work are solely those of the author and do not necessarily reflect the views of the publisher, and the publisher hereby disclaims any responsibility for them.

Any people depicted in stock imagery provided by Getty Images are models, and such images are being used for illustrative purposes only.
Certain stock imagery © Getty Images.

Print information available on the last page.

Rev. date: 12/03/2019

To order additional copies of this book, contact:
Xlibris
1-888-795-4274
www.Xlibris.com
Orders@Xlibris.com
798919

To my wife, Karen: my confidante, my partner, my ultimate editor, my source of strength, and most of all my best friend who has always stood by my side.

A NEW PERSPECTIVE

Frankly, the old models of managing and leading people are quickly fading away. The speed of business in the new millennium requires an accelerated level of execution unthinkable only five years ago. Technical organizations, in particular, depend on creativity and intellectual horsepower to meet this challenge. People are their primary asset. If they lose them, or can't attract them to begin with, they squander their competitive edge. This course teaches managers of technical professionals how to deliver results—that matter—through others. It demonstrates the vast differences between management and leadership and concurrently assists the recipient in implementing behavioral changes that makes them more effective on the job.

As you study each of the following lessons in this program, you will learn leadership skills vital to attracting, retaining, and inspiring these topnotch technical professionals. Such a restless group of self-reliant people play by a different set of rules than those with which you may be familiar. This particular self-study program will aid you in avoiding misunderstandings and conflicts by teaching you what the newest generation of technical professionals wants and needs. To solve that complex riddle, you will discover how to effectively meld their requirements with your organizational goals. In essence, this approach will broaden you in becoming more of a leader and less of a manager.

PREREQUISITES TO CONSIDER

You should be, or should aspire to be, in a position of leadership overseeing technical professionals (that is, engineers, scientists, doctors, programmers, lab technicians, lawyers, aircraft mechanics, financial analysts, architects, or anyone whose position requires a strong technical expertise). If you are not currently in that type of position, ideally you will need to anticipate a leadership role within ninety days of completing this course for optimum results. Intrinsically, we have a tendency to lose what we don't use, so consider your own situation before you embark on our extensive leadership journey.

SYLLABUS AND TABLE OF CONTENTS

Note: Following each lesson, you will find an assignment dedicated to the topic of that lesson, a multiple-choice quiz, accompanied by the answers, and frequently asked questions (FAQs) regarding the subject matter discussed. It is to your advantage to complete all assignments, quizzes, and read the FAQs to assist in your self-study and learning. Additionally, it is recommended that you immediately take the Pre-Test in the Appendix beginning on page 269. Afterwards, check your answers and come up with a percentage score reflecting your correct answers.

Once you finish the course, take the Post-Test on page 305, score it, and compare the results to your Pre-test to determine your new level of knowledge. If necessary, go back and re-study any areas where your scores may not be up to par. Enjoy the course.

Lesson	**Topic**	**Page**
Lesson One	Generation X: Who They Are and What they Want	1
Lesson Two	World Class vs. Traditional Organizations	22
Lesson Three	Management and Leadership: Seeing the Difference	42
Lesson Four	A New View of Leadership	66
Lesson Five	Keeping Your Eye on the Ball	90
Lesson Six	The Meaning of Meaning	111
Lesson Seven	Taking Stock of You	132
Lesson Eight	What The Young Technical Professional Wants From Their Boss	154
Lesson Nine	Becoming a Better Communicator	173

Lesson Ten	Learning to Let Go and Develop Others	197
Lesson Eleven	Leading Organizational Change	219
Lesson Twelve	Building a High-Performance Environment	241

APPENDIX

	Basis	**Page**
Pre-Test	Testing Your Current Knowledge of the Topic	269
Test Answers	Determine How Well You Did	281
Post-Test	Testing Your New Level of Knowledge of the Topic	305
Test Answers	Determine How Well You Did	317
Links	Further Study and Research on the Internet	319
Readings	Gen X and Classic Leadership For Further Research and Study	331
Index	Reference Specific Course Content	335

YOUR AUTHOR

Irv Gamal, M.A., is President & CEO of Insight Systems™ Group, a Southern California consulting firm specializing in leadership and organizational development. Irv brings forty-six years' of experience as a business owner, corporate manager, consultant, university instructor, executive leadership coach, and facilitator to this course for your benefit. His knowledge of proven techniques, his practical approach to leadership principles, and his flair for writing, have created an invaluable and agreeable learning experience.

As a management consultant and executive coach, Irv has worked with such companies and organizations as Activision Blizzard, Alcoa, Apple, The American Red Cross, AT&T, Beckman Coulter, City of Newport Beach, Department of Defense, DirecTV, Fluor Constructors International, General Motors, Hennessey's Taverns, Hughes Electronics, Johnson & Johnson, Little River Casino Resort, Mazda Motors of America, Microsoft, Monster Cable, Motorola, Oakley, Pacific Financial Companies, Pasadena Police Department, Phelps Dodge Mining Company (Freeport McMoRan), Raytheon Systems, Seagate Technology, Sol Casinos, Taco Bell (Yum Brands), T-Mobile, UCLA, Verizon Communications, Wells Fargo, Western Digital, Whirlpool, and Yamaha Corporation of America to name a few.

Irv has been an Adjunct Leadership Coach with the Center For Creative Leadership (CCL) in La Jolla, California since 1993. CCL was rated by BusinessWeek Magazine as *one of the top leadership research and development think-tanks worldwide.* Further, Irv was an instructor for seven years at P.O.S.T.'s Command College, where future police chiefs and other public safety leaders throughout California learn timeless and contemporary leadership principles.

As you study the subject matter of this course, you'll particularly enjoy the numerous personal anecdotes, case studies, and illuminating examples Irv weaves into the rich content that literally brings this timely topic to life. You will not only find this approach especially meaningful, but highly applicable to your circumstances. The course is a fully integrated, well orchestrated program, complete with quizzes, frequently asked questions (FAQs), suggested activities, Internet links, recommended readings, and a pre and post-test.

PREFACE

In the latter part of the Fall of 2001, following the savage terrorist attacks of 9-11, I was approached by an online education organization. They were interested in having me develop a comprehensive leadership course for ultimate dissemination worldwide. I agreed to consider their offer, but felt that such a course could best be designed with a focus on a more specific audience. Given the pronounced consternation existing then and the palpable challenges facing Western Civilization, I firmly believed we needed to up our game in the entire technology arena.

No one doubted that we produced world-class technology in the United States. We certainly did. Nonetheless, we didn't necessarily have world-class leaders managing front-line people who brilliantly created that breathtaking technology. Sadly, we often succeeded in spite of ourselves.

Over the span of many years, I've coached technical managers in a wide variety of companies and government agencies. Although most of them possessed stellar credentials and were wizards handling technology, they often went begging when it came to dealing with people. Interpersonal skills as a broad set of competencies was frequently missing in action or stillborn. Obviously, these managers were smart people who were not originally drawn to professions requiring these abilities. In fact, many of them were clearly not hard wired to excel at these soft skills we called, Emotional Intelligence. As a result, they repeatedly lost talented people to competitors, and those who stayed behind coped the best they could. The repercussions varied, of course, but project deadlines were habitually missed, creativity suffered, costs increased, and products were recalled, etc.

So, after mulling over these unwelcome factors, I suggested writing a self-study, thoughtfully integrated, online leadership program that would face these issues head-on. One nagging problem we could quickly solve with this strategy was that many of these technical managers had little exposure to leadership training—especially training they could take at their own convenience. Fittingly, our course would be titled, "Leadership Skills For Managing Technical Professionals." My proposal had instant appeal to this online distribution group and so the project was given the green light and launched.

In the early part of 2002, "Leadership Skills For Managing Technical Professionals" was officially kicked off and was eventually offered at 730 colleges and universities throughout the world. The course would continue into 2008—a total of six years—after which I finally decided to pull the plug. During that time, hundreds of technical managers completed the program, and the feedback we received from them was very gratifying. In essence, we achieved our original aim of helping them to become better leaders.

Since that time, the program has sat in my archives collecting dust and has not seen the light of day. From time to time, though, I've had colleagues and friends familiar with the content tell me I should publish the course for future generations of technical managers. I initially balked at this idea since, to be blunt, as many of the people noted, the generation that was focused on and some specific situations are plainly out of date. Yet, simultaneously, the concepts, tools, principles, processes, models, theories, advice, etc., are ordinarily timeless.

In that spirit I have accordingly changed my mind and decided to publish the course with most segments intact, except for those which are no longer relevant and have been expunged. I see this endeavor as a two-step process: (1) The first pass will be to have a record of the original course published with slight modification (as noted). (2) The second phase will be to update all items that are not timely and publish a second edition of the course downstream. This latter effort will be much lengthier and require signifiant effort on my part. However, I am fully committed to seeing this through.

Irv Gamal
Laguna Niguel, California
September 2019

INTRODUCTION

The working environment has probably changed more within the last ten years than in the previous thirty. There are four overarching changes that have had a paramount affect on how business is conducted today. To begin with, we have become a global economy with competitive pressures leveraging dramatic transitions in first, second, and third world countries alike. For example, consider the tremendous industrial growth in China and how they have become one of America's largest trading partners. The literal flood of goods from China have exerted downward pressure on prices of similar products and intensified the need to simultaneously improve domestic productivity and lower internal costs.

Secondly, we have become far more dependent on technology and those who understand it, in all areas of the economy. High tech pervades almost everything that is designed, manufactured, inventoried, shipped, etc. It has a strong presence in the administration and delivery of most services as well; this is true whether we're talking about banking, auto repair, health care, retail, and so forth.

Not only do we require people who are infinitely comfortable with technology, but we need them 24/7/365. This drives the third major trend: like Las Vegas, our economy never sleeps. The work frequently must go on without stopping. In some cases, it's analogous to a relay race, where the work is handed off from one person to another. As a case in point, some software companies employ software developers in India because they can pay lower salaries for some of the best talent in the world. Developers in the U.S. may labor the entire day on a project and then email their work to a counterpart in India at the end of the day. And so it goes. Thus, the pace of business has quickened as a result of this. Companies must move swiftly when it comes to making decisions, executing strategies, launching products, etc. If they delay, they could likely lose a significant competitive advantage and pay dearly for it.

The fourth change is the influx of Generation X (those people born between 1965 to 1984) into the labor pool. This restless group of independent people are apt to question authority and play by different rules. Their paradigm of the working environment is far different from the baby boomers who comprise the bulk of management. These differences invariably lead to misunderstandings and conflict.

Furthermore, Gen Xers demand greater freedom on the job and more say-so in shaping their career. Traditional methods of leading them yields poor to mediocre results and considerable frustration on all sides. Understanding their needs and how to effectively lead them has become an issue that many organizations now face. It simply isn't going to go away. Some managers wonder whether a softening economy will have an affect on Gen Xers. No doubt it could increase the available body of attractive talent. However, the values of this generation, like any other, are firmly imprinted within them. Only minor behavioral modification could realistically be expected. Additionally, the demand for their services could fluctuate, but long-term it will continue to increase.

Collectively, these four changes conspire to create a need for a special kind of leadership. Coupled with interpersonal skills, leaders who understand generational differences, who realize the global nature of the economy, who commit to the pace of business, and who embrace technological innovation can be the winners in the years ahead. So too—without a doubt—will be their organizations.

LESSON 1

GENERATION X: WHO THEY ARE AND WHAT THEY WANT

CHAPTER 1 — INTRODUCTION

> *"In case you're worried about what's going to become of the younger generation, it's going to grow up and start worrying about the younger generation."*
>
> —Roger Allen

Welcome to my course on Leadership Skills for Managing Technical Professionals. I'm Irv Gamal, and I'm delighted that you could join us for an exciting voyage of discovery as you learn more about leadership and sharpen these vital skills. Throughout the length of my career as a corporate manager, consultant, college instructor, and leadership coach, this topic has never been more relevant to your success. Why is this so?

Actually, it's because of numerous factors which can act as barriers keeping you from doing your absolute best. Among these factors are traditional career paths, generational differences, the global economy, confusion over management, leadership, and the pace of organizational change, etc. Each of these things can muddy the water and, collectively, make the leader's job seem overwhelming. Yet, it needn't be so. For example, let's briefly examine one of the first issues regarding the traditional managerial career path.

The majority of managers of technical professionals rise through the ranks into positions of leadership. They invariably have wonderful technical know-how. However, they concurrently possess limited expertise or comfort in managing and leading a group of very bright people. Maybe you feel the same way about your immediate situation. If you do, you're in the right place, so relax. You see, the major objective of our course is to build your understanding, comfort, and ability to lead technical professionals, no matter what their field or endeavor.

In this course we'll be exploring the most critical issues facing technical leaders today. You can easily view the topics of each lesson in the syllabus to gain a sense of our overall direction. As you progress with each lesson, you'll build upon your previous knowledge and probably notice greater confidence in your skills as a leader. So let's get moving. Our starting point in lesson one will be with generational differences and more specifically, Generation X.

Most members of the newest generation of technically savvy employees were born between 1965 and 1984—the core group between 1965-1975. This is America's thirteenth generation, usually referred to as Generation X, or Gen Xers—a more commonly held nickname. Perhaps you are a member of this generation as well. If you are, you'll likely identify rather quickly with some of the characteristics we'll discuss in subsequent chapters. If you're not, the topic should be invaluable in furthering your understanding of the crucial differences within this group of people.

LESSON OBJECTIVES

As we begin our exploration of how to best lead technical professionals, our primary focus in this lesson is to explain what underlies the bulk of Gen Xer needs. Secondly, we'll see how these needs can effectively be met by organizational leaders like yourself. Remember though, when recounting information about any generation, the facts pertain to approximately 80% of the group. The remaining 20% do not necessarily reflect the same features; in fact, they could be dramatically different. This is just human nature, and these percentages play out similarly whatever generation you might be talking about.

The Baby Boomer generation, born between 1946-1964, was 76.7 million strong. No matter what their age, they had a profound impact on the country's economy because of their sheer size. The irony of Gen X is that their strength lies in their scarcity. They are a generation of 44.5 million people and, until recently, simply not numerous enough to fill all the available jobs in the U.S.

Furthermore, Gen Xers are motivated in ways that vary from traditional Baby Boomer expectations. They tend to look upon organizations from a different perspective, frustrating older managers whom they say, "Just don't get it!"

CHAPTER 2 — WHO ARE THE GEN XERS AND WHAT MAKES THEM TICK?

The majority of this generation grew up in two-income families, where both mom and dad worked. This contrasts markedly with 75% of the traditional families of the 1950's characterized by stay-at-home mothers. Educated parents of Gen Xers worked hard so they could afford the luxuries of life. On the other hand, parents with limited education or training both worked so the family could survive. Plus, as many as forty percent of the Gen Xers were the children of divorce.

The consequence of all these factors was scores of latchkey kids who became very self reliant in taking charge of their day-to-day lives. Often they attended day care and then came home to an empty house. Since they infrequently had close supervision, they don't like it as grown-ups. Approximately 12 percent of elementary and 30 percent of middle school children rarely saw their parents during the day. This is three times higher than it was for the Baby Boomers.

MEDIA-SHAPED VALUES

Because Gen Xers had limited adult supervision growing up, their values were often shaped by influences other than their parents. For the first time in our history, the media may have contributed more to a generation's basic values than their immediate family. Gen Xers spent considerable time watching MTV, CNN, playing video games, and, within the last several years, using the Internet. More than any previous generation, this group was affected to a greater depth by the mass media and high technology.

For example, many Gen Xers were exposed to high technology at a very early age. This was especially true of Gen Xers from affluent homes who may have had access to a personal computer when they were as young as five or six. By the time they were teenagers, they may have mastered the intricacies of numerous software programs, including actually writing program code. Very likely they were also at home on the Internet, familiar with popular video games, and perhaps they had their own cell phone or pager. In other words, as I pointed out in Chapter 1, they became very savvy with all kinds of technology.

Other environmental forces exerted significant leverage on this generation as well. During the late 1980's and early 1990's, many companies were laying off literally tens of thousands of employees. Blue chip organizations like AT&T, IBM, and Hewlett-Packard, that had always celebrated life-long employment, were enticing people to leave with fancy severance packages. Most often companies simply handed out pink slips with cold detachment, pushing people into the ranks of the unemployed.

THE CONSEQUENCES OF HYPOCRISY

Gen Xers observed these practices while simultaneously hearing companies eulogize loyalty to their employees. Compounding this, they read a myriad of mission statements that promoted teamwork, yet realized internal competitiveness and political maneuvering were consistently rewarded. They heard their workaholic parents talk about the importance of quality time, but seldom interacted with them. All of this hypocrisy was firmly rejected by Gen Xers. This is at the root of much of their jadedness about organizations in general.

Essentially, they don't trust organizations to have their best interests at heart. Their loyalty is to themselves and their lifestyle, not to some huge Fortune 500 company. When Baby Boomer managers chastise them because they've lost their loyalty to the company, Gen Xers wryly grin because the loyalty was never there in the first place. The old social contract between companies and their employees faded away with widespread layoffs more than a decade ago. Any remaining loyalty is viewed as quaint, and just as outdated as bell-bottoms and love beads from an earlier time and place. Does this sound familiar to you?

CHAPTER 3 — HOW GEN XER VALUES TRANSLATE INTO REAL-TIME NEEDS

Understanding any generation is never easy and there will eternally be generational differences. Sometimes, however, the differences are magnified and this has likely been the case for Generation X. From the mid to late 1990's, the labor force was squeezed to the point where anyone who wanted a job was working. Unemployment in some regions was less than 2%, and the number of people entering the work force was the lowest it's been since 1940. Our overheated economy produced enormous competitive pressures to recruit the best and the brightest of this generation.

This competitive environment for people created severe labor shortages that sometimes brought out the best and the worst (as opposed to the best and the brightest) in Generation X. It became commonplace for companies to offer signing bonuses—occasionally $25,000 or more. This is the premium a nephew of mine received when he began his career with a leading Silicon Valley Company at age 22. Frequently added to these bonuses were tempting stock options, lucrative employee benefits, and other desirable perks that made Gen Xers look greedy and mercenary.

Some critics of this generation have asked if a slowing economy and just the normal process of aging will change the behaviors of Gen Xers. I'm certain that these things can affect them as they might with anyone. Exactly how this would evolve into actions individually or collectively is hard to say. So for now, let's focus on the present situation and maybe extrapolate a bit from there.

GEN X TIME HORIZONS

Typically, Gen Xer time frames tend to be one to three years. When they start a new job, they don't commit to be there until they retire, as did the Greatest Generation (those who lived through the great depression and who won World War II). This term for the parents of the Baby Boomers was coined by Tom Brokaw in his best selling book by the same name. The limited time horizon for Gen Xers may eventually expand as job opportunities diminish in a contracting economy.

Nonetheless, Gen Xers have little interest in climbing the corporate hierarchy. They view this ladder of promotions as a long-term commitment and that goes against their grain. Moreover, as an employee moves into the ranks of management, they might initially earn less money and concurrently have to work longer hours. Gen Xers value their time above all else. Their quality of life is a big issue for them, and they refuse to sacrifice their family, lifestyle, or personal principles for any job.

What they do prefer are a variety of lateral stretch assignments that are short-term, challenging, and which help grow their skill sets. They like projects that have a beginning and an end, hence a sense of closure and accomplishment. They are very concerned about job satisfaction and will hop from one organization to another with little hesitation if their needs are not being met.

As I noted above, time off (with or without pay) is right at the top of their list of priorities. They covet this time to savor their interests, spend time with their family, or do nothing at all. They refer to this as hanging, while Baby Boomers used to call it hanging out. Gen Xers have little patience for dreary organizational cultures that grant limited time off. They'd rather go elsewhere to work.

SOUGHT AFTER PERKS

Having witnessed their parents' surrender of family life, the resulting divorces and other related problems, they are overly sensitive to the costs of blind ambition. This is why they are attracted to companies that have liberal vacation policies, flexible schedules and telecommuting opportunities. Gen Xers are not nine-to-five people, nor do they wish to wait five years for a three week vacation.

Security to a Gen Xer means being highly marketable. Having skill sets that employers emphasize enables the Gen Xer to command a higher salary and to quickly obtain an appealing position. Because they don't intend on staying in an organization for longer than possibly three years, fast track entry into training and development becomes very important.

Gen Xers don't buy into promises, but rather look for actions that demonstrate intentions. Their attitude is similar to the revealing line from the movie, Jerry McGuire: "Show me the money!" They may not stick around for a year waiting for assurances to come to fruition. It appears that the more competent they believe they are, the more secure they become. Why do they feel this way? To answer that, we need to revisit some of their history so you can more clearly see the cause and effect relationships.

Some researchers suspect Gen Xers are one of the most insecure generations to come along in many years. This almost seems like an immense contradiction in impressions considering their recurring displays of bravado. However, when you weigh their experiences in this light, it begins to make some sense. For example, forty percent of them were the children of divorce. Even if they didn't grow up in a broken home, many of their friends did. So they were surrounded by peers who likely were from single-parent households or had step parents. As a consequence, they view marriage as a somewhat risky proposition.

In addition, you probably recall that they observed many organizations laying off vast numbers of employees. So, obviously, you couldn't trust that relationship either. Institutions, like marriage and corporate life, that were viewed by older generations as built on a foundation of solid bedrock, were looked upon with wariness by Gen Xers. Is it any wonder, then, that they may have feelings of insecurity and look towards themselves for their ultimate peace of mind?

This is why Gen Xers are not attracted to company 401K plans, or traditional pension plans. Aside from not intending to be there long enough to vest in most plans, they dislike the fact that these retirement programs are not within their immediate control. They prefer self-directed IRA's that are portable. That way, when they leave, they can take their savings plan with them to their new location. The same logic applies equally well to their health insurance. They wish for insurance plans that are readily transferable.

LESS SOCIAL SKILL

Gen Xers spent more time interacting with technology in their youth than they did interacting with each other. As a result, their interpersonal skills are not as highly developed as the Baby Boomers. Gen Xers are more informal, less team oriented, and don't particularly like structured social functions. Because they're less gregarious, they commonly go home to their families after work instead of going out socializing with coworkers. On the other hand, they are more likely to attend a spontaneous pizza blast that commemorates the end of a successful project than to come to the company's annual Christmas Party.

They expect diversity to be equitably reflected in the work environment because chances are they grew up with it at school. This is a diverse generation with Caucasians actually in the minority. Most Gen Xers are Hispanic, Asian, and African-American. Their outspoken support for diversity often leads them to compare the racial complexion of the organization with the community in which it resides. If they detect any substantial gaps in the ethnic make-up of the organization, you can expect to hear about it.

Gen Xers want to know what's expected of them. They want clear goals and defined expectations. They will assertively, and sometimes aggressively, probe not only what outcomes are anticipated, but what the performance standards are. They are hungry for feedback and appreciate coaching and mentoring from the boss and others in higher level management. They dislike leaving this to chance. Although they don't subscribe to lots of structure, this is one area where they relish it.

Invariably, the delicate matter of compensation ultimately arises. I previously pointed out the signing bonuses, stock options, and trendy perks that Gen Xers enjoyed during the ego inflating 1990's. Many of them received oversized paychecks very early in their careers and this caused resentment among older workers who thought they hadn't paid their dues.

Gen Xers tend to be knowledgeable about industry-specific compensation levels and practices. Marketplace earnings information and related comparisons data are easily available on the Internet. The average Gen Xer wants to be paid based on his or her performance and with marketplace rates tied in as a reference point. They'll use this information as leverage for negotiating raises, bonuses, and other desired rewards.

Human Resource professionals find it increasingly difficult to keep sensitive salary information confidential anymore. This obviously exacerbates the whole situation governing rewards and compensation. Notwithstanding, the whole question of equity and fairness will probably become a little easier to manage as jobs become harder to find in a recessionary economy that's been unfolding since at least March of 2001.

CHAPTER 4 — HOW SHOULD LEADERS RESPOND TO GEN XER NEEDS?

Organizational leaders will need to be more creative in their approach to managing this unique group of people. New system-wide policies will be required allowing more flexibility in scheduling, telecommuting, and time off. There is actually a grass roots effort that has emerged nationally, drumming up interest in paid sabbaticals for corporate employees. Although this has long been a tradition in academia, it never favorably crossed over into the private sector.

Nonetheless, it readily plays to one of the most basic needs of Gen Xers. Time off is viewed as a key factor for strengthening a marriage, a family, and improving one's overall quality of life. Sabbaticals give an individual time off to do appreciable personal reflection and see the big picture. No one will argue that it's a time for renewal and revitalization. Yet, it can be very expensive for an organization to fund and, frankly, this might not be the best time to promote it. The jury's still out on this one, but you can expect to hear much more about it in the future.

In lieu of sabbaticals, more liberal vacation policies can offer parallel benefits. Gen Xers are not afraid of hard work and frequently put in hefty amounts of hours. But unlike their workaholic Baby Boomer parents, they know when to put on the brakes. When they do so, they'll demand time off to take care of their personal and family needs.

REDEFINING SUCCESS

Leaders will have to respond to this, allowing them their time off. This gesture can prevent unnecessary and expensive turnover, and keep people from burning out on the job. Another step that will be necessary is to redefine what success means in an organization or individual's career. Career development shouldn't only be measured vertically, but can likewise be assessed on a horizontal or lateral scale.

Dual career paths will appropriately become the norm in most organizations. In other words, if someone wants to stay a software developer, an engineer, or a scientist, they will have that option. They needn't move into management to prove to themselves and others that they have achieved success. It may realistically be entirely inappropriate. As a case in point, how often have you observed an outstanding engineer, or scientist, or technician, etc., morphing into a very mediocre manager.

Lateral assignments, challenging projects, and ad-hoc troubleshooting can all meet the needs of Gen Xers for variety, personal growth, and stimulation. Some organizations have previously created Corporate Fellow positions for those who have achieved a position of recognized mastery. This is somewhat akin to the emeritus designation in the academic setting. No matter how the career path is eventually designed, compensation will need to be commensurate with a technical professional's mastery of their assignments. We must never lose sight of the issue of fairness or equity.

FORMALIZED, FAST-TRACK DEVELOPMENT

As Gen Xers increase their know-how, they'll require formalized development activities to accelerate their growth. Fast-track entry into training programs within the first six months of their tenure is very important. As they continue to learn and improve, the training should become tougher and more sophisticated. Higher levels of proficiency should always be recognized by certificated training programs that are both challenging and relevant.

Complementing this indispensable training, all leaders must sharpen their one-on-one coaching skills. Gen Xers want to be nose-to-nose and toes-to-toes with key decision makers. This obviously includes their boss. Their immediate supervisor should spend an ample amount of time furnishing feedback about their performance, being emotionally supportive, and assisting the individual to improve their overall competence.

One last thought for you: Gen Xers like to be kept in the loop and not in the dark. They want access to important information, but not necessarily data dumps. Information should readily be available to them in a distilled form, so the most salient points are communicated. Gen Xers do like brevity, but some of them may want supplemental data with more depth. Leaders who provide a meaningful format that can meet these separate needs will have more satisfied, informed employees.

CHAPTER 5 — CONCLUSION

As you can see, Gen Xers present organizational leaders with challenges that can readily be misunderstood. Generational differences have existed throughout history and will likely continue. However, organizational leaders who don't understand this generation will create considerable frustration for themselves and their technical employees.

The Baby Boomers were America's largest generation, whereas, the Gen Xers are one of the smallest in modern times. Gen Xer's number 44.5 million people born between 1965-1984. Their scarcity in a booming U.S. economy led to intense competition for their services. Lucrative salaries, signing bonuses, and numerous perks were offered as the norm during the 1990's.

Because of the particular needs of Gen Xers, leaders will need to be responsive in ways that are likely unfamiliar to them. In fact, several of these needs might cause Baby Boomer managers some discomfort. Gen Xers want more time off, fast-track entry into training programs, lateral assignments, coaching and mentoring, portable IRA's and health insurance, and access to information. In the final analysis, the more these needs are met, the better organizations will be at attracting and retaining Gen Xer technical professionals.

LEADERSHIP SKILLS FOR MANAGING TECHNICAL PROFESSIONALS

LESSON ONE ASSIGNMENT

Interview three people, one from the Greatest Generation (grew up during the depression and reached maturity before the end of World War II), one from the Baby Boomer's Generation (born between 1946-1964), and one from Generation X (born between 1965-1984). Try to single out three individuals you believe are good examples of people who grew up in these three different eras. Don't seek people who may fall outside that representative 80% we talked about early in the lesson.

Ask them the following questions and pay close attention to their answers. Look for clues in their answers that tell you about their underlying values. Also, you may have to peel the onion back to get to these deeper layers. In other words, someone might say in answer to question one, that the most important criteria was working for a big company. You might need to probe why. Ultimately, you may discover that security was their key issue, and for them it meant working for a big company which was less likely to go out of business.

1. What was the most important criteria for you in taking a job when you were in your thirties (or twenties for a Gen Xer)?
2. How did you generally measure your level of career success?
3. How important was company loyalty, that is, your loyalty to the organization and vice versa? Why?
4. What usually was or is your top challenge at work?

Solutions: Listen for subtle and not so subtle differences in their answers. For example, members of the Greatest Generation will probably look for security and fair pay in a job. Tenure and position will likely also rank high with them, where company loyalty was a very important characteristic. Top challenges for the Greatest Generation might be satisfying the boss—like a good soldier.

Baby Boomers will likely be sensitive to interesting work and promotional possibilities and measure career success by how high they climbed the organizational ladder. Loyalty was originally somewhat important, but it diminished over the years. Getting the job done no matter what was likely one of their greatest challenges.

Gen Xers will look for organizations that will allow them challenging projects and flexible policies. Company loyalty will rank low. Success will very likely be measured by their competence and marketability. Top challenges may center on life-balance issues, taking care of themselves, having enough time off.

LESSON ONE MULTIPLE-CHOICE QUIZ
(Answers on the Following Pages)

1. When recounting facts about any generation, the information generally pertains to approximately what percentage of the group?

    A. The entire generation.
    B. About 80% of the people.
    C. One standard deviation from the mean, or 68% of the people.
    D. About 20% of the people.

2. Gen Xers tend to be very skeptical about trusting organizations to have their best interests in mind. Why?

    A. They watched a lot of TV portraying organizations as big and impersonal.
    B. They distrust anyone over thirty.
    C. Most of them had stay-at-home moms who encouraged them to avoid big organizations.
    D. They witnessed the hypocrisy of mass layoffs, lukewarm teamwork, and poor quality of life for their parents.

3. Gen Xers are very self-reliant and customarily dislike close supervision. Why?

    A. They had very little close supervision growing up and seldom had to answer to authority.
    B. Their values closely reflect the Greatest Generation's.
    C. Most of them are well educated and can think for themselves.
    D. Because heated competition for their services made them in short supply.

4. Security to a Gen Xer is primarily being highly marketable. Why?

   A. So they can command higher salaries and quickly find a position.
   B. They don't save enough money and live paycheck to paycheck.
   C. They don't take good care of themselves, so they're insecure with their physical well being.
   D. They're more interactive with one another than previous generations. Consequently, they're better at networking.

5. Gen Xers ardently support diversity. And most of the members of this generation are from minorities.

   A. Most of the members of this generation are actually Caucasian.
   B. The vast majority are Hispanic, African American, and Asian.
   C. Most Gen Xers are currently liberal undergraduates who would likely encourage Affirmative Action policies.
   D. Most of the members of this generation are foreign nationals attending schools of higher learning on student visas.

LESSON ONE MULTIPLE-CHOICE QUIZ
(Answers)

1. When recounting facts about any generation, the information generally pertains to approximately what percentage of the group?

   A. The entire generation.
      Incorrect.
      There will always be exceptions to the information.

   B. About 80% of the people.
      Correct.
      About 20% of the make-up of a generation will be the exception to the rule.

   C. One standard deviation from the mean, or 68% of the people.
      Incorrect.
      One standard deviation will usually strongly exhibit the characteristics. Others will also, but not quite as strongly.

   D. About 20% of the people.
      Incorrect.
      This indicates that 80% of the generation will be the exception. This is too high a number.

2. Gen Xers tend to be very skeptical about trusting organizations to have their best interests in mind. Why?

   A. They watched a lot of TV portraying organizations as big and impersonal.
      Incorrect.
      Although they did watch quite a bit of TV growing up and this helped imprint some of their values, it didn't create their overall attitude toward organizations.

B. They distrust anyone over thirty.
Incorrect.
This is more of a throwback to the 1960's and the Baby Boomers.

C. Most of them had stay-at-home moms who encouraged them to avoid big organizations.
Incorrect.
Most of their moms worked and many of them were in day care.

D. They witnessed the hypocrisy of mass layoffs, lukewarm teamwork, and poor quality of life for their parents.
Correct.
Many of them became jaded at what they saw as gross violations of words and actions within organizations.

3. Gen Xers are very self-reliant and customarily dislike close supervision. Why?

A. They had very little close supervision growing up and seldom had to answer to authority.
Correct.
Forty percent were the children of divorce and many grew up in single parent households. Those who lived in an intact family still were in child care because both parents worked.

B. Their values closely reflect the Greatest Generation's.
Incorrect.
Their values are very much unlike this generation.

C. Most of them are well educated and can think for themselves.
Incorrect.
Certainly more of this generation are college educated than before. However, but this is not the reason for their self-sufficiency.

D. Because heated competition for their services made them in short supply.
Incorrect.
Although there weren't enough of them available in the 1990's to fill all of the technical positions, this is not why they are self-reliant.

4. Security to a Gen Xer is primarily being highly marketable. Why?

A. So they can command higher salaries and quickly find a position.
Correct.
They intend to stay for 2-3 years in an organization and will quickly leave if their needs are not being met. Also, they consider the possibility of layoffs.

B. They don't save enough money and live paycheck to paycheck.
Incorrect.
Although their savings rate is poor compared to other generations, this is not the primary reason for their mind set.

C. They don't take good care of themselves, so they're insecure with their physical well being.
Incorrect.
Older Baby Boomers seem to have more physical activity, but this is not the reason for Gen Xers to feel the issue about security.

D. They're more interactive with one another than previous generations. Consequently, they're better at networking.
Incorrect.
This group has less favorable interpersonal skills than older generations. They're better interacting with technology.

5. Gen Xers ardently support diversity. And most of the members of this generation are from minorities.

   A. Most of the members of this generation are actually Caucasian.
      Incorrect.
      Caucasians represent a minority position in this generation.

   B. The vast majority are Hispanic, African American, and Asian.
      Correct.
      Many of the Gen Xers grew up in a diverse environment, so this is natural for them.

   C. Most Gen Xers are currently liberal under-graduates who would likely encourage Affirmative Action policies.
      Incorrect.
      Unquestionably, as we pointed out, many of this generation are college educated. The bulk of this generation have completed their earlier college studies. If they are working on an advanced degree, it's usually while they are working full time.

   D. Most of the members of this generation are foreign nationals attending schools of higher learning on student visas.
      Incorrect.
      Indeed many students attending colleges and universities in the U.S. are using student visas. But this is not the correct answer.

LESSON ONE FREQUENTLY ASKED QUESTIONS

Q: Will members of this generation (Gen Xers) become more conservative and less outspoken as the economy slows and as they age?

A: The normal process of aging has a tendency to make any generation more conservative in their lifestyle and in their decisions. As people get older, they usually become less willing to take certain risks. They begin to develop a broader perspective that changes some of their views.

Additionally, as the world economy contracts, companies will find profitability harder to come by. Shrinking margins will lead to larger layoffs and the ranks of the unemployed will swell. People will be less likely to jump ship or complain to management if things are not totally suited to their needs.

Q: Won't some members of Generation X want to climb the organizational hierarchy?

A: Of course, just not in the same numbers that we're used to seeing. It was typical among Baby Boomers to measure success by moving up through the ranks of management. It's not so with this generation as a general rule.

LESSON 2

WORLD CLASS VS. TRADITIONAL ORGANIZATIONS

CHAPTER 1 — INTRODUCTION

> *"People consider it axiomatic that a company exists to return profit to its shareholders, that even a not-for-profit exists to return benefit to its shareholders, and must have a healthy margin in order to survive. But all of the visionary companies we studied - all of them major profit-makers - are about something else, something beyond profit."*
>
> —*Jim Collins, Noted Author*

In our first lesson we closely examined the newest generation, Generation X, that's making its mark within organizations today. We discussed what makes members of this generation tick, how their values translate into real-time needs, and how leaders need to respond to them. Now, however, it's time to segue to a much broader view and focus at the organizational level. In particular, I'd like to talk about what has come to be called "world-class organizations."

When you hear the term, world-class organization, what immediately comes to your mind? Perhaps you think about companies that do it better than anyone else. In other words, they seem to set the standards by which other companies gauge themselves. They are the companies (or organizations) that other companies benchmark in order to improve certain elements of their own make-up. This could reflect their desire to improve their quality, leadership, human resource practices, customer service, manufacturing processes, marketing, etc.

If you were thinking along these lines, you're right on target. Let me ask then, what are some of the companies that you would place on your best practices list? Some examples of companies that often make the "A list" (a world class status list) because of something special they do are Disney, FedEx, GE, Hewlett-Packard, Coca-Cola, Southwest Airlines, Intel, Charles Schwab, Pfizer, MBNA, WalMart, Toyota, Apple, etc. Most of these monikers are so well known they are household names. But maybe not all, like MBNA, the Delaware-based credit card specialists.

OUR OBJECTIVE IN THIS LESSON

All of the companies above do things that are envied by others in their industries. Frequently, they are the pacesetters, the fiercest competitors, and the leaders that others want to emulate. What is it that they do to achieve this recognition or status? Generally, it appears that the answer to that question is fairly simple. They offer better quality, like Toyota, or attention to detail, like Disney, or reliability, like FedEx. These attributes have become legendary! Often, though, the truth lies much deeper than it seems and requires a more concentrated analysis.

That being the case, our objective for this lesson is to reveal what world-class organizations are, what some of them actually do to achieve their earned reputations, the benefits they obtain from it, and how they adeptly communicate to meet the challenges presented by America's newest generation, the Gen Xers.

CHAPTER 2 — WHAT LIES AT THE HEART OF BEING WORLD CLASS?

When considering what it takes to be world class at anything, you might look at what it takes to make the Olympics. It takes passion, drive, perfectionism, focus, tenacity, vision, pain, and sacrifice. This is quite an impressive list of traits, wouldn't you say? Becoming a star athlete <u>overnight</u> just doesn't happen in the real world, does it?

Achieving and maintaining world class status <u>is</u> relentless and is nicely captured in Lexus's positioning statement, "The Relentless Pursuit of Perfection." It's a never ending proposition and there are no guarantees. You can never let down your guard, never rest on your laurels, and never allow yourself to coast. If you do, you'll lose your edge and you'll no longer be a world class performer. Also, you can't automatically assume that you'll always make the team even if you keep at it. Sometimes you have a bad year no matter what you do. Periodically things are beyond your control. There's an ebb and a flow to everything in life.

The bulk of these analogies apply equally well to world-class organizations. The "tech wreck" of 2000, the recession of 2001, and the tragedy of September 11 have had their combined ill affects on the global economy. As a result, many world-class organizations struggled through 2001 with decreased revenues, lower profits, declining market share, and a depressed stock price. In total, this doesn't necessarily mean that they still aren't world-class organizations. It depends on what they have or haven't done to get where they are, and what they will truly do about it.

For example, Sears used to be a world class, retailing powerhouse. Like McDonald's, Sears stores were located everywhere. It actually was where America shopped, but that coveted market position was won by WalMart some time ago. WalMart is the world's leading retailer with 2001 annual revenues exceeding $193 billion versus Sears far distant $40.9 billion. Sears has had serious merchandising problems for many years that they haven't suitably addressed.

As a result, they continue to lose market share, as their reputation is scuttled. Sears gave up their leading position primarily because they didn't do the right things.

SO WHAT DOES WORLD CLASS REALLY MEAN?

Now, many people might not consider a discount retailer as a viable candidate for a world class title. World class designations aren't only reserved for organizations which possess a trendy technology or operate in an industry with lots of sizzle. WalMart achieves world class status because of many significant factors at which they excel. As an example, they designed state-of-the-art inventory control and vendor/supplier ordering systems. They maintain consistent, low pricing strategies. They've initiated innovative community-oriented programs, and they create strong bonds of loyalty with their employees and customers. The bottom line here is that world class status does not depend on business or industry classification. It can exist just about anywhere where you have organizations doing the right things right. Sometimes, however, you get companies doing the right things in the wrong manner.

Certainly one of the biggest business news events of 2001 was Enron's debacle, declaring bankruptcy on December 2. To my knowledge, this was the second largest bankruptcy filing in U.S. history. Enron, with over $55 billion in assets, was the sixteenth largest company in the world. For many years, Enron was considered the darling of Wall Street, and from most vantage points, a world class performer. Yet its stock plummeted from $80 to 80¢ a share in only 12 months. So many people lost so much, congress is investigating what went wrong. What generally did go awry?

This question is worth spending some of our time to explore. We usually associate world-class organizations with talented people, advanced technology, creative strategies, applied innovation, consistently high quality, effective internal systems, well regarded products and services, etc. Furthermore, world-class organizations must unceasingly demonstrate utmost integrity, act in concert with their values, promote an openness in their culture, and give people something to believe in and care about.

Enron shined when it came to talent, creativity and innovation. They evolved from an energy company to an on-line commodities trading company with annual revenues approaching $100 billion.

Enron designed e-business systems that enabled them to grow their on-line trading exponentially. Their skill was so compelling that only a short time ago everyone wanted Enron stock in their portfolio.

THE CRITICAL INTANGIBLES

What most people overlooked, including supposedly savvy Wall Street analysts, SEC officials, and large investment managers, was Enron's lack of integrity and openness. Enron was heavily involved with unsavory investment partnerships, complicated financial arrangements, and other dubious business deals hidden from full public disclosure. Many of these will likely be found to be laden with conflicts of interest, exorbitant risk, and possibly outright illegal acts committed by senior management. A good portion of their business arrangements were barely mentioned as footnotes in their financial reports.

Integrity, values, openness, something to believe in and care about. These intangible features must be coupled with some of the other tangible characteristics that define world class. Without that critical linkage, you wind up with *the chaos of an Enron.* So world class is a seamless merging of tangible and intangible properties—or characteristics—in a variety of industries that sets an organization apart from the pack.

We must always be aware of the whole picture when evaluating an organization and not be swayed by their mastery of a handful of factors. Keep in mind that the tangibles are always easier to observe. When we are aware of both the tangibles and intangibles in an organization, we won't likely fall prey to a case of the Emperor's New Clothes. This was exactly what happened with Enron.

CHAPTER 3 — HOW WORLD-CLASS ORGANIZATIONS PERPETUATE THEIR CULTURE

Years ago, when I was in college I worked part time at Disneyland and had a chance to meet Walt Disney on several occasions. The second time I met Walt, as he liked to be called, it was 3:30 a.m. during my lunch break at a graduation all-night party. This was three months after our first meeting which lasted about three minutes. Walt spent plentiful time at Disneyland and truly loved his creation.

I was standing in line in the Employee's Cafeteria, when Walt approached and recognized me by name. He asked about my college activities and how I was enjoying my work at Disneyland. We talked for several minutes and then he departed, greeting others also waiting for their meal. As he exited, I looked down for my name tag and then realized that I had left it back on the ride. I was astounded. There were over 8,500 employees at Disneyland. How could he have possibly remembered my name?

AN IMPORTANT LESSON

To this day, I have never forgotten that incident and the important lesson it taught me. When Walt died in December of 1966, there wasn't a dry eye in the park. Walt genuinely made everyone feel important and gave them something to care about. Each employee in the organization, from sweepers to managers, made every effort to make the Disney experience a truly memorable one. They rarely failed to do so.

Disney's current Chairman and CEO, Michael Eisner, still gets involved in the details. This is in spite of the fact that the Disney organization is significantly larger than back in Walt's days. Sometimes Eisner gets criticized for his insistence on focusing on the "small stuff." Eisner believes that attention to detail is a hallmark of Disney's culture. No doubt the organization has strong strategic anchors, but it always goes the extra mile to insure that in their theme parks, movies, or other entertainment venues nothing gets overlooked.

Disney invests heavily in training all of their people in the values, traditions, and practices of their culture. For example, in their theme parks they have a whole vocabulary which explains relationships with each other, their guests, and their work. Employees are called "cast members," customers are "guests," uniforms are "costumes," doing your job is "being on stage," etc. The company has always had a policy of promoting from within. I personally know people who began their career there as college students, and are still there today in middle and senior management positions around the world.

The company even has an Alumni Club offering discounts, package tours, a newsletter, and reunions. It's consummate fun and perpetuates a culture that's literally handed down from one generation to another. To summarize from Disney's example, we can say that companies with strong cultures make people feel important, give them something to care about, pay attention to detail, invest heavily in training, have a common language, promote from within, and even reach out to those who have left.

Consider for a moment if your company had an alumni association, would you join and participate? If the answer is "no," that tells you something important, doesn't it? On the other hand, if the answer is "yes," celebrate your good fortune!

APPLE AND INNOVATION PLUS

We've talked about a number of companies from a variety of industries. Let's now address a high tech company that has achieved world class status although they have endured very difficult times along the way: Apple Computer. The January 14, 2002 issue of Time Magazine features Steve Jobs on the cover with the new, revolutionary iMac. While Apple only controls about 4.5% of the U.S. personal computer market, they've always had a profound influence on the overall industry. In fact, Apple seemingly started the personal computer industry back in 1976 when they created the Apple I.

Unfortunately, Apple has played a remote secondary role with their Macintosh® operating system in contrast to the monumental size of the Windows® platform market. While Microsoft has dominated in their marketing and strategic business acumen, Apple has historically shown formidable strength in their innovation. Apple's recent release of the iPod, a pioneering music player which can hold over 1,000 songs, is another illustration of this.

Steve Jobs has become an icon inseparable from Apple. His attention to detail parallels Eisner's. Perhaps even more so. He's been accused of being pathological with his urge to send apparently completed projects back to be completely redone. Yet, the loyalty and commitment he commands from Apple staff are admirable. He's always been a terrific cheerleader.

Moreover, Job's ability to communicate his abstract visions enable his technical wizards to mold their magic. Much of Apple's success is the aftermath of their people's belief in what they're building. They see their work as important and ground breaking. It's comparable to the old story of the three masons who are asked what they are doing. The first answers, "I'm laying bricks." The seconds replies, "I am putting up a wall." The third says, "I am building a cathedral." Obviously the last mason will be the best at his craft. Apple people are building cathedrals and the company emphatically instills that unfaltering belief.

Even Jobs's penchant for control doesn't derail the empowering of Apple engineers and designers to stretch the limits of their imagination. Hence, Apple has become synonymous with creativity. The company's strategic advantages are at the very least fourfold: (1) their ability to push the envelope on design, (2) their innovative technology, (3) a willingness to take risks, and (4) resiliency in bouncing back from difficulties.

With the vast majority of computer manufacturers circling the wagons in 2001, Apple is moving ahead with the opening of retail stores and entry into consumer electronics. These bold tactics are typical of this unique company—an organization repeatedly underestimated by their competitors. Obviously, the jury is still out on how effective these actions will eventually be. Nonetheless, you must give them credit for their courage and distinctiveness.

IRV GAMAL, M.A.

CHAPTER 4 — HOW WORLD-CLASS ORGANIZATIONS ADEPTLY COMMUNICATE

Each January, Fortune Magazine publishes a special issue that features the 100 best companies to work for. It always makes for interesting reading, especially the segment that chronicles what the companies do that differentiates them. For instance, in the January 2002 issue, MBNA was listed as the 26th best employer in the U.S. One of their unique characteristics is that when an employee gets married, they get an extra week of vacation. Beyond that, they have six full-service child care centers available. They even offer college scholarships of up to $32,000 for their employees' children.

Obviously, MBNA has strong family-centered values. College tuition has risen far faster than the Consumer Price Index, so scholarships can be a very attractive benefit to concerned, cash-strapped parents. As seductive as the perks and benefits are in Fortune's detailed article, they frequently mask a much deeper commitment that these companies have for their people.

As an illustration of this, when Malden Mills factory in Lawrence, Massachusetts burned to the ground a few years ago, CEO Aaron Feuerstein kept every employee on the payroll. It took at least a month before the company was partially operating in temporarily quarters. That was not only an incredibly sincere gesture by top management, but also a very expensive one. Most organizations wouldn't even ponder it. Regardless, the loyalty that kind of act fosters cannot be bought for any sum of money.

SIX KEYS OF COMMUNICATIONS

As you probably have noticed, there is considerable variance in the practices, cultures, perks, products or services, etc., of world class companies or organizations. Yet, there are numerous commonalities as well, like commitment. We've discussed many examples throughout this lesson. One we haven't talked about in quite enough depth is the importance and prevalence of an underlying infrastructure of communication. All of these organizations have a resolute connection with their people constantly reinforced through communication. They never take this bond for granted.

Look closely and you'll soon discover two-way, open lines of communication woven throughout the systems of these companies. The type of communication vehicles and the media utilized are as varied as the organizations themselves. One thing we can ordinarily be assured of is that each organization uses multiple approaches. Still, most follow six important keys for successfully reaching out to their people and especially the Gen Xers.

1) Listen. Most of the top organizations realize that what they don't know could hurt them, so they listen. They do annual employee opinion surveys, attitude surveys, focus groups, etc. Alaska Airlines CEO John Kelly flies randomly selected employees in from around the world for small group sessions twice a month. Many companies, like Microsoft, rely heavily on email to gauge what their people are thinking. They even have a newspaper, Microsoft News, which modifies its content based on reader comments.

2) Show people you're listening. The *best of the bunch* provide feedback on what they learn. One organization I consulted with many years ago, issued a monthly newsletter called "Feedback," explaining how they were addressing what they learned from surveys. Kinkos established a comprehensive communications system with all of their 850+ branches. This included: two-way telephone news lines, broadcast faxes to get news out within two hours, and a newsletter publishing answers to FAQs—frequently asked questions.

3) Never underestimate the power of face-to-face communication. As a matter of course, organizational leaders make themselves accessible and visible. In early 2002, President Bush was conducting interactive town hall meetings across the country. Gen Xers want to be nose-to-nose and toes-to-toes with key organizational leaders. The *personal touch* plays directly to that need.

4) Let them hear it from you. This means that people want to hear about their company from their company and not the Wall Street Journal. AT&T Wireless in Seattle would send a seven minute

monthly corporate update to all employees in their voice mail. Alaska Airlines used a two-way telephone news line to keep thousands of employees up to date on critical company issues. The messages would be updated twice weekly, or more often depending on changing events. Their employees came to rely heavily on these updates and their prompt participation in accessing the news line was impressive.

5) Encourage interaction. People need a venue for sharing information, asking questions, getting answers, and feeling that they can trust their organization. These mandates can be handled in a variety of ways and often are. Ed Vick, outgoing CEO of Young & Rubicam Advertising, greeted employees in the lobby of their Manhattan building on the Monday following the September 11 attack. The response from his employees was overwhelming.

6) Make your managers accountable for communications quality. GE's ex-CEO Jack Welch was both feared and revered as a leader, especially when he was facilitating one of his "workout sessions." These sessions became famous within GE—or infamous, depending on your role in them. It was Welch's way of establishing accountability, eliminating bad habits, and getting to the bottom of acute organizational issues.

An action workout was a method of compressing a protracted re-engineering process into a short span of time—often no more than a week. GE would gather together key managers and team members to tear apart a working process and make radical recommendations for change. The discussions could frequently become very intense, but commonly led to dramatic breakthroughs within GE divisions. Other organizations began to take notice of GE's success and adopted similar practices.

Communications can run the gamut all the way from spontaneous, interactive town hall meetings to fancy, edited video productions. Sometimes world-class organizations have nontraditional methods for staying connected to all of their people. Others prefer more traditional venues like newsletters, special bulletins, or slick company magazines. Whatever their choice or combination of choices, they pursue communications with a religious fervor that crystallizes meaningful bonds with their employees.

CHAPTER 5 — CONCLUSION

Becoming a world-class organization is a coveted achievement that only a few are able to master. They are the ones that set the standard for others to follow. It takes enormous passion, drive, and tenacity to make this special group. Like any other organization, they will have to deal with the normal up swings and the down swings of market cycles.

When the market is strong and profits are healthy, life is easier. When storm clouds start gathering and the waves of change are not favorable, world-class organizations learn to effectively tack. Those that don't, wind up with significant problems like Sears, Xerox, Gateway, or worst yet, Sunbeam, Polaroid, or Chiquita Brands. The latter three all eventually filed for bankruptcy protection from their creditors.

World class means doing the right things right. It doesn't matter what business these organizations are in. It's all about how they conduct their business. Thus WalMart is world class and a trendy high tech outfit might not be.

World-class organizations do a superb job of managing both tangible and intangible factors. Tangible elements include things like talented people, advanced technology, creative strategies, products and services, etc. The intangibles are more difficult to spot, but include integrity, values, openness, and something to believe in and care about.

Although the best organizations are different in many ways, there are underlying similarities. Aside from a marriage of tangible and intangible factors, they possess a complex infrastructure of dynamic communications. World-class organizations reach out for their people, and in turn, allow them appropriate channels for feedback. They don't take anything for granted. The perceived genuine concern yields levels of commitment, achievement, and quality that are the envy of most others.

LESSON TWO ASSIGNMENT

Visit any of the web sites listed for outstanding organizations in this lesson and read about a company that you favor doing business with. This must be an organization that you believe is truly excellent at what they do. You could choose any type of organization where you purchase a particular service or product(s).

Try to uncover information about the company that helps explain why they do their job so well. Organize your findings within several main categories:

1. Organizational Culture
2. People Development
3. Business Strategy
4. Service/Product Quality
5. Organizational Practices/Policies
6. Communication

As you'll soon discover, there will be some overlap between categories, but don't worry too much about that. Try as best as you can to fit your information within the assigned categories.

After you've had a chance to arrange the results of your research, answer the questions below:

1. How does your information compare with what we discussed in the lesson?
2. Would you consider this organization to be world class? Why or why not?
3. What does this organization do differently from their competitors that sets it apart?
4. What is the central reason that you prefer this organization to others?
5. If this is a public company, would you invest in them? Why or why not?

LEADERSHIP SKILLS FOR MANAGING TECHNICAL PROFESSIONALS

LESSON TWO MULTIPLE-CHOICE QUIZ
(Answers on the Following Pages)

1. What do we mean by a world-class organization?

   A. A company that has global operations.
   B. A company that generally makes the news.
   C. An organization that sets the standard for others to follow.
   D. A high tech, trendy organization.

2. Enron failed because they didn't manage their intangibles. What do we mean by that?

   A. They weren't paying enough attention to their on-line trading business.
   B. They lacked integrity, openness, and honesty in disclosing their business dealings.
   C. They out sourced their intangibles to other companies.
   D. Enron's intangibles didn't need to be managed. They were self perpetuating.

3. Why is it important for companies to give their employees something to believe in and care about?

   A. Because it makes people feel they are doing something important and that makes them feel important.
   B. People are isolated today and need a cause.
   C. People believe most organizations are self serving and this won't work.
   D. Because the pressures of work are more intense and stressful than ever.

4. What do we mean by saying Steve Jobs is an icon inseparable from Apple?

   A. Jobs' picture appears on the Macintosh desktop.
   B. When you think of one (i.e., Jobs) you cannot help but think of the other (i.e., Apple).
   C. He has a golden parachute arrangement in his contract.
   D. Jobs over controls everything done at Apple.

5. Effective communication underlies everything world class companies do. Why is this so?

   A. We are a media-oriented society and expect it.
   B. It lets people know they are valued by the organization.
   C. Many marketing executives gain control over this internal process and they are strong communicators.
   D. They recognize the value of newsletters.

LEADERSHIP SKILLS FOR MANAGING TECHNICAL PROFESSIONALS

LESSON TWO MULTIPLE-CHOICE QUIZ
(Answers)

1. What do we mean by a world-class organization?

   A. A company that has global operations.
   Incorrect.
   Although a world-class organization may operate worldwide, that's not the criteria for being world class.

   B. A company that generally makes the news.
   Incorrect.
   Sorry, you may read or hear about them in the news, but that's not on the mark.

   C. An organization that sets the standard for others to follow.
   Correct.
   The standard may be in one or a variety of areas, like: customer service, quality, on-time delivery, etc.

   D. A high tech, trendy organization.
   Incorrect.
   World-class organizations may be found in any industry, and might be very low tech.

2. Enron failed because they didn't manage their intangibles. What do we mean by that?

   A. They weren't paying enough attention to their on-line trading business.
   Incorrect.
   Enron did an excellent job in expanding their trading business.

B. They lacked integrity, openness, and honesty in disclosing their business dealings.
Correct.
Enron did a great job managing their tangibles. They had talented people, applied technology, effective internal systems, etc. They failed with the intangibles.

C. They out sourced their intangibles to other companies.
Incorrect.
You cannot out source intangibles.

D. Enron's intangibles didn't need to be managed. They were self perpetuating.
Incorrect.
Intangibles are either managed or mismanaged. In Enron's case, they performed poorly in this area.

3. Why is it important for companies to give their employees something to believe in and care about?

A. Because it makes people feel they are doing something important and that makes them feel important.
Correct.
When people believe they are performing important work that translates into commitment.

B. People are isolated today and need a cause.
Incorrect.
Although the sense of community is less than it used to be, this is not the best reason.

C. People believe most organizations are self serving and this won't work.
Incorrect.

Many companies may be viewed that way. People do want to believe their company is different and want to support their choice to work there.

    D. Because the pressures of work are more intense and stressful than ever.
Incorrect.
Although this is likely the case, that's not the best answer.

4. What do we mean by saying Steve Jobs is an icon inseparable from Apple?

    A. Jobs' picture appears on the Macintosh desktop.
Incorrect.
There are his detractors who probably think he'd want that. Sorry, this isn't the right answer.

    B. When you think of one (i.e., Jobs) you cannot help but think of the other (i.e., Apple).
Correct.
Steve Jobs founded Apple in 1976 and returned to rescue it in the 1990's. Apple is part of his identity and vice versa.

    C. He has a golden parachute arrangement in his contract.
Incorrect.
Very likely is true, but not the right answer.

    D. Jobs over controls everything done at Apple.
Incorrect.
Oops, although Jobs is known for his high control, he still can empower members of his team.

5. Effective communication underlies everything world-class companies do. Why is this so?

    A. We are a media-oriented society and expect it.

Incorrect.

Certainly we rely on the media for a lot of our information today. However, that's not the right response.

B. It lets people know they are valued by the organization.
Correct.
People discover that the organization genuinely cares about them.

C. Many marketing executives gain control over this internal process and they are strong communicators.
Incorrect.
Gong. Not your best shot, try again!

D. They recognize the value of newsletters.
Incorrect.
Newsletters are but one approach of many. They may be integrated with numerous other communicative tools and strategies.

LESSON TWO FREQUENTLY ASKED QUESTIONS

Q: Do world-class companies ever fail?

A: Unfortunately, world-class companies sometimes grow old and stodgy, just like people. For example, Polaroid was a world-class performer with an incredible technology about fifty years ago. With the advent of digital photography, they saw their market position being eroded to the point of extinction.

Xerox, whose name became synonymous with photocopying, is in serious trouble. They were a world-class company, but not at the moment. That's why we say staying at the top of your game is relentless. If a company becomes lax, it's only a matter of time before a competitor overtakes them.

Q: Can other organizations that are not world class gain commitment from their people?

A: Sure, and there are many of them out there. It's always a matter of degree. Some organizations which never make the media "radar screen" do a great job in many areas. They may falter on some other pivotal factors and that might keep them from being an industry leader. Overall, they probably do just fine.

LESSON 3

MANAGEMENT AND LEADERSHIP: SEEING THE DIFFERENCE

CHAPTER 1 — INTRODUCTION

> *There is a great difference between knowing and understanding: you can know a lot about something and not really understand it.*
>
> —*Charles F. Kettering*

This is an intriguing quote. As we get started with this lesson, I want you to occasionally refer to what Charles Kettering has said. This is especially true regarding what this discussion is all about—"Management and Leadership: Seeing The Difference."

Leadership is a big issue today. Of course, it's always been a big issue, but sometimes we lose sight of its importance. During the Civil War, General Robert E. Lee took over command of the Confederate Army from General Gustavus Smith. Smith had command for about one day; unfortunately though, he "froze at the wheel." He didn't know what to do, so he did nothing. Confederate President Jefferson Davis had the foresight to know and understand he had the wrong man in the job and he acted quickly. The rest is history.

Robert E. Lee earned his place permanently in the nation's memory. Gustavus Smith is lost to the ages. You may ask, okay, that's great, but what's this have to do with me? I'm a supervisor or manager of technical professionals—the boss. I've got a job to do with all the accompanying deadlines and pressures. The truth of the matter is that it has everything to do with you. Bosses have subordinates, and leaders earn followers.

Do you know what the attributes of a subordinate are compared to that of a follower? A subordinate usually does what they are told. They perform according to their view of what you want done, moderated with what they are willing to do. On the other hand, a follower is someone who is adamantly devoted to living up to what they believe their leader wants from them. They are passionate about their performance. They have a spirit of ownership that prompts them to go the extra mile in delivering results.

OUR OBJECTIVE IN THIS LESSON

It's easy to see which is better. World-class organizations don't obtain their stature by having a legion of subordinates on board. Among other things, they chiefly foster leadership within their ranks which, in turn, begets many followers. So, we can say that achieving world-class status absolutely depends on effective leadership. They go hand in hand.

The objective of this lesson is to point out the imperative nature of leadership. We'll talk about the importance of management too. You can't run an organization without it. Nevertheless, management is not leadership, and some people use the terms interchangeably because they don't understand the extraordinary differences between the two. After this lesson, you'll know what the distinctions are. We will also explore the underlying nature of organizations and how effective leaders respond to it. Additionally, we'll begin to lay a foundation for future lessons by which you'll be able to judge your own leadership skills and decide what to do to strengthen them.

CHAPTER 2 — WHAT IS IT THAT MANAGERS DO?

As we said above, many people use the words "management" and "leadership" as if they were the same thing. There's little doubt that given the task, the vast majority of managers could explain what management is all about. However, when it comes to elaborating on what leadership is, these individuals might have some difficulty agreeing to what it is that leaders actually do, or what constitutes what we call "leadership."

The problem exists primarily because of where the emphasis has been for most of the last 100 years—squarely on management. There are courses in management, majors in management, management development, management workshops, management retreats, etc. On the other hand, the topic of leadership is relatively new, especially when it is expanded beyond the one context where we're most familiar. That is, viewing leadership at the top of the organization.

We inherently recognize that we need strong leaders charting our course at the top: those like Robert E. Lee or Jack Welch. But, unfortunately, we may not see the necessity for them beyond that. In the old organizational paradigm, this point of view was widely held and in most cases it acceptably worked. Yet, in the world of the 21st century, it is no longer functional and will hastily undermine an organization's attempts to respond to external forces in the global economy.

Even though you're probably more familiar with management principles than those of leadership, we'll begin by *placing management under the microscope.* This is to level the playing field and keep all of us together as we delve deeper into these diverse concepts.

THE FIVE FUNCTIONS OF MANAGEMENT

At its simplest level, management is about planning, organizing, controlling, directing, and staffing. Managers need to plan for the future, both long-term and short-term. They need to plan for contingencies as well. This is especially incontestable now more than ever. For instance, how would an organization operate during specific crisis situations? Or how can they back up and protect all of their precious data? Or how would they conduct business during a lengthy power failure? The list could go on and on. Indeed, whatever the salient concerns are, they deserve thoughtful, detailed planning.

Organizing has to do with marshaling the resources of an organization to bear on the challenges it faces. Resources fall into five categories, sometimes referred to as the Five M's. It's a real easy way to remember them. The first "M" concerns <u>manpower</u>, or people. I surmise this term is probably not politically correct, so forgive me. I'm more concerned about you remembering it than its correctness. Enough said. So, this "M" is about staff, employees, or people who are needed to get the job done.

The second "M" is about <u>money</u> or budget. How much do you have and what do you actually need? Financial resources are the lifeblood of an organization. Money allows us to purchase other resources or fund the hiring of additional staff to meet our management obligations. The third "M" stands for <u>machines</u>. This is about any type of equipment that might be mandatory. This can run the gamut from a single cell phone to a towering crane unloading steel shipping containers in the harbor.

The fourth "M" refers to <u>materials</u>, which could be anything other than machines and equipment. Materials may be books, surveys, reports, blueprints, depositions, journals, CD's, directories, etc. The fifth or final "M" implies <u>methods</u>, standard  operating procedures, or processes that the organization can utilize. Methods might be traditional, established practices or protocols, or they can be new, innovative techniques of dealing with a particular circumstance. In summary, the Five M's are the *fodder* of the organizing responsibility of management.

There are very few things ever initiated by a manager that do not insist upon some element of control. Without the controlling function, actions or events can suddenly overtake us and go amiss. Monitoring what's going on is an integral part of preventing this. Try to imagine driving a car blindfolded. You would likely think this is a completely ridiculous invitation. But it's frankly no more ridiculous than any manager who implements a program and then moves on to another priority without vigilance of any kind to the former.

Monitoring something presupposes that you may have to change it. In other words, you could discover that what you assumed would happen never did. Well, what do you do now? Without knowledge of where you are—i.e., some type of check point or milestone—it's pretty hard to get to your ultimate destination. Appropriate controls keep processes on track and alert us to potential problems.

Managers also provide direction to their people. They let them know what the goals are and help move them along the right path. When there is a lack of direction, people become frustrated and anxious about their performance. They are not sure what's important and subsequently adopt a "no news is good news" mind set. It becomes the embodiment of the *management by exception philosophy*. This is a style of management characterized by pointing out what's wrong. It's negative reinforcement at its worst and doesn't work well at all.

So, what's best? Well, for starters, letting people know what you expect. Providing structure to their job in the form of goals, expectations, and deadlines is essential. Yet, how these goals are set will vary according to their needs. We'll talk more about that later. For now, recognize that people want direction and that is part of what a manager does. If you avoid giving adequate direction, your people might feel like they're spinning their wheels, or see themselves on a rudderless ship. Neither one is very appealing.

Lastly, managers must have ample staff to do the necessary work.

Many organizations today have laid people off without accurately measuring the impact on individual workloads. As a consequence, the work pressures people bear have increased dramatically. Since payroll is frequently a large, visible expense, it's also one of the most vulnerable to cutbacks. This action fuels the jadedness Gen Xers have for large organizations. It also amounts to a loss of intellectual talent that might not be easily replaced in the future.

The staffing function pertains to not only having enough people, but placing the right people in the right positions. This matching of people to skill sets required is not rocket science. But sometimes things don't go right, or people plateau in their work performance or attitude. AT&T has a unique approach for solving this issue called *Resource Link*. Resource Link is an internal program that connects plateaued employees with short-term assignments that complement their talents. Thus, valued employees who ordinarily would leave the company are retained. A unique approach for sure and apparently a winner for AT&T.

CHAPTER 3 — THE UNDERLYING NATURE OF ORGANIZATIONS

Certainly the events of September 11, 2001 will forever endure in the history books as one of America's greatest tragedies. What's truly remarkable about leadership is that adversity often sparks it. Sometimes people whose leadership skills appear only to be mediocre rise up to the occasion. Currently, this certainly seems to be the case with George W. Bush.

When Bush first visited the destruction at ground zero in New York City, one of the workers shouted that he couldn't hear him speak. Without hesitation, the President hollered back, "I can hear you. The world hears you, and the people who knocked these buildings down will hear from all of us soon."

Bush demonstrated an uncanny instinct for what the American people needed to hear during those early days of the terrorist crisis. People wanted plain talk, comfort, and an honest assessment of the situation, and hope for the future. The President delivered well on all counts.

During the darkest hours of World War II, when England was engulfed in the mass bombings of the German Blitzkrieg, Winston Churchill rallied his people. In the short run, he promised the stark reality of "...blood, toil, tears, and sweat." But he held to the belief England would prevail "...however long and hard the road may be." The British resolutely stood behind Churchill and valiantly fought the Axis powers until they were reduced to a heap of rubble in 1945. Such is the power and influence of leadership.

I've always told my students that anyone can man the helm when the sea is calm. When the ocean looks like glass, i.e., when things are going well, just about anyone can appear to lead. It's fairly easy since the demands are usually moderate. However, when the wind whips up and the swells toss you about like a piece of driftwood, you'd better have a seasoned skipper at the wheel. Otherwise you wind up with a catatonic Gustavus Smith instead of a take-charge Robert E. Lee.

IMMERSED IN AN ORGANIZATION'S CULTURE

What these examples above all have in common has a lot to do with people and the underlying nature of organizations. Someone once proposed that a fish doesn't know it's in water until you take it out. In essence, a fish does not have the capacity to consider that the world is different beyond its own environment. The same logic applies equally well to organizational life—especially if you've been a part of such a system for many years.

Although we have the mental capacity, sometimes when we've been immersed within an organizational system for a while, we forget that things are done differently elsewhere. We begin to accept certain unquestioned assumptions regarding the way we relate to others, communicate with them, solve problems, work as a team, handle interpersonal conflict, lead others, etc. For instance, readily sharing information with employees or empowering the rank-and-file is a way of life in some organizations. Although this is a generic example, these two overarching practices would be strongly indicative of a progressive company culture. As a rule of thumb, we would find these actions would be appreciated by the bulk of people who earned their living there.

Organizations have a way of quietly superimposing their values on us. Like a current in a river or an ocean, these values run deep within us and, to a large degree, determine the types of behaviors we engage in...for better or worse. The behaviors which are valued are generally rewarded by the organization; whereas those frowned upon are frequently punished or ignored. Enron, previously discussed in Lesson 2, is an excellent example of this phenomena.

The company's stated values, symbolized by the acronym "RICE," were Responsibility, Integrity, Communication, and Excellence. RICE was ubiquitously displayed throughout Enron and management consistently reminded employees of its importance. In practice though, people were rewarded on the basis of "origination" or how much business they brought the company. Making money was apparently the only thing that genuinely mattered at Enron and most employees soon learned that.

ORGANIZATIONS AS LIVING ENTITIES

As complex as large organizations are, they are <u>first and foremost</u> a collection of people working together. In fact, we could go so far as to say that if you take the people out of an organization, all you'll have left are empty buildings with fixed costs. All of the systems, processes, policies, standards, protocols, and trade secrets will mean little without that ultimately irreplaceable ingredient—people.

Therefore, we can earnestly say that organizations are intrinsically people. Isn't this so? Let's carry that thought to a higher level. We can then reasonably claim that organizations are biological entities. They are "living, dynamic creations" that lend themselves to analysis organically. Look at the two terms: <u>organically</u> and <u>organization</u>. What do you see that is similar? They both contain the prefix *o-r-g-a-n*. So, what is a living organ? We'll, it's something that's alive, dynamic, and ever changing. Interesting?

Please bear with me as I progress with this discussion. There are several very significant arguments here that you will need to know and understand. In fact, it's of even greater relevance to people who come from technical backgrounds. This is because they've probably had minimal exposure to many of these notions. To continue, I want to briefly examine some facets of human personality without getting into a lengthy, tangled dissertation on the topic. So, I will try to keep this as simple as possible.

At its most basic level, there are three components that compromise human personality. These are: how you think, how you feel, and how you act. How you think is related to human hardwiring or temperament, combined with intended coping behaviors. Temperament, for the most part, is primarily inherited from your parents. It has a lot to do with individual preferences like how you process information. Are you more analytical or are you more inclined to be intuitive?

Another example of preferences has to do with whether you are an extrovert or an introvert. Extroverts obtain their energy from the external world of people and things. Introverts gain energy from the internal world of thoughts and reflection. Intended coping behavior reflects your perceptions of the expectations of significant others in your external environment. Got it? I know that's a mouthful; keeping it simple is not always as fruitful as I'd like it to be.

How you feel is associated with your character, your values, beliefs, mores, and the norms of society you accept. It's the seat of your most fundamental emotions. Most of all, it's aligned to learned behavior and what you've experienced in life. Now it gets even more fascinating. The interaction of how you think and how you feel produces overt, observed behavior. This leads us to the most salient question at this juncture: which has the greater influence on your behavior, <u>your thinking</u> or <u>your feelings</u>? Which one would you vote for?

CASTING YOUR VOTE

If you voted for thinking, your opinion coincides with the majority of other managers. Lamentably, you would also be incorrect. Reflect on this for a moment. How often have you known intellectually what to do about something, but diverged 180 degrees because you felt like it? When was the last time you withdrew from confronting someone even though you recognized that wouldn't solve the problem? Or, perhaps you lost your temper with someone who broke a promise or made a major mistake. You did this in spite of knowing that you shouldn't.

That's the way people are. Most of what we do is based on feelings. Fully as much of eighty percent of human behavior is premised on what we feel. Afterwards, or occasionally beforehand, we rationally justify it to ourselves or others.

Since we formerly agreed that organizations are all about people, then the driving force of organizational life must also be emotional, and not rational! Consequently, the underlying nature of organizational life has everything to do with emotions. The most effective leaders understand this at a visceral level. And what they do is *manage the emotions of the organization*. As a matter of fact, this will become our most seminal definition of leadership: **Managing the emotions of the organization.** Remember this: it will be one of the most meaningful maxims you <u>must</u> embrace as a leader!

CHAPTER 4 — WHAT LEADERS DO—THE BIG PICTURE

In Lesson 2, I gave the example of Malden Mills' CEO Aaron Feuerstein and what he did when the factory burned down. He kept everyone on the payroll when the company effectively wasn't even making any money. What do you suppose was the greatest emotion people had when the factory burned down? Perhaps fear, anxiety, or insecurity. They likely worried about how they would pay their bills, put food on the table, or merely take care of their family. Feuerstein gave them the security they needed when they needed it most. In other words, he managed the emotional needs of the organization.

You might ask what about his security? Wasn't he insecure? Wasn't he wondering how he was going to meet his own obligations? Of course, but leaders can't cry on their follower's shoulders. In a sense, leaders act as the emotional storehouse for their people. They must absorb a lot and deal with it in a suitable manner. Envision, for instance, a father whining to his young children about the terrible stress he's under at work. You can easily see the inappropriateness of this behavior.

In reality, the emotional dynamics involved in both parent-child relationships and leader-follower relationships are quite similar in many ways. They are each in an authority type relationship. Some of the same rules apply (although I'm not suggesting that your people are children and should be treated that way). However, managing those dynamics means paying attention to your own limitations, fears, or doubts that linger within you. We'll talk more about this later.

YOUR LEADERSHIP BANK ACCOUNT

As a supervisor or manager, you have a leadership "bank account." You may have never known this before. Every time you do something well as a leader, a deposit is made in your name. And every time you do something inappropriate, a withdrawal is made. For example, with everything you do or say, there is a result and a consequence. We can look at it this way:

Leadership Effectiveness = Results + Consequences

Imagine the following scenario: you want one of your direct reports—that's what I call subordinates—to complete a task he or she abhors. Because they resist, you berate them in front of others. They grudgingly comply and finish the task exactly as you wished. Are you effective as a leader? What do you think?

Actually, you have been successful in getting the task done, but you have been very ineffective as a leader. You now have a problem in your relationship with this direct report; thus, a withdrawal has been made from your bank account. Everything a manager does carries with it some kind of consequence—good or bad. Also, everything you say or do carries with it a message about you. It's comparable to the attachment of an email. The email is analogous to what you say or do, the attachment labels who you are as a person. In this vignette, you would be viewed as a belligerent, humiliating boss.

THE BEST AND THE BRIGHTEST

The three smartest presidents in the last century were Jimmy Carter, Herbert Hoover, and Woodrow Wilson. Does that surprise you? They each had tremendous intellectual horsepower, were quick studies, and could recount volumes of detailed information without notes. What else do all three have in common? They all failed as presidents. During Carter's administration, interest rates soared, the economy tanked, and Americans were taken hostage when the U.S. Embassy in Iran was overrun. Things looked so bad for awhile Carter blamed it principally on us. He said Americans suffered from a general malaise in their spirit.

Actually Jimmy Carter may have been right. Nonetheless, he didn't understand it was his behavior that primarily caused this apathy and it was his job to get the nation moving again. Ronald Reagan eventually did just that. Ironically, Reagan wasn't nearly as bright as Carter, Hoover, or Wilson. But he was the great communicator who could connect with all segments of our society. People readily understood and embraced his vision of America and the world. Besides, Reagan had dogged determination to keep going regardless of the obstacles or problems. Was he effective? I think he was very effective and I'm sure historians will bear this out.

So what did Reagan actually do? He was boundlessly optimistic and concurrently blunt in his realism. Remember, he referred to the Soviet Union as an "Evil Empire." He had a vision that he echoed at any opportunity. He was tenacious about what he desired. He never relented for a nanosecond. All of these components are about leadership. Leaders don't have to be the brightest, nor do they have to be the absolute best. But they do have to understand who they are, what their followers need, and how to credibly meet those needs.

Just like Reagan, George W. Bush is a "down home guy." Not as articulate as Reagan, Bush says what he thinks in simple, meaningful ways. He knows that and he's okay with it. He is trusted by even diehard democrats to say it like it is. When you're hedging on everything like Bill Clinton, and argue that, "...it depends on what the meaning of is is," you create distrust.

Warren Buffett, who heads Berkshire Hathaway, and is considered America's foremost investor, applies similar leadership principles. When Berkshire Hathaway took a massive loss in 2001, he wrote to the company's managers. He said, "Even with tax recoveries our loss is huge. Nevertheless, it's one Berkshire can easily bear..." He went on to say, "In short, you do the managing, and I'll do the worrying."

Buffett, whose personal fortune has been estimated as high as $16 billion (2002 value), knew his people needed reassurance. They needed to know he was smart enough to keep the company viable. His recognition of the gravity of the situation coupled with his confidence made for a powerful, effective statement. Buffett is an excellent leader who embodies the essential qualities of leadership.

He might have had some significant reservations about the company's immediate prospects, but he played that close to his chest.

Leaders need to be able to not only manage others, but they need to manage themselves. This is that part of the emotional dynamic we noted earlier. When Jimmy Carter succumbed to his own frustrations, he said the people were at fault. He didn't manage himself. He certainly didn't manage the emotions of the American people either. They needed a leader they could believe in and Jimmy Carter wasn't fitting the bill.

A curious epilogue to this story is worth noting. No one will customarily argue the inherent goodness of Jimmy Carter—the man. His personal commitment to world peace, his work with Habitat For Humanity, his continued service to the U.S. government, etc., is beyond reproach. But that is not the issue. Carter is and always has been a good man. Sadly, he was not a good president, or a good leader. Period.

CHAPTER 5 — CONCLUSION

As you can now see management and leadership are necessary for organizational life, but certainly they're not synonymous. Using the terms as if they both meant the same thing doesn't make any sense. Managers must plan, organize, control, direct, and staff. All of these functions are vital to administering to the complexities of organizations.

Becoming a world-class organization depends to a large degree on the quality of leadership within. World-class organizations create followers rather than just subordinates. Subordinates, or direct reports, do as they're told, whereas followers often go the extra mile in getting the job done. They have greater zeal for their job viewing it more as a mission than only as a paycheck.

The five M's of the organizing function pertain to: manpower—people, money, machines, materials, and methods. These are the critical resources that must be marshaled by managers to achieve results. Resources will always be scarce because everyone in the organization competes for them. Therefore, managers must do a good job in protecting them and using them wisely.

People are what organizations are all about; that is, without them all you have are empty buildings with fixed costs. In reality, emotions are the driving force of human behavior. The dynamic integration of how we think and how we feel leads to overt behavior. However, feelings influence our actions far more than thinking. Therefore, since organizations are really all about people, they are emotional in nature. Hence, the underlying nature of organizations is biological. They are living, dynamic, and ever changing.

The broadest definition of effective leadership is managing the emotions of the organization. In its finest sense, this is the <u>essence</u> of leadership. Certainly, leaders need to do other things to augment this in carrying out their duties and obligations. We'll take this up in our following lessons.

LESSON THREE ASSIGNMENT

Think of the best boss you ever had. What is it that you remember most about him or her? Write out several paragraphs describing them. After you've written your synopsis, answer the questions below regarding what your description says about how they:

1. Communicated with you
2. Challenged you
3. Was fair to you
4. Was a role model
5. Was honest and ethical
6. Created trust and openness
7. "Walked their talk" (acted according to their promises, values)
8. Showed they cared about you

Overall, how did they make you feel about you? Altogether, how did they make you feel about them? Did they manage your most important emotional needs? What did you learn from them? What did you learn from this particular activity?

LESSON THREE MULTIPLE-CHOICE QUIZ
(Answers on the Following Pages)

1. What are the five functions of management?

   A. Problem solving, decision making, setting priorities, asking the right questions, and managing conflicts.
   B. The 5-M's.
   C. Managing: the boss, yourself, your direct reports, your peers, and those external to the organization (such as, vendors, suppliers, customers, etc.)
   D. Planning, organizing, controlling, directing, and staffing.

2. The 5-M's are part of the organizing function of management. What are they?

   A. Managing our major mission without making mistakes.
   B. Manpower, Money, Machines, Materials, and Methods.
   C. In real estate, they say price is all about location, location, and location. In management, organizing is all about money, money, money, money, and money.
   D. 5-M stands for never having more than five major goals at any one time.

3. Managers who provide inadequate direction may later discover that their direct reports...

   A. Become frustrated and anxious about their performance.
   B. Are happier with the lack of structure.
   C. Collectively have risen to the occasion in spite of it.
   D. Don't care one way or the other.

4. Why is it important that an organization reward the values they exalt?

A. It's not important. They should reward the values they value and not necessarily those they extol.
B. So they are walking their talk. That is, they have integrity.
C. They should pay for performance and not worry about values.
D. Because the best companies do that.

5. What do I mean by managing the emotions of the organization?

   A. Offering an Employee Assistance Program for the rank-and-file.
   B. Listening and showing empathy to employees.
   C. This is the essence of effective leadership: responding to the predominant emotional needs that exist at any given time.
   D. Adults are children grown larger, and a boss needs to treat them more as a parent would.

LESSON THREE MULTIPLE-CHOICE QUIZ
(Answers)

1. What are the five functions of management?

    A. Problem solving, decision making, setting priorities, asking the right questions, and managing conflicts.
    Incorrect.
    No doubt all of these things are important to a manager, but these are not the five functions.

    B. The 5-M's.
    Incorrect.
    The 5-M's are part of the organizing function of management.

    C. Managing the boss, managing yourself, managing your direct reports, managing your peers, and managing those external to the organization (vendors, suppliers, customers, etc.)
    Incorrect.
    These are not functions, they are constituencies.

    D. Planning, organizing, controlling, directing, and staffing.
    Correct.
    Good, these are the functions we discussed.

2. The 5-M's are part of the organizing function of management. What do they stand for?

    A. Managing our major mission without making mistakes.
    Incorrect.
    Good luck, but this is not likely to happen in the real world.

    B. Manpower, Money, Machines, Materials, and Methods.
    Correct.
    Great, you were paying attention!.

C. In real estate, they say price is all about location, location, and location. In management, organizing is all about money, money, money, money, and money.
Incorrect.
Enron's dubious example would support this, but obviously their philosophy was misguided and illegal.

D. 5-M stands for never having more than five major goals at any one time.
Incorrect.
Perhaps this is not a bad idea, but it's nevertheless incorrect.

3. Managers who provide inadequate direction may later discover that their direct reports...

A. Become frustrated and anxious about their performance.
Correct.
People want to know what's expected of them. They also want a reference point by which to gauge their performance.

B. Are happier with the lack of structure.
Incorrect.
The key words in the question are inadequate direction. This should tell you that it's simply not enough.

C. Collectively have risen to the occasion in spite of it.
Incorrect.
It's possible that a few people may actually do this. However, this is the exception and not the rule.

D. Don't care one way or the other.
Incorrect.
People are generally not apathetic when it comes to performance issues that could affect their perceived security.

4. Why is it important that an organization reward the values they exalt?

   A. It's not important. They should reward the values they value and not necessarily those they extol.
   Incorrect.
   Hypocrisy undermines trust, performance, and profitability.

   B. So they are walking their talk. That is, they have integrity.
   Correct.
   Organizational integrity contributes to the emotional health of an organizational culture.

   C. They should pay for performance and not worry about values.
   Incorrect.
   Organizations get what they reward, not what they value.

   D. Because the best companies do that.
   Incorrect.
   Right behavior for the wrong reason. Sure, the best companies do it. They do it because it's the right thing to do.

5. What do I mean by managing the emotions of the organization?

   A. Offering an Employee Assistance Program for the rank-and-file.
   Incorrect.
   Sorry, that's off target.

   B. Listening and showing empathy to employees.
   Incorrect.
   No doubt this is critical, but not quite the right answer.

   C. This is the essence of effective leadership: responding to the predominant emotional needs that exist at any given time.
   Correct.
   Great! This is what I want to hear.

D. Adults are children grown larger and a boss needs to treat them more as a parent would.
Incorrect.
Uh, oh. You weren't tracking with important points in the lesson. Go back and study it again!

IRV GAMAL, M.A.

LESSON THREE FREQUENTLY ASKED QUESTIONS

Q: How can leaders tell if they're managing the emotions of the organization?

A: The higher a leader is positioned in an organization, the more difficult it is to learn how people actually feel. This is because employees are frequently nervous about disclosing information that could hurt their career or job security. Therefore, anonymous feedback is the best measure of how a manager is doing. This can be accomplished through 360 degree feedback assessments administered through Human Resources or an outside consultant — preferably the latter.

Another method is utilizing employee opinion surveys, but these generally are non-specific in pinpointing a particular manager's strengths or weaknesses. Other metrics are revealing, but again more obtuse in locating exactly where the problems are. Examples of these are: turnover, quality, customer service, employee grievances, re-work, productivity, and so forth.

Q: Why is it that technical professionals have a more difficult time with the "softer skills' than MBAs or those who had an education emphasizing the Liberal Arts?

A: Good question. There are really two parts to this though. First off, MBAs used to have as difficult a time because their education and expertise emphasized areas like financial analysis, strategic planning, economics, management, etc. In fact, Liberal Arts majors would historically surpass MBA's in the long haul with their leadership effectiveness. This was because they were more proficient with their soft skills. They needed some time to learn the management areas and eventually were literally a bit more effective than MBA's.

Graduate schools of Business began to recognize this and incorporated topics such as Organizational Behavior, Interpersonal Skills, and Communications into their curriculum. This closed the gap. Secondly, Liberal Arts majors tended to be effective in the softer skills for the same reasons. They likely took courses focusing on those areas and already possessed average or better interpersonal skills.

Technical Professionals, on the other hand, had little or no exposure to interpersonal skill topics. Their training and job experience was directed to scientific or technical challenges. Once they enter into management, the skills sets required dramatically change to their disadvantage.

LESSON 4

A NEW VIEW OF LEADERSHIP

CHAPTER 1 — INTRODUCTION

> *The truth is that there is no appropriate model for business except business itself. Business is not a diversion. It reflects the character of life itself; complex, difficult, susceptible to success and failure, sometimes unruly, always challenging, and often joyful.*
>
> —*Warren Bennis*

Warren Bennis, noted author, former university president, professor, and management guru, is right on the mark. Business indeed reflects the character and complexity of life itself. It's a mirror of the times we live in. The excitement and intensity of business can be the ultimate adrenaline rush hour. In his book, <u>Why Leaders Can't Lead</u>, Bennis notes that just as a human being needs brainpower to function, organizations need leadership to suitably operate.

It's deplorable that we often are disappointed by the quality of the leadership we spot in many companies. If there were a Leadership Hall of Shame it would be teeming with the pictures of ill-fated leaders who miserably failed. Their downfall might be the result of a few terminal errors, or sometimes many glaring deficiencies. It might be the outcome of debasing arrogance, inflated egos, lack of integrity, outright greed, rigid inflexibility, cold detachment, or "you name it." These are several of the most common reasons that top leaders plunge disgracefully from their lofty pedestals.

OUR OBJECTIVE IN THIS LESSON

The price of leadership failure is steep. Obviously, the greater the responsibility the individual has in an organization, the more acute is their impact. Frankly, there have been too many leadership failures. In this lesson, we'll spotlight things that could get in the way of your career advancement causing you to derail.

Derailment has several disheartening facets. For example, you might be passed over for promotion and find yourself plateaued, or demoted, or worse yet, terminated. All are forms of derailment and, obviously, should be avoided. Bad as they are, you'll learn many of the intrinsic reasons for derailment are often self-imposed.

We urgently need more effective organizational leaders with "staying power." Because leaders are made, not born, our central emphasis in our lesson will be on strengthening areas vital for your leadership success. We will discuss "The First Dimension of Leadership: Building Trust and Commitment" expanding on the thinking shared in previous lessons. We'll examine more specifically what leaders do in this area to manage the emotions of the organization.

CHAPTER 2 — THE FOUR LEADERSHIP DIMENSIONS

Warren Bennis characterizes four major competency areas of leadership as: (1) Managing Trust; (2) Managing Attention; (3) Managing Meaning; and (4) Managing Oneself. I've placed them in a slightly different order from Bennis. I ranked trust first because that's the foundation upon which everything else is built. If you don't establish trust, nothing else will be long lasting. It will be a house of cards. You might envision a model as the one below, moving in a counterclockwise manner.

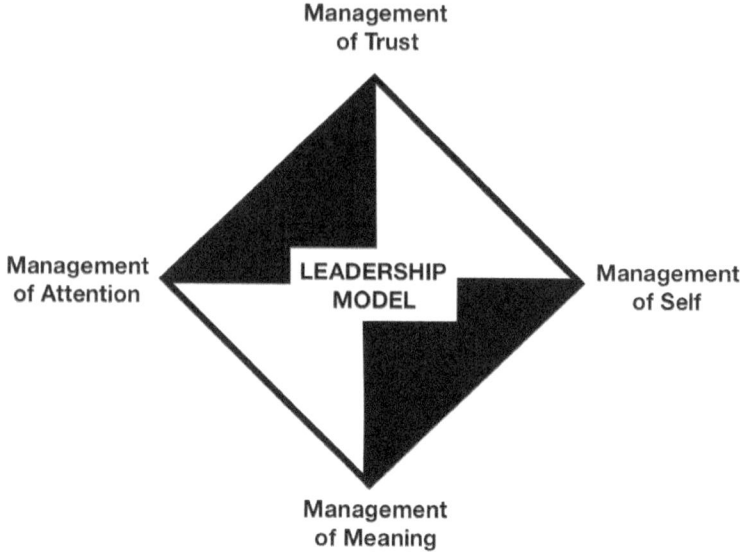

Each of the following three lessons will deal with one specific portion of the Bennis model. For example, in Lesson Five, "Keeping Your Eye on The Ball," we'll carefully scrutinize the Management of Attention. Lesson Six will examine the Management of Meaning, and Lesson Seven, the Management of Self. So, that's the game plan for us to follow in the next several lessons.

Now, let's roll up our sleeves and dig into what the first of these competencies "looks like," allied with what leaders exactly do. Initially, I want to take the Darth Vader perspective and delve into the *dark side of leadership.* Think about what occurs when trust is lacking in the work environment. Have you ever worked in an organization where you didn't trust management, or your peers, or even your direct reports? What was it like? Not too pleasant for you, was it?

WHEN TRUST AND COMMITMENT IS LACKING

I can remember working in a large company many years ago that was in the midst of a significant business contraction. The stock price nose dived, layoffs were rampant and two engineers tragically committed suicide. It doesn't get much worse than that.

In the meantime, senior executives were holding meetings to assure employees that the company had turned the corner and layoffs would be curtailed. People left those meetings shaking their heads wondering what these guys were smoking. There was no credibility, limited work was performed, and there was a glut of anxiety. Employees were pumping out resumes as fast as the photocopiers could run.

When people work in environments where trust is lacking, they eventually become dysfunctional. Stress, suspicion, fear, anger, depression, etc., abound. The less trust that is present, the more emotionally toxic the climate. Aside from overall declines in individual performance, people become more litigious, or opt for union certification. There's a rising trend in the country for technical professionals to sign up for union representation. Where it used to be primarily a blue collar attribute, unions are now vigorously seeking the ranks of the professionals.

Typically, people will work to about the 20-30% level of their potential when they are motivated principally by fear. Oddly enough, studies have shown that people can actually perform at this low level and still keep  their job. It's quite a formidable task to raise performance when fear is the cardinal agent. That's why it's so hard to turn around companies that are in a virtual tailspin.

Trust and respect are the underpinnings of all relationships. When people know they are trusted, and they can trust in return, strong feelings of confidence, commitment, ownership, and cohesiveness begin to emerge. Managers who are evasive, manipulative, or use intimidation as the basis of their style will witness some of these classic negative behaviors in their people:

- Avoidance
- "Yes people" (Tell you what they think you want to hear)

- Risk aversion
- Abject compliance
- CYA ("Cover your...")
- A myriad of excuses
- Finger pointing and blaming others
- Subversion or sabotage
- The possibility of violence
- "Management as the enemy" mind set

Obviously, these kinds of behaviors require very close supervision, otherwise little will get done. That eats into a manager's time and prevents them from attending to things they might find more challenging and satisfying. Work becomes a daily tug of war and loses most of its luster.

CHAPTER 3 — INITIAL GUIDELINES FOR BUILDING TRUST

So, how do you begin to turn this around and build trust in an organization? Here are some important guidelines:

- Have high integrity
- Show you care, exhibit concern
- Be reliable and behave in a consistent manner
- Follow up on your promises
- Be straightforward and aboveboard
- Provide needed <u>and</u> <u>timely</u> support

INTEGRITY

We've talked before about the nature of integrity. I would like to say that it should go without question, but periodically we lose sight of this virtue. Suffice to say, integrity is to trust as oxygen is to human life. The relationship is that crucial. Once more, I'll maintain that integrity is walking your talk. What you say and what you do must be one and the same. Some of the prior guidelines will help build and reinforce your integrity too.

Your reputation is a measure of how people view your personal integrity. It's so significant that we might say it's sacred. It was once referred to as your "sacred honor." A damaged reputation, on the other hand, is nearly impossible to repair. So you must guard and defend your reputation as you would anything that is valuable.

For example, consider the reputation of the following companies and the trust you place in their products or services: Firestone, ValueJet, Enron, Tyson Foods, K-Mart, or Arthur Anderson. As an epilogue to their crash in the Florida Everglades a few years ago, ValueJet acquired another airline and went so far as to change their blemished name. What do you think will happen to Firestone? Or Arthur Anderson? Contemplate how hard you've worked in your career to establish your reputation. Much of it is a result of your integrity.

CARE AND CONCERN

Another way to shape trust is by showing <u>authentic</u> concern for people. Concern must be genuine and demonstrated, that's why I underline the word, "authentic." *When people feel you are concerned about them, they are concerned about what they do!* Simple axiom, but a very powerful one. It's one that's well understood by the managers in companies who excel in their quality and/or customer service.

A neighbor of mine is a project manager for a company that manufactures drones for the Department of Defense. Before these were in vogue (prior to 9-11), their business was dismal. Instead of laying off employees, the president of the company gave them a choice of cutting back on their hours by 20% and taking a commensurate pay cut. They opted for this second choice unanimously. By the way, the company's president reduced his hours and took the same pay cut.

After about two years of tough times, their business picked up. Everyone was back working full time at full pay. As revenues soared, so did raises and bonuses. No one was ever let go and the company is prospering. Because people, including my neighbor, believed that this company cared, their loyalty is monumental. So are profits.

What have you personally done lately to show your employees you care? Do you presume your employees believe you are concerned about them? Managers can show they care in a number of meaningful ways.

One of my previous graduate students—we'll call him Rob—owned a moderate-sized high tech manufacturing company with two plants, one in Southern California and the other in Northern California. The first plant was located in the southern part of the state where the company was originally founded. One of his early professional hires worked his way up to Manufacturing Manager and was relocated to Silicon Valley where he helped open the second plant.

Rob approached me one day after class to share a problem that was unquestionably bothering him. He said that he had brought a new General Manager on board for the Northern California facility. After a few months on the job, he wanted to terminate the Manufacturing Manager, Rob's long-term veteran, for insubordination. The GM said that this individual was trying to run his job, continually telling him what to do. Rob asked the GM to hold tight and wait until he could look into the situation.

Rob was caught on the horns of a real dilemma. He didn't want to undermine the GM, but neither did he want to lose a senior employee who contributed so much to the company's success. He asked me what he should do. I told him to let the GM know he will talk with his direct report and also visit the northern California plant within the week to meet with both of them. He immediately talked with the Manufacturing Manager and discovered that he was making a number of needed suggestions that the GM clearly didn't want to hear. Consequently, he was frustrated, demoralized, and considering leaving. Rob and I talked again soon.

This was a typical case of a misunderstanding between two strong managers spinning out of control. One felt his boss didn't care and the boss felt he was being bossed by a subordinate. I suggested Rob send the Manufacturing Manager's wife a letter sharing his admiration for the man. Also to recount his recognition of how much the man's wife sacrificed moving her family to Silicon Valley and giving her emotional support to her husband throughout his career. Rob was incredulous that I would suggest him writing such a letter. He said,

"Nobody does that!" My response was, "Exactly! Isn't that a shame?" He ultimately gave in to my recommendation.

About a week later, he flew up to San Jose and met with the GM over lunch. They discussed the situation and Rob shared what he had deduced from the situation. Rob told the GM he was doing a terrific job and had his full support, but wanted to work through this sticky plight together. The GM agreed and they arranged a meeting for the three of them. Prior to that meeting, Rob had dinner with his Manufacturing Manager who was visibly sentimental.

He revealed that he had come home the day before and his wife was reading the letter from Rob while sobbing. When his wife explained the letter was from Rob, he assumed he was fired. When he read it, he was so profoundly touched, he wept as well. He felt vindicated, cared for, and valued by Rob. His self-esteem was back intact and his commitment to the company was higher than ever before. The aftermath of the meeting, among the three of them, was to resolve the problems and finally put the difficulties behind them.

RELIABILITY AND CONSISTENCY

Part of reliability is following up on your promises. If you're prone to forget what you say, make notes to yourself. The key is not to forget what you commit to—you see, a promise is a commitment. If you can't deliver on a commitment, let people know why. At the very least, you then show them they were important enough to warrant your follow through.

Reliability is a factor we ought to be able to "hang our hat on." For example, when you look at your car's speedometer, you expect it to be accurate, i.e., reliable. What if it were correct today, but tomorrow, it vacillated plus or minus 15 miles per hour? You'd never be able to trust any of its readings. How would you respond if you were being followed by a police car on the freeway? How would you feel? Reliability enables us to drive at a safe and legal speed trusting the data we have to be right.

The complexities of our society mandate reliability in all areas of our lives. Try to imagine what your life would be like if your bank wasn't reliable, or your power company, or your doctor, or your broker, or your computer, etc. Think about what the run on banks did to society during the early part of the depression. How about the affects of the power crisis in California during 2001? Just as reliability is critical for a higher standard of living, it's essential for a higher standard of leadership. If we're unreliable in our behavior, our leadership is way below par.

Having a moody boss is one of the most insufferable experiences imaginable. Some people have compared it to being seasick. You feel you're going to die, but you're afraid you might not! Mood swings are terminal behaviors. Managers who are constantly moody throw other people off balance. Employees never know if you're going to be in a good or bad frame of mind.

People avoid moody managers. These managers eventually find themselves cut out of the communication loop—isolated from information. They generally receive low marks for their people skills and their peers don't like working with them either. Being consistent in your behavior is preferred. Maintaining an even keel is best, but not always achievable. This is especially evident in high pressure situations. If you maintain "your cool" while facing stressful events, you'll fare much better with others.

CHAPTER 4 — SECONDARY GUIDELINES FOR BUILDING TRUST

Straightforwardness

As Secretary of Defense, Donald Rumsfeld receives numerous kudos for his straightforwardness. He doesn't hedge his comments, waffle in his opinions, or use a bucketful of qualifiers. Rumsfeld has enormous credibility as a leader. He is trustworthy because he says it like it is. The same may be true for you. How do you handle communicating delicate or volatile information? Do you hold back out of fear or concern how others will react? Or do you have the personal convictions to say it "with the bark on." You might ask for some feedback about this from some of your colleagues.

Sometimes straightforwardness can come across with a humorous edge. Long regarded as having a mammoth-sized ego, Donald Trump was interviewed for a Fortune Magazine article. Over-inflated egos, you'll recollect, can often lead to a one-way ticket out the door. Trump, however, has never denied his intense love affair with himself. When asked by a journalist if he had the biggest ego in America, Trump said, "I hope not." Then for a time he mulled over who might have a bigger ego. Finally, unable to come up with an alternative, he forthrightly elected himself.

Although Donald Trump would not be considered a fitting model of leadership, his candor is well appreciated. Harry Truman, who came to be known as "Give 'em Hell" Harry, kept a motto on his desk that expressed a basic philosophy he lived by. It said, "The Buck Stops Here." Plain and simple. It would be difficult to misunderstand what President Truman had in mind.

Being straightforward frequently takes a healthy burst of courage. I've found that many managers dislike confrontation of any kind. They feel uncomfortable with it and prefer an atmosphere of harmony, even if it's a facade. Andy Grove of Intel refused to pay homage to "yes men" and always surrounded himself with intelligent dissenters. He termed this tactic *constructive confrontation with associates.* He believed that disagreements would help Intel's leaders ferret out the truth in any particular context.

We have a habit in our society of avoiding saying anything that might be offensive. It's called being politically correct. We don't want anyone to feel bad about anything. So, we hide the truth behind terms or words that obscure what really is. We don't lay people off; we right size, or down size. We don't put someone on probation; we place them on a development plan. We don't suspend someone; we place them on administrative leave. We don't demote someone; we reorganize or restructure. We don't fire someone; we outplace them.

The list goes on and on. It permeates every aspect of our society, our thinking, and our ability to communicate truthfully. When Rudy Giuliani was asked what the death toll would probably be at the World Trade Center disaster, he laid it on the line, from the heart, and said, "…more than any of us can bear." His honesty and strength of character earned him the admiration and respect of millions of people around the world.

SUPPORT AND TIMELINESS

A study conducted some time ago by Hewlett-Packard disclosed valuable findings about project managers. They concluded that the most significant factors separating average from exceptional project managers was their ability to motivate, coach, support, and lead team members. Providing expedient support was one prominent criteria.

This action requires that managers remain aware of how their direct reports are doing. If you delegate a task or project and then rarely check back to review progress, you'll not be able to aid them. Support can be offered in many ways. You may give someone a verbal vote of confidence, or send them to a workshop, or enlist a peer's cooperation for them, or furnish material resources. All are examples of support.

However, when the support is given too late, it will be viewed unfavorably. People will react by saying, "It's about time!" This is equivalent to being served an appetizing dinner that's been lingering in the kitchen until it's cold. Timeliness is just as important as the very support that's offered.

The level of emotional support a manager provides is frequently an offshoot of their expectations and personal style. Your expectations for a direct report's performance are communicated in many subtle ways. It's conveyed by what you say, how you say it, the amount of your attention, your responsiveness to them, etc.

For example, you might say to one of your people, "I know you'll do well on this project." That's a strong message of support and people know it instinctively. Contrast that to a manager who says, "You'll probably have difficulty with this." What do you think the outcome will be in the latter case?

Robert Rosenthal, a behavioral scientist from Harvard conducted a famous study in San Diego, California a number of years ago. Rosenthal passed himself off as a psychometrist, someone who administers psychological tests, to a school superintendent. He convinced the superintendent that his "company" had developed a series of psychological tests for children that could identify success in later adult life. The superintendent was excited and arranged for Rosenthal and his staff to work with four fourth grade teachers.

Rosenthal flew out from the East Coast with several graduate students—his alleged staff—and met with the four teachers. They set aside a day where over 100 4th grade students would be taking a variety of tests—IQ, personality inventory, aptitude, etc. Once, this was done, Rosenthal gathered up all the tests and took them back to his hotel room where he threw them all out—except for the IQ tests which were scored.

Then his staff set up four hats on a counter and dropped the names of all students from each class in the individual hats. They arbitrarily reached in and pulled out the names of four students from each hat, for a total of sixteen. A few days later, they were back at the school meeting with the four teachers.

They told them they had scored all the tests and sixteen students were singled out as having high potential as "bloomers." The teachers urgently wanted the names of these children, but Rosenthal made them sign binding nondisclosure agreements before he shared that information. There was some surprise, yet essentially the teachers accepted what they had been given.

One year later, Rosenthal returned and tested the children again. They were now in the 5th grade and most of them were still there. Out of over 100 children, sixteen had an increase in their IQ. It happened that it was the <u>exact</u> sixteen that he had predicted would bloom. When the teachers were informed of the true nature of the experiment, they were shocked. They swore, to a person, they never violated the terms of the confidentiality agreements. Rosenthal believed them and I do too. If you believe them as well, then what do you think went on in those classrooms during that year?

To begin with, the teachers' expectations changed and therefore their behavior followed. They were far more supportive of the bloomers than the other students. They gave them more attention, more "atta boys" and "atta girls," more feedback, more encouragement, more challenges, etc. The children trusted the teachers, their positive messages, and lived up to them. The results were incredible, but proved that support is a powerful mechanism in helping fashion the performance of others.

CHAPTER 5 — CONCLUSION

In this lesson, you were introduced to a leadership model developed by Warren Bennis. Bennis believes that there are four major dimensions to leadership effectiveness: managing trust, managing attention, managing meaning, and managing one's self. Although I placed them in a different order, they manifest Bennis's thinking.

Trust and respect are the foundation of all human relationships. Together, they yield confidence. Without trust, you cannot establish any type of meaningful connection with another person. Therefore, that becomes the first point of discussion with this model and the basis of our lesson.

When trust is lacking in an organization, all types of dysfunctional behaviors begin to show up. These behaviors add to the emotional turmoil already existing in the organization. As a bad situation worsens, the organization will eventually see declines in quality, customer service, and ultimately, profits.

Trust can be established through a number of characteristics and behaviors consistently reinforced by organizational leaders. They are:

- Have high integrity
- Show you care, exhibit concern
- Be reliable and behave in a consistent manner
- Follow up on your promises
- Be straightforward and aboveboard
- Provide needed support and do so promptly

We looked at a number of examples and their implications of each of these throughout the chapters in this lesson. I encourage you to examine your own behaviors and attitudes in light of these factors and make whatever adjustments may be desirable.

IRV GAMAL, M.A.

LESSON FOUR ASSIGNMENT

Assessing How Much You Think Others Trust You

Circle the number that best reflects your evaluation of how you think you do in each of the areas below. A "10" is excellent, a "5" would be average, and a "1" is poor. Those areas where you score yourself low should be targeted for improvement. Also, keep in mind that these are your ratings. The closer you're in touch with your impact on other people, the more likely your ratings reflect the ratings of others.

If you want to take this to a higher level, you might print this out for others and ask them to anonymously rate you. Then compare your "self" and "other" ratings. Where are the biggest gaps? What are the best and worst surprises for you?

1. Makes realistic promises and keeps them
   1   2   3   4   5   6   7   8   9   10

2. Demonstrates integrity and respectable behavior
   1   2   3   4   5   6   7   8   9   10

3. Puts others before himself/herself
   1   2   3   4   5   6   7   8   9   10

4. Follows through on all commitments
   1   2   3   4   5   6   7   8   9   10

5. Is competent and consistent in conduct
   1   2   3   4   5   6   7   8   9   10

6. Admits personal mistakes and what he or she doesn't know
   1   2   3   4   5   6   7   8   9   10

7. Fosters open and straightforward communication

    1 2 3 4 5 6 7 8 9 10

8. Maintains confidences and sensitive information

    1 2 3 4 5 6 7 8 9 10

9. Allows others to ask difficult and challenging questions

    1 2 3 4 5 6 7 8 9 10

10. Is honest and "aboveboard" with his or her answers

    1 2 3 4 5 6 7 8 9 10

11. When delegating, provides meaningful and timely support

    1 2 3 4 5 6 7 8 9 10

12. Upholds the company's written code of ethics (if applicable)

    1 2 3 4 5 6 7 8 9 10

LESSON FOUR MULTIPLE-CHOICE QUIZ
(Answers on the Following Pages)

1. What are the four dimensions of the Bennis Model?

   A. Length, width, height, and time.
   B. The Management of trust, attention, meaning, and self.
   C. Avoidance, risk aversion, abject compliance, and excuses.
   D. Managing, writing, teaching, and consulting.

2. I make the comparison that integrity is to trust as oxygen is to human life. Why is integrity so critical?

   A. It's not. This was an unfortunate exaggeration.
   B. Without integrity, there is no chance of trust. Without trust, there are no worthy, long-lasting relationships.
   C. Most of the air we breath is actually nitrogen, so, likewise, integrity plays a secondary role related to trust.
   D. Virtue is back in style, so it's politically correct to say integrity is critical.

3. Why is it important that managers comply with the same standards they ask of their employees? Recall the company president who cut his own hours and pay.

   A. So that managers will be viewed as martyrs.
   B. So that they do not establish a double standard which undermines trust.
   C. It makes good "copy" in the press.
   D. Company policy may dictate it.

4. Can a manager who generally doesn't return phone calls be perceived as reliable?

A. No.
B. Yes.
C. Only if they are the CEO or COO.
D. Yes, as long as it's a personal call.

5. Political correctness...

   A. Exists only in the academic environment.
   B. Occurs every four years during major elections.
   C. Only occurs within the ranks of managers.
   D. Is a form of censorship and undermines straightforward, honest communication.

LESSON FOUR MULTIPLE-CHOICE QUIZ
(Answers)

1. What are the four dimensions of the Bennis Model?

   A. Length, width, height, and time.
   Incorrect.
   Sorry, wrong course. Physics 101 is down the hall!

   B. The Management of: trust, attention, meaning, and self.
   Correct.
   Exactly. Go to the head of the class.

   C. Avoidance, risk aversion, abject compliance, and excuses.
   Incorrect.
   These are not dimensions; they're dysfunctional behaviors.

   D. Managing, writing, teaching, and consulting.
   Incorrect.
   Oops, you may have been reading Bennis's biography. Right man, wrong answer.

2. I make the comparison that integrity is to trust as oxygen is to human life. Why is integrity so critical?

   A. It's not. This was an unfortunate exaggeration.
   Incorrect.
   Better go back and re-read this lesson. You missed a vital point!

   B. Without integrity, there is no chance of trust. Without trust, there are no worthy, long-lasting relationships.
   Correct.
   Good, we're tracking with one another.

C. Most of the air we breath is actually nitrogen, so, likewise, integrity plays a secondary role related to trust.
Incorrect.
Without oxygen, we die. Without integrity, there is no trust. It plays a primary role—always!

D. Virtue is back in style, so it's politically correct to say integrity is critical.
Incorrect.
Virtue is back in style because it is observed less and less. Let's hope it's here to stay. Integrity is a virtue and it's vital to society because without it our institutions, relationships, and agreements fall apart. This has nothing to do with political correctness.

3. Recall, for example, the company president who cut his own hours and pay. Why is it important that managers comply with the same standards they ask of their employees?

A. So that managers will be viewed as martyrs.
Incorrect.
That doesn't rate so high in our culture.

B. So that they do not establish a double standard which undermines trust.
Correct.
We all need to live by the same rules. When we inaugurate an elitist environment, we create a "we/them" attitude.

C. It makes good "copy" in the press.
Incorrect.
Certainly, it does look good publicly for any organization. However, this is not why you do it.

D. Company policy may dictate it.

Incorrect.

This may be true. But, alas, it's not the right answer.

4. Can a manager who generally doesn't return phone calls be perceived as reliable?

   A. No.
   Correct.
   There's a reason we have voicemail. We don't call it *disregarded mail.* There's the anticipation of a returned call when we leave a message. Especially if the outgoing message promises such a call back. Managers who don't follow up violate expectations and look bad.

   B. Yes.
   Incorrect.
   Managers who don't return phone calls are not reliable. They abuse their position and violate the caller's expectations.

   C. Only if they are the CEO or COO.
   Incorrect.
   It doesn't matter who they are. We expect all managers to return phone calls—it's a common courtesy.

   D. Yes, as long as it's a personal call.
   Incorrect.
   Again this is wrong. It could be an emergency call. A manager who neglects personal calls might be perceived as neglectful of his family, uncaring, manipulative, etc.

5. Political correctness…

   A. Exists only in the academic environment.
   Incorrect.
   Nope, you'll find it everywhere.

B. Occurs every four years during major elections.
   Incorrect.
   It probably intensifies during election years among politicians. Yet, it remains an ongoing force to be reckoned with throughout our society.

C. Only occurs within the ranks of managers.
   Incorrect.
   All people are prone to it, although some managers have certainly taken it to new lows—as opposed to heights.

D. Is a form of censorship and undermines straightforward, honest communication.
   Correct.
   I'll probably get nasty letters, but this is the correct answer.

IRV GAMAL, M.A.

LESSON FOUR FREQUENTLY ASKED QUESTIONS

Q: What do you do if you're already working in an organization where there is considerable distrust of management?

A: I'm assuming that you are referring primarily to senior management. With anything we consider, there is always a price and a prize. When weighing what to do, you'll want to look at where you are in the "food chain" and what prizes you are getting? What other prizes are you promised, in what period of time, and can you bank on that? Furthermore, you must carefully consider what price you are paying for working there. What are your stress levels? How is your emotional and physical health being affected? What about your close relationships?

All of these need to be evaluated. If you are desperately unhappy with your present situation, then the compass is pointing out the door. The longer you wait, the more perilous your situation will become.

Q: Why do we seem to have such a lack of integrity in our leaders today?

A: Remember what Bennis said: Business is a reflection of the character of life itself. We've inherited the liberalism of the sixties with all the firmly rooted feel-good philosophies. Many of those selfish, me-first, baby boomers who believed in those principles are in positions of leadership today where they influence the activities of others.

Integrity was replaced by what you could get away with. It ran all the way up to the Oval Office in the White House during the Clinton Administration. We see it with Enron and all other "Me, Inc." organizations that push the limits of good virtue.

Q: Is trust really that important, or are we just being a bit Pollyannaish?

A: Aside from the fact that trust is basic to all relationships, that civilized society cannot function without it, trust is also profitable and perpetuates economic affluence. Most third world economies are dominated by institutions that are not trusted by the general population. The most successful economies in the world happen to also have the highest rankings of trust from their citizens. These countries would be the United States, the United Kingdom, Germany, and Japan.

LESSON 5

KEEPING YOUR EYE ON THE BALL

CHAPTER 1 — INTRODUCTION

> *"When we started this company, we were out to change the world. And we did that. We put the Internet in the hands of normal people. We kick-started a new communications medium. We changed the world."*
>
> —*Jamie Zawinski, Netscape*

There's an old saying, "If you don't know where you're going, any road will get you there." When leaders and organizations operate haphazardly, without identifying an ultimate direction, they promote mediocre commitment and waste most of the limited energy that's available to them.

Jamie Zawinski—the twentieth person hired at Netscape—appeared to possess a bold passion for his work at Netscape, judging by his statement above. This level of zeal didn't happen by fluke or accident. It occurred because of the remarkable leadership of both CEO Jim Barksdale and technology wizard Marc Andreeson. Each of these individuals were evangelistic about their belief in Netscape. Their celebrated all-hands meetings were often compared to Southern tent revivals. Employees came out of those sessions spirited "believers," with staunch emotional ties to the company.

Nonetheless, there are never any guarantees in business. Netscape was eventually purchased by America Online—AOL—and a portion of the company was sold off to Sun Microsystems. But for four exciting years, from 1994-1998, the company reigned as a bright, shining star in Silicon Valley.

Without their powerful vision they would never have achieved their outstanding success. You might think that this success was not so spectacular since it was limited to only four years. However, if Netscape hadn't changed the world, then it's likely you currently wouldn't be utilizing the Internet for work or play.

THE OBJECTIVE OF OUR LESSON

In Lesson Four we introduced Warren Bennis's model of the leadership dimensions and discussed key elements of Managing Trust. With trust as our foundation, we're now ready to move ahead and study the Management of Attention. This lesson will concentrate on "Keeping Your Eye on the Ball." In other words, knowing what's truly important by identifying what your vision is and never losing sight of "it."

For sure, these are tall orders and ones not easily attained. However, without vision, you're hopelessly lost—adrift on a sea of uncertainty without a compass, a rudder, or a paddle.

CHAPTER 2 — ATTENTION, THE SECOND OF FOUR LEADERSHIP DIMENSIONS

Leaders ignite others to action by communicating a powerful vision of the future. They also "bind" themselves to their vision so that they come to represent the vision themselves; it appears almost inseparable from them. Such an impression helps convey commitment, tenacity, and belief in the rightness of their choice. Jim Barksdale was a charismatic leader who embodied all of these traits. Some have said that Netscape was a company founded with the undying energy of a brilliant and precocious staff who had no doubt they were transforming the world forever.

I worked as a consultant for a leading aerospace manufacturer for about five years. I happened to be meeting with a group of senior project managers when we embarked on a discussion of the early space program. I learned that several of them had been young engineers when President Kennedy announced in 1961 that we were going to the moon by the end of the decade. What I didn't realize, and they soon informed me, was that approximately 85% of the necessary technology didn't even exist at the time.

Just imagine that only 15% of what was needed to travel to the moon had been invented. We didn't even know what we didn't know. Yet, Kennedy's vision was so compelling that NASA made it a reality. On July 20, 1969, Neil Armstrong amazingly made history by stepping foot onto the surface of the moon.

Are visions powerful forces for change? What do you think? For instance, Netscape engineers envisioned changing the world through technology. AOL's vision is more aligned with changing the world through media. Their cultures clashed with one another. When this occurs, there's monumental emotional turmoil. Most company watchers believe that the acquisition of Netscape by AOL was an unmitigated disaster. For many of Netscape's pioneers, that may have been the reason most of them left.

VISIONING VERSUS VISIONARY

Many managers are in a real quandary when it comes to visioning. They think they're expected to be great visionaries like a Howard Hughes, Henry Ford, Walt Disney, Sam Walton (WalMart), Fred Smith (FedEx), or a John Kennedy. They say to themselves, "I've got a spouse, 2.5 kids, a mortgage, and too much credit card debt.

I'm an Engineering Manager; I'm not a Bill Gates." If you're feeling a little intimidated by limited visioning skills, it's entirely okay. The fact is the majority of technical managers feel the same way you do. So, ease up on yourself.

I don't expect you to single-handedly write a breathtaking Vision Statement. Yet, it's not uncommon for technical people to sell themselves short regarding their ability in this area. Let me share with you what I mean by this. Do you have a sense of what you'd like the future to be for your organization or your unit within the organization? Are you aware of some of the most significant emerging trends in your field? Can you guess the implications of some of these trends downstream? How could these repercussions affect your organization, your people, and maybe you, personally?

Some of these things are so visible you may take them for granted, without a whole lot of thought. Others run much deeper, requiring more probing and analysis. Conditions, tendencies, or patterns of this sort are like currents in a river. Felt, yet not easily seen.

Let's do a little experiment with something we're all familiar with to see how this might work. What can you predict about the future of television? What will it probably look like, what features might it have, how will we likely use it, and what could you expect regarding costs? Project this approximately five years out into the future. What did you come up with?

Here's how I view it: TV's will become flatter, bigger, more interactive. HDTV, movies on demand, and home theaters will be widespread, satellite reception will be commonplace, and costs will decrease. Did you think of some features that I didn't suggest? Was this TV scenario so difficult to forecast? Of course, there will assuredly be other variables impacting television that cannot possibly be foreseen today. That's just the way it is.

Since you're on a roll, if you're game, let's try another. What can you predict about automobiles over the next five years? Just off the top of my head, I would predict there will be more combustion/electric hybrids, mastery of fuel cell technology, and increased utilization of plastics and lighter materials. In addition, there will be smaller "city cars," some "Smart Roads" for trouble-free driving, and some brands like Oldsmobile, Buick, Mercury, Daewoo, Mitsubishi, etc., will disappear. What did you come up with?

A SENSE OF PURPOSE

Sometimes these "guessing games" can be fun. It doesn't have to be a management or leadership drudgery to draft a Vision Statement. Basically, it's kicked off with some of the things we're doing right here. When groups are starting out to create their vision, they typically ask *why* it's important—although they already know it is. They've seen many examples of how visions mobilize people to action. But what does a vision actually do?

Visions provide a sense of purpose for members of an organization. It spells out the desired destiny for a group, company, or organization. Have you ever heard of someone retiring after a fulfilling, successful, life-long career and then dying within the first year? Ever wondered what happened to them? Chances are they lost their sense of purpose and reason for living. That's how powerful a sense of purpose is. It transcends the individual and becomes bigger than we are. It creates a positive energy of its own that begins to permeate all the actions of those who embrace it.

CHAPTER 3 — GETTING STARTED WITH YOUR VISION

As we launch into this topic, I'd like to briefly address one of the most common myths about leadership. In particular, I'd like to tackle the whole aura surrounding the nature of individual charisma. Earlier on, we examined some of the "self-talk" you might be having. Frequently, managers compare their personal traits or characteristics with famous business or political figures and they come away feeling apprehensive.

Part of this is the fault of writers, teachers, and the media. I am among the guilty parties and throw myself on the mercy of "the court." The reason we're jointly guilty is that many of the people we use as examples to make specific points are very charismatic.

They have presence, bearing, and are newsworthy in some respect. They could be historical persons or business leaders who you have read about. However, they also give the false impression that to be successful as a leader, you must have a charismatic personality.

Nothing could be further from the truth. In fact, in his newest book, Good To Great, Jim Collins explains what he terms Level 5 Leadership. Collins, co-authored the national best seller, Built To Last: Successful Habits of Visionary Companies. In his latest research, he initially investigated 1435 companies and found 11 that moved from being average to becoming great. These companies met very rigorous criteria Collins and his research team established to identify "greatness."

Collins states unequivocally that great companies can only come from Level 5 Leadership. What is Level 5 Leadership? Ironically it's not charismatic leadership as you might expect. The qualities of a Level 5 Leader are personal humility and an iron will. That doesn't mean that these leaders are stubborn or inflexible. Rather, it means they have firm convictions and an absolute belief in their vision.

Now, these leaders also have qualities of Levels 1-4, which we'll talk about in another lesson. Be assured, though, that none of those qualities has anything to do with charisma. If you think of yourself as more on the quiet side, then you're like Darwin Smith who turned Kimberly-Clark into the world's leading consumer paper products company. Under his stewardship, Kimberly-Clark stood head and shoulders above their competition, Proctor & Gamble and Scott paper. They outsold Proctor & Gamble and ultimately bought Scott Paper.

VISIONING PROCESS OPTIONS AND EXAMPLES OF STATEMENTS

The processes for developing visions vary depending upon the preferences of an organization's leadership. Sometimes the founder or CEO will solely craft the Vision Statement. Other times, the Senior Management Team may do this. Occasionally, the task is done in concert with all stakeholders within a unit or organization. The latter approach obviously takes much longer, but it's easier to gain buy-in from the very beginning.

No matter what course of action you pursue, rest assured that you don't have to go it alone. If you honestly assess your skills and deduce that this is not your most striking aptitude, then obviously you need to draw others into the process. Additionally, I'll help you by spotlighting a detailed goal-setting process you can follow in the next chapter.

Whatever you eventually come up with must make sense, be understandable, and be clarified into explicit employee actions. There are some dreadful pitfalls that you must avoid at all costs. Don't do what Disneyland Operations did a few years ago when their Vision Statement was unabashedly featured in the Orange County, California Register:

> "Enable our cast to deliver a premier world-class guest experience by providing actionable business, financial and scheduling solutions in a growth environment through truth-seeking analytics, A-Z processes that stick, and targeted training materials and communication."

Huh? Dana Parsons who wrote the regular newspaper column where this appeared, asked if this Vision Statement started off as a doodle on a cocktail napkin. What does it mean? Does it make any sense to you? Can anyone really understand it? For example, what are truth-seeking analytics? Is that an algorithm, lie detector, or perhaps Sodium Pentothal? The real truth is no one can really make heads or tails of this. We can only hope that the folks at Disneyland

Operations, a bona fide first-class outfit, changed this zany Vision Statement quickly.

Let's look at other examples of Vision Statements that do meet our three criteria. The first is from the Princeton Plasma Physics Lab: *"To create the innovations which will make fusion power a practical reality."* That's short and sweet, isn't it? It certainly makes sense. It's understandable and it can be translated into specific, individual actions.

Here's another vision sample from Ionics, a leading provider of purified water and purification equipment, *"Preservation and enhancement of our environment and quality of life is the ultimate legacy one generation can bequeath to future generations."* A little different from the one above, but, nonetheless, one that can affect the behavior of organizational members.

Advanced Technology Laboratories has this as their Vision Statement: *"To be a world-class resource of advanced computing technology, software development, software demonstration and field test, and software transition for our government and Lockheed Martin customers."*

Let's try one more, from the Air Force Research Laboratory, *"We defend America by unleashing the power of innovative aerospace technology."* So there you have a number of different examples from various high technology, public and private sector organizations. Many of these examples were brief, concise, and very focused. Vision Statements can be longer, but that doesn't mean they're any better. Furthermore, they should never be longer than three or four sentences. If they are, the meaning may get lost in the excessive wording.

In the next chapter, we'll provide a more detailed approach for you to follow in working this through your group of direct reports.

CHAPTER 4 — A PROCESS FOR DEVELOPING AND ALIGNING YOUR VISION

We've all seen the generic science fiction movie where a space colony is established on some far distant, barren planet. In most cases, these colonies experience a series of dreadful calamities that combine for an evening of stimulating mental escape and rousing entertainment. Suppose though, that you could actually set up a colony representing your company or unit in another star system. Who would you choose to personify the most important qualities or values of your group?

To put it another way, who among your people might represent a "genetic slice of your organization?" This question was similarly posed by Jim Collins, in an article in the <u>Healthcare Forum Journal</u> a number of years ago. Indeed, it's a very interesting thought that could yield many rare insights.

You might select a number of people from varying levels of your organization. Perhaps a top flight secretary, a senior engineer, a young, dynamic supervisor, a street-smart middle manager, a project scheduler, a unit liaison with Human Resources, etc. It doesn't matter who they are, but *what they are* by knowing your organization and being firmly committed to its core values and beliefs. This is <u>the key</u>, and a good starting point in revisiting your values and purpose as an organization.

As we launch into this discussion, I'd like to borrow on the work of both Gregory Bateson and Robert Dilts by applying their model of human behavior to organizations. They developed a model comparable to what I've depicted on the following page.

In their paradigm, the levels in the middle have an influence in both directions, but a change on a higher level will have greater impact on those below. Thus, a group's identity, *or their vision* of how they perceive themselves, will create more leverage for their future than anything else. The starting point, though, for developing a Vision Statement and aligning it with the organization should begin with the environment.

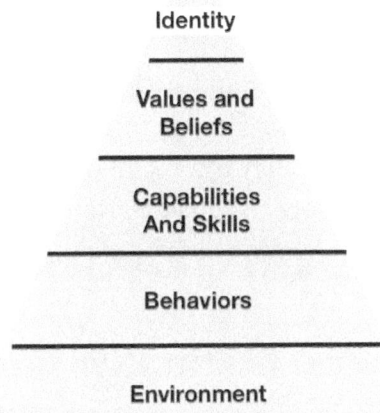

Once you have this exemplary group of perhaps 5-7 people, begin by considering what the future business environment might look like. What's likely to occur in your industry five years ahead? If you're part of a larger enterprise, consider how your organization might respond to that. What will your company likely do in that scenario and how could that affect your group? What would be the ideal outcome for your people?

Let your imagination run a little wild here. Even if your business is in a terrible downturn, remember that adversity can foster creative solutions. Masaru Ibuka wrote his famous nine page business philosophy in a bombed out building in central Tokyo in 1946. If you're wondering who Ibuka is, he started a company called Sony.

IDENTIFY FUTURE BEHAVIORS

Given the nature of what the environment will likely be, what kinds of behaviors will your organization require? Suppose you're managing a group of very independent research scientists exploring applications of the Human Gnome. The scientific and business environment will likely be fiercely competitive, global in scope, driven by profits, and involve strong egocentric personalities, etc. This will no doubt require effective synergies at every organizational level.

Consequently, internal competitiveness and rivalry will need to be replaced by collaboration and cooperation. Individualism will be subjugated by teamwork. The lone wolf will now have to travel with the pack. As you weigh the likelihood of certain conditions evolving, explicit behaviors will have to flourish, be reinforced, and be rewarded. How would you describe those behaviors? List them out in your group.

IDENTIFY FUTURE CAPABILITIES AND SKILLS

Once you know which behaviors are desired and mandated, what kinds of skills and capabilities will underlie them? If we piggyback on our example above, then some specific things do come to mind. For instance, collaboration and cooperation require some of the following talents and characteristics:

- Negotiation and conflict resolution skills
- Communication and listening skills
- Straightforwardness and a willingness to share
- Flexibility and open-mindedness
- Organization and follow-through
- Customer service (where one's colleagues become customers)

As you observe this list, it should occur to you that the skills—like negotiations—should be taught, coached, and evaluated. On the other hand, characteristics—like open-mindedness—ought to be evaluated during performance reviews and individual coaching sessions.

COMMIT TO CURRENT AND FUTURE VALUES AND BELIEFS

First off, it's essential to study the core values of the organization and recommit to them. If they were originally well conceived, they probably remain as valid now as they did in the past. Traditionally, these never change. However, you might still ask if you'll need some other values and beliefs in the future that transcend what you presently have? If you're inviting different behaviors, will any different values be necessary? If not, then that is wholly acceptable.

Let's examine how this works in one well-known company. 3M has always prided itself on the basic values of innovation, encouragement of persistence, and a tolerance for failure. They yearned for their people to have the capacity to "tinker," to explore ideas, and to pursue whatever esoteric concepts interested them. So, they backed that up with a behavioral philosophy called their "15 percent rule": employees have fifteen percent of their time to spend on whatever they want to innovate. It's all intricately linked together into a workable framework, from values to capabilities to behaviors.

DEFINING THE IDENTIFY OF YOUR GROUP OR ORGANIZATION

If your organization or group were dissolved right now, what services or products would immediately disappear? Without your organization what would be lost, perhaps forever? The answers to these questions helps explain why you exist. Now compare this with the changing environment, new behaviors, new capabilities and skills, and all your authentic values and beliefs. What will be the purpose and identity of your organization?

Push the envelope here, don't be boxed in by conventional thinking. Keep in mind, Sony had their philosophy <u>before</u> they had any of their successful products. As you reviewed your core values earlier, you may have been reluctant to change them, and they may never change. Sometimes core values are timeless. Yet strategies, improvements, and innovation never stops. It's relentless.

Your Vision Statement needs to embrace this identity: strong values and beliefs united with a push for exciting, future achievement. Don't get locked into "survival mode" or a survival mind set. Although it's clearly desirable, survival is not particularly inspiring to most people.

Let your group help you here. You may want to delegate some of this writing to people in the group who are better "wordsmiths" than you.

CHAPTER 5 — CONCLUSION

The passion expressed by Netscape's Jamie Zawinski at the beginning of this lesson can only be ignited through personal conviction. It can't be mandated, purchased, or induced by management policy. Such zeal is the result of a profound belief in something of a higher magnitude. Survival or its converse, making enormous profits, are not compelling enough to precipitate it.

Such is the power of a Vision Statement. Are Vision Statements altruistic and sometimes a bit fluffy? The Air Force Research Laboratory's vision, *"We defend America by unleashing the power of innovative aerospace technology"* may seem so on the surface. But I'll bet it has an overwhelming positive influence on the entire organization. If we glimpse at the results of the air war in Afghanistan, we can only conclude that the United States did in weeks what the entire Soviet military was unable to do in ten years of warfare. Certainly the Air Force contributed significantly to that overwhelming success.

A Vision Statement lets everyone know what the purpose is of the organization. It implies what are some of the core values and helps everyone to establish and focus on top priorities. It enables organizational leaders to keep their eye on the ball. Yet, in spite of all this, some leaders shrink from the task of defining a vision because they feel unqualified to do it.

In this lesson we shared a simple process to empower leaders to orchestrate the writing of a vision and concurrently align it with the organization or unit. This is an effort best done in concert with other stakeholders who are reliably committed to the organization and its central principles. The bottom line is that when it comes to drafting a Vision Statement, you need not go it alone.

LESSON FIVE ASSIGNMENT

Find two or three organizations that you regard highly. They might be companies you do business with as a consumer. Or perhaps your company uses one as a supplier, another is a customer, the third is a worthy competitor, etc. Once you have settled on these organizations, do the following:

1. Document their individual Vision Statements.
2. What core values and beliefs do they adhere to as an organization? Ask some of their people if it's not completely clear from their Vision Statement.
3. What capabilities and skills have you typically observed in their employee's behavior? How does this compare to their core values?
4. Ask their people if they are trained in those skills. Check on whether they are evaluated and held accountable for certain behaviors, characteristics, and knowledge.
5. What does the organization anticipate in their future business environment? What trends do they see? What challenges will they need to overcome? Does their Vision Statement effectively address their anticipated future environment? Do you see some potential problems for themselves several years down the road? Do they have some organizational "blind spots?"
6. What did you learn from this assignment about these organizations?

LESSON FIVE MULTIPLE-CHOICE QUIZ
(Answers on the Following Pages)

1. Many technical managers feel ill at ease when it comes to being visionary. Why is this so?

   A. It's not in their job description.
   B. They compare themselves with great visionaries in the media and come up short.
   C. They missed this course in their undergraduate work.
   D. They equate visioning with being a prognosticator like Nostradamus.

2. Charismatic leaders are essential to crafting and implementing an effective organizational Vision Statement. Do you agree or disagree?

   A. Agree. Without them there can be no passion.
   B. Agree. Only a charismatic leader has the credibility to get people to believe in the vision.
   C. Disagree. Leaders who practice nepotism fare much better.
   D. Disagree. Level 5 Leaders are not charismatic, but extremely effective.

3. A sense of purpose is so strong, people…

   A. Will actually die if they don't have one.
   B. Will say they have one even if they don't.
   C. Will avoid it at all costs because it's threatening.
   D. Will demand it in their benefit package.

4. Vision Statements are almost always written by the Chief Financial Officer. Is this correct?

A. No. They're written by the Board of Directors.
B. Yes, after Enron it's needed.
C. Yes, but together with their staff.
D. No, it's often written by or with others, like the CEO, organizational founder, or designated group.

5. An example of aligning your Vision Statement would be...

A. Adjusting the camber and toe.
B. Making sure all margins are even on the final printed copy.
C. Supporting the Vision Statement through training, coaching, and performance evaluation.
D. Straightening the framed Vision Statement on your office wall.

IRV GAMAL, M.A.

LESSON FIVE MULTIPLE-CHOICE QUIZ
(Answers)

1. Many technical managers feel ill at ease when it comes to being visionary. Why is this so?

    A. It's not in their job description.
    Incorrect.
    Perhaps that's so, but it's not the underlying reason.

    B. They compare themselves with great visionaries in the media and come up short.
    Correct.
    Unfair comparison, but, nonetheless, the correct one. Visioning is a process that can be learned.

    C. They missed this course in their undergraduate work.
    Incorrect.
    Interesting guess. I'll bet you know it's the wrong one.

    D. They equate visioning with being a prognosticator like Nostradamus.
    Incorrect.
    Who really knows about what they think of this historical demigod.

2. Charismatic leaders are essential to crafting and implementing an effective organizational Vision Statement. Do you agree or disagree?

    A. Agree. Without them there can be no passion.
    Incorrect.
    Charismatic leaders can add some zip, but if they don't build a strong organization, the best Vision Statement means nothing.

B. Agree. Only a charismatic leader has the credibility to get people to believe in the vision.
Incorrect.
Not so. Other leaders, who are not charismatic, are often more effective in getting people to believe in their visions.

C. Disagree. Leaders who practice nepotism fare much better.
Incorrect.
Their favorite movie might be "The Godfather," but family-oriented organizations often have as much difficulty with Vision Statements as anyone else. Sorry, nothing personal.

D. Disagree. Level 5 Leaders are not charismatic, but extremely effective.
Correct.
Non-charismatic Level 5 Leaders who have personal humility and an "iron will" take their companies from being good to being great.

3. A sense of purpose is so strong, people…

A. Will actually die if they don't have one.
Correct.
Many retired, successful people perish soon after they leave organizational life if they don't find another sense of purpose.

B. Will say they have one even if they don't.
Incorrect.
I suppose this could occur, but it's not the right answer.

C. Will avoid it at all costs because it's threatening.
Incorrect.
Are drawn to it rather than running away from it.

D. Will demand it in their benefit package.

Incorrect.

This could start a new trend. In the meantime, your answer is wrong.

4. Vision Statements are almost always written by the Chief Financial Officer. Is this correct?

   A. No. They're written by the Board of Directors.
   Incorrect.
   Most boards would be bored to do this.

   B. Yes, after Enron it's needed.
   Incorrect.
   A lot is needed after Enron. Unfortunately, this is not something in high demand by anyone, especially CFO's.

   C. Yes, but together with their staff.
   Incorrect.
   This could happen if the CFO was writing a Vision Statement for their financial group and not the entire organization.

   D. No, it's often written by or with others, like the CEO, organizational founder, or designated group.
   Correct.
   Much better and on target.

5. An example of aligning your Vision Statement would be...

   A. Adjusting the camber and toe.
   Incorrect.
   You may need to rotate your perceptions.

   B. Making sure all margins are even on the final printed copy.
   Incorrect.
   I'm afraid your answer is hard to justify!

C. Supporting the Vision Statement through training, coaching, and performance evaluation.
Correct.
This is part of aligning values and beliefs with capabilities and skills.

D. Straightening the framed Vision Statement on your office wall.
Incorrect.
There's almost nothing worse than asymmetrically framed documents on an office wall—except for, of course, a bad answer like this one.

LESSON FIVE FREQUENTLY ASKED QUESTIONS

Q: What's the secret to writing a good Vision Statement?

A: The best advice is don't try to tackle this alone. Get other people involved with you. As in our lesson, the participation of a small team of employees and members of management generally works well. Furthermore, keep the wording brief and make it understandable. If people are confused by it, their efforts will likewise be diffused and wasted. Vision Statements must be clear-cut and furnish a defined sense of purpose. If it's a bit altruistic, so be it. Don't worry about it. People like to hang their hats on causes, ideas, and principles that are much bigger than they are.

Q: What's the difference between a Mission Statement and a Vision Statement?

A: We haven't talked about missions, but they are anchored in the present and primarily proclaim the business an organization is in. Also, Mission Statements may reveal some pivotal elements of an organization's culture. That is, cherished values, behaviors, and practices. They are usually lengthier than a Vision Statement too.

LESSON 6

THE MEANING OF MEANING

CHAPTER 1 — INTRODUCTION

> *"I'm tired of dreaming. I'm into doing at the moment. It's, like, let's only have goals that we can go after."*
>
> —*Bono, U2*

Bono, megastar of the rock group U2 is out to change the world. Ironically, he's not a flash in the pan as many might suppose. He's a dedicated man with a vision of changing the plight of millions of poor, indigent people in Africa. He has translated his vision into tangible goals, and lobbies endlessly for them with political and religious leaders around the globe. Stay tuned because there <u>will likely be</u> further developments from Bono, a man the late John Kennedy might regard as a realistic idealist.

In our previous lesson, we talked about the power of vision and how it helps us to keep *our eye on the ball*. This is the second dimension, called "The Management of Attention," within Warren Bennis's model of leadership. In Lesson 3 we first introduced the Bennis model and emphasized the significance of building trust. We will continue this exploration and show how the other dimensions can readily apply to you as a leader.

Like any person with a passion, Bono understands that trust is foundational to building support for his long-term vision. He had to establish his credibility and overcome shortsighted perceptions of being just another rock star with a fleeting cause. Bono's insights, knowledge, and political giftedness enabled him to do this. Yet, visions don't become reality until they are translated into meaningful and practical goals.

THE OBJECTIVE OF OUR LESSON

The focal point in this lesson will be with the Management of Meaning. You're probably asking at this juncture, "Okay, what does that actually <u>mean</u>?" Good question. What it implies is what I stated above. It's so important, it's worth repeating: *intangible visions* must sooner or later be translated into *tangible goals*. Then—and only then—we can align people with salient actions, provide them with needed direction, and communicate in a compelling manner. All of this adds up to achieving results—the bottom line for leaders. This is exactly, in the final analysis, what Bono is seeking as well.

CHAPTER 2 — "PUTTING LEGS" ON YOUR DREAMS OR VISION

How many times have you dreamed about that great vacation to Europe, or maybe hitting it big in the state lottery? Or perhaps buying that new sail boat and abandoning civilization for a year? Or maybe you'd rather climb that precarious mountain peak in the Alps, or possibly win that sought-after promotion?

Whatever, your dreams might be, they are indispensable because without them, life loses an important element of delight. Your zest for living rapidly flies out the window. In fact, one big difference between people who are "young-at-heart" and others who are considered "over the hill," is the loss of their dreams.

Suppose, for example, we drew a linear continuum with these two polar descriptors ("young-at-heart" vs "over the hill") placed at opposite ends. Guess where leaders without a vision would fall? Where would you position yourself?

Unfortunately many people go through life unclear about what they want, but knowing pretty much what they have isn't it. You see, your dreams act as a sort of vision of what the future could realistically become. However, one of the big stumbling blocks is figuring out what it is you really want. Many people don't take the time to refine their vision and probably spend more time thinking about their weekend than planning out their life.

John Goddard wasn't one of them. When he was fifteen years old, he wrote out 127 goals he wanted to accomplish before he died. The year was 1940. By 1972, when he was 47, he had achieved 103 of his original quests, as reported in a Life magazine article entitled, "One Man's Life of No Regrets." The article quickly became one of the most requested reprints in the celebrated history of the magazine. Below are listed some of the goals Goddard wrote on his yellow pad of paper.

Sail the Following Rivers
- The Nile River
- The Amazon River
- The Congo River
- The Colorado River

Study Primitive Cultures in:
- The Congo
- New Guinea
- Brazil
- Borneo
- The Sudan
- Australia

Climb:
- Mt. Everest
- Mt. Aconagua, Argentina
- Mt. McKinley
- Mt. Huascaran, Peru
- Mt. Kilamanjaro

Photograph:
- Iguacu Falls, Brazil
- Victoria Falls, Rhodesia
- Sutherland Falls, New Zealand
- Yosemite Falls
- Niagara Falls
- Retrace the travels of Marco Polo and Alexander the Great

Explore Underwater:
- The Coral Reefs of Florida
- The Great Barrier Reef of Australia
- The Red Sea
- The Fiji Islands
- The Bahamas

Visit:
- The North and South Poles
- The Great Wall of China
- Panama and Suez Canals
- Easter Island
- The Galapagos Islands
- Vatican City
- The Taj Mahal
- The Eiffel Tower
- The Tower of London

Swim in:
- Lake Victoria
- Lake Superior
- Lake Tanganyika

Miscellaneous:
- Become an Eagle Scout
- Dive in a submarine
- Land on and take off on an aircraft carrier
- Play the flute and the violin
- Follow the John Muir Trail

MAKING THINGS HAPPEN

I've listed a meager 43 of the original 127 goals Goddard had. What do you think about these mighty aspirations? Goddard told the Life reporter who interviewed him that, "...all the adults I knew seemed to complain, 'Oh, if only I'd done this or that when I was younger.' They had let life slip by them. I was sure that if I planned for it, I could have a life of excitement and fun and knowledge."

John Goddard achieved his vision of becoming a world-renowned adventurer, explorer, author, and lecturer. His achievements are truly remarkable and no doubt are inspiring. Nonetheless, they were not accidental; they were dreams or visions to begin with which led to goals, then actions, and finally the experiences themselves.

So what's all this have to do with leaders like yourself and your vision? We've already spent an ample amount of time talking about Vision Statements and their impact on people. We know that leaders who have difficulty crafting a vision can work with their direct reports to develop one. But, where do you go from there?

Simply put, you need to put "legs" on your dreams or visions. Someone once said a dream without a plan is just a wish! So, in order to make them happen you must draft individual goals. Like Yogi Berra said, "When you come to a fork in the road, take it!"

CHAPTER 3 — WRITING S.M.A.R.T. GOALS

Goals should be written so that they are S.M.A.R.T. This is an acronym which stands for the following characteristics or criteria:

- **S**pecific
- **M**easurable
- **A**ction-oriented
- **R**ealistic and attainable
- **T**ime bound

Specific means that your goal is detailed enough to be focused and understood by others. For example, "increase productivity" is vague and too general. However, "increase the lines of code written per hour" is right to the point.

Measurable goals are *quantified*. A standard of comparison is provided for determining how successful you have been in achieving the goal. Thus, your earlier goal becomes "increase the lines of code written per hour by 15%." The 15% is the addition of a *measurement or metric* that becomes the "yardstick" for assessing this accomplishment.

Action-oriented means that the goal indicates an activity, a performance, an operation, or something that leads to output or results. It tells you what will be done to reach the goal. The word, "increase," tells you that your people must write more code than what they did before.

It must also be *realistic or attainable,* which means that if your goal is so outlandish, your direct reports will lose their will to even attempt it. If you said they would write 80% more code per hour, this might seem unreasonable and inconceivable. So why even be motivated to begin?

The other side of the coin is also true. That is, if a goal offers too little challenge, then the level of motivation is generally low from the get-go. For example, if you wanted to increase the number of lines written by only 5%, this might be so easy to attain, that your programmers would be unwilling to go for it.

For instance, take a look at the model below.

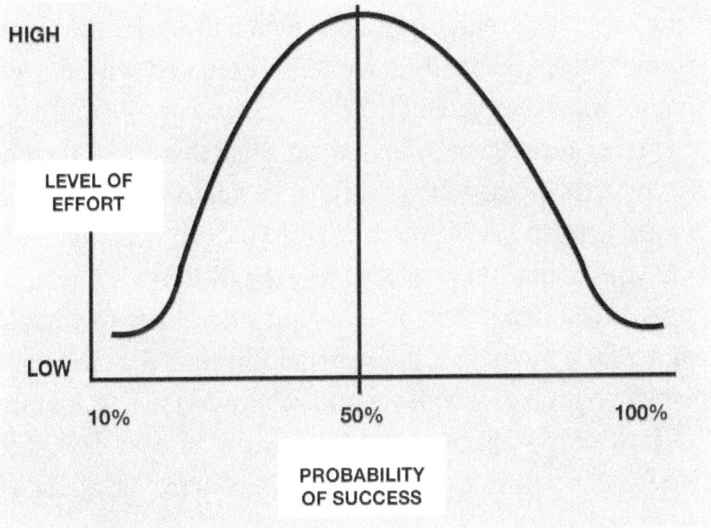

The highest levels of personal effort or motivation tend to occur when people perceive their probability of success as being about 50/50. Interestingly enough, if the prospect of success is viewed as either too low or too high, effort is slight. Too often leaders foolishly believe that their people are truly committed to pursuing the "low hanging fruit." Research indicates that this isn't the case. The best thing leaders can do is to present challenges that are *framed* somewhere at the fifty percent level of success.

GOALS ON STEROIDS

On the other hand, some leaders have urged the adoption of huge organizational "stretch goals." These are goals that demand monumental levels of achievement from everyone. Because of the unceasing intensity, there is no time whatsoever to catch your breath. I judge these to be *goals on steroids*. They often create havoc within an organization and activate negative repercussions for years to come.

Some of you might say that I'm now talking out of both sides of my mouth. Wasn't John Goddard's original 127 goals stretch goals?

You're raising a fair objection. You're also paying attention and I appreciate that. Goddard's goals were immensely challenging; no one will dispute that. But remember, he had an entire lifetime to achieve them. Stretch goals normally have to be executed within a year or two. That's a big difference in time.

The final criteria, *Time bound,* means that there is some schedule regulated by a time when the goal must be achieved. Deadlines help to give a priority to people's actions. If you can accomplish a goal whenever you would like, it's easy to put off doing it forever. Time constraints encourage people to move their activities to completion.

Imagine for a moment if the Internal Revenue Service stipulated that you pay your taxes whenever you get around to it, rather than by April 15 (or the appropriate calendar day of the year closest to that date). How many people would comply? Of course, you already know the answer to that!

CHAPTER 4 — REFINING YOUR GOALS AND ALIGNING YOUR ACTIONS

Whenever you are thinking about implementing something new, you must plan for it. Goals are the vehicles that first help you and your direct reports to move forward. We've seen the importance of being goal oriented. Moreover, we've examined the S.M.A.R.T. Goal criteria to help you write credible goals. Now, let's springboard ahead by refining your understanding of goals and aligning your actions. These steps will make all of your future planning *much clearer and easier.* Guaranteed!

Once you define the metric within your goal, the question you must ask is what is the <u>least</u> amount of that measurement that would constitute success. For example, if your goal is to increase the lines of code written by 15%, would 12% still be legitimate? What about 11% or 10%? You might reply that 11% would be okay, but anything less would not be sufficient.

MINIMUMS AND MAXIMUMS

Thus, the 11% represents what we call the Minimum Standard of Performance (MSP), the lowest limit of what you're willing to accept as a benchmark of your success. It's the least amount of your goal you will tolerate and genuinely consider yourself to be successful. *(Note: it may in some cases be the same as the goal, but not necessarily so).*

Next, we should heed the uppermost limits of performance or what is called the Maximum Allowable Performance (MAP). This number portrays a determination of how much of your goal you could achieve before it starts causing you problems. Sometimes, there is no upper limit, yet often there is.

However, you need to test the water and weigh whether this is indeed the case. For instance, consider what happens when the airlines overbook a flight. They have to entice volunteers to give up their seats. If they can't get enough people to do this, they either have to increase the "ante," or bump people from the flight. Sometimes flights get delayed while they are doing this and the end result is a lot of very unhappy travelers.

To return to our original example, speculate about what percent increase in the development of lines of code might start causing you potential problems. If you increased written code by 30-40%, what could happen? Perhaps you foresee the deterioration of quality or excessive overtime payroll hours. Whatever the case might be, the organization will suffer some costly pain.

At what level would such pain become intolerable? Suppose you settled on 25%. This would then be the Maximum Allowable Performance. Now our range of success is a gradient from the MSP of 11% to the target metric of 15% to the upper limits of 25%. Anything from 11% to 25% will be considered a successful and welcomed effort.

CONSTRAINTS AND RESTRAINTS

The subsequent activity is to identify constraints and restraints that might keep you from reaching your goal. Constraints are blockages that you cannot change, such as government regulations, competition, minimum wage, interest rates, weather, etc. Even though you cannot change them, you need to know what they are so you can action plan with them in mind.

Restraints are blockages that can be changed, but they do take some effort on your part. Lack of enough budget, inadequate training, and poor interdepartmental communications are examples of restraints that some supervisors or managers occasionally have. You will need to know which restraints must be handled and which you can live with for your action planning to be successful.

Some leaders perceive every restraint as a constraint. They erroneously believe they have to live with them as they are. It's essentially an unquestioned assumption. Don't fall into this dreadful trap. Thoughtfully mull over all of your presumptions about your constraints and restraints, keeping the differences in mind.

At this point, it's time to gauge the status quo in relation to the goal. Of course, the goal is really what you want to focus on as you move ahead, yet you must recognize your point of departure—and that is your current situation.

Why is this so important? Because only then can you specify action steps you need to take to move from the status quo to your ultimate goal. Action steps are written as small goals along the way. An action step might be making a phone call, writing a letter, retrieving a file, reading an article, taking a class, etc. List out key action steps for each goal necessary for you to ultimately achieve your vision.

You'll also need to plan with any hurdles in mind. If your action planning currently feels awkward or uncoordinated, don't fret. Remember, learning is a process of study and practice to create new habits. The more you use these ideas, the better you'll become as a planner and the easier it will be for you to manage successful organizational implementation.

ALIGNING OTHERS TO YOUR PLAN

You can easily teach your direct reports these same steps so they can write out goals and action steps that support the group's vision. *When they are involved they are more committed.* Hopefully, you remember this key principle from previous lessons.

I have frequently asked my students if they know their boss's major goals. Seldom do more than 25-30% of them indicate they do. This is deplorable. How can direct reports ever support their boss's efforts when they're in the dark about what's critical? Simply put, they cannot. That's what's called *Mushroom Management*. That is, keeping people in the dark and hoping they'll grow. This is ideal for mushrooms, but not for people.

Therefore, communicating your vision, or the group's vision, and your most important goals is at the heart of your effectiveness. Moreover, you'll need to do this in a compelling manner. Sharing a vision and goals in  a monotone voice without any *spark* will fall on deaf ears. Many technical leaders I've worked with over the years have not been the best public speakers. They might be a bit shy, introverted, and uncomfortable in front of a group—even a small group of their own people. So, they avoid public speaking to everyone's detriment.

If this sounds a bit like yourself, what can you do about it? Well, there are choices available if you want to sharpen your presentation skills. You could ask for help from your HR Department. They may have some internal coaches available to work with you. You might attend some local college workshops. Or you could inquire about Toastmasters International which has working groups scattered throughout the world.

Toastmasters is recognized as one of the best in developing executive presentation skills. Check them out for yourself and determine if that is what's right for you. Then commit to attend for at least one year. That's what it takes to really develop some formidable skills sets in this vital area.

CHAPTER 5 — CONCLUSION

Goals help give meaning to and bring visions to life. They translate the intangible Vision Statement into tangible organizational reality. They enable leaders to attain results—the bottom line for why leadership is mandatory for organizational survival.

Goals enabled John Goddard to achieve a life of high adventure. In his adolescence, Goddard outlined 127 major goals he was determined to accomplish. By the time he was 47, he had already fulfilled over 80% of them. He eventually achieved 111 of 127 before his death at 88. By anyone's standards, this was truly remarkable. Nevertheless, the impressive focus that we obtain through a goal orientation is accessible to everyone.

Like anything else, there are certain rules that apply to correctly writing goals. We call this S.M.A.R.T. Goal Criteria. Goals need to be **S**pecific, **M**easurable, **A**ction-oriented, **R**ealistic and attainable, and **T**ime bound. Without living up to these touchstones, goals become limp statements of desired outcomes.

Refining a goal requires an assessment of the Minimum Standard of Performance (MSP) and the Maximum Allowable Performance (MAP). These are the lower and upper limits of what would be acceptable as a measure of success. Accordingly, achievement generally lies on a continuum or gradient rather than just a narrow point on a target.

Constraints are factors that cannot be changed, whereas restraints are elements that can be changed, but with some effort. Some leaders see all restraints as constraints. The converse might also be true, but to a much lower degree.

Many leaders do not share their most important goals with their direct reports. This is shortsighted and not even mediocre management, let alone leadership. Communicating visions and goals must be done in a manner that creates some excitement and buy-in. Leaders must believe in what they say and learn or sharpen skills that enable them to meet this central need.

LEADERSHIP SKILLS FOR MANAGING TECHNICAL PROFESSIONALS

LESSON SIX ASSIGNMENT

Write out three goals you will achieve in the next year. Each goal will target a different area of your life. They should address the following:

1. A professional goal: After you complete the next lesson (Lesson 7), craft a goal that will make you more effective in your professional life. This must be something that's within your control, focuses on either a strength or a weakness, and will increase your vitality as a leader.
2. A relational goal: This goal can be written immediately to improve a relationship somewhere in your life. Thus, it can be in your personal life or your professional life. You make the choice. However, it must be a significant relationship that will contribute to your overall quality of life.
3. A personal goal: Something that will increase the joy and meaningfulness of your personal life. Again, it must be something within your control. If you want to wait until you finish Lesson 7 to do this, that is entirely okay. At that point, you should have more information that could prove helpful.

Remember, goals should be written so that they are S.M.A.R.T. This is the acronym we spoke about earlier which stands for the following characteristics or criteria:

- **S**pecific
- **M**easurable
- **A**ction-oriented
- **R**ealistic and attainable
- **T**ime bound

When you have completed each of these goals, discuss them with key people depending on the goal. For instance, your boss or a confidante would be invaluable in providing feedback on the professional goal. Your spouse or a best friend could be a good sounding board on relational or personal goals.

Take stock and get a sense of how you did at the end of the year. What level of achievement was made? What did you change for the better? How did this goal make you a better person? How do you feel about what you did?

Has the quality of your life improved? Has anything become worse? What are your next steps?

LESSON SIX MULTIPLE-CHOICE QUIZ
(Answers on the Following Pages)

1. Who was John Goddard?

   A. A rocket scientist.
   B. A religious leader.
   C. A remarkably accomplished adventurer, driven to achieve difficult, esoteric goals.
   D. A well-known CEO in the theme park business.

2. Why is a dream or a vision without a plan just a wish?

   A. Because dreams or visions provide hope for the future.
   B. Plans rob us of the innocence of simple wishes and are not to be desired.
   C. Plans put "legs" on dreams and wishes and move them towards becoming reality.
   D. Plans are too structured, too businesslike and ruin the underlying spirit of dreams and visions.

3. What does the acronym, S.M.A.R.T., stand for?

   A. Structured, Maximum, Allowable, Results, and Tenacious.
   B. Specific, Measurable, Action-oriented, Realistic (or attainable), and Time-bound.
   C. It means that people who write goals are SMART. Period.
   D. Some Managers Are Really Tough.

4. Level of effort appears to have a lot to do with perceived probability of success. When is a person's motivation to achieve at the highest level?

A. People are optimally motivated to achieve when they see their chances at approximately 50/50.
B. When they go after the "low hanging fruit."
C. When they see their chances as one in ten.
D. When they are entrepreneurial and can do their "own thing."

5. How do constraints differ from restraints?

A. Restraints are factors that cannot be changed. Constraints can be.
B. Constraints are induced by managers above, while restraints come from the people below.
C. Constraints are factors that cannot be changed. Restraints can be with some effort (sometimes lots of effort).
D. Constraints are issues that arise from the government, while restraints emanate from the business community.

LEADERSHIP SKILLS FOR MANAGING TECHNICAL PROFESSIONALS

LESSON SIX MULTIPLE-CHOICE QUIZ
(Answers)

1. Who was John Goddard?

    A. A rocket scientist.
    Incorrect.
    Nope, that was Robert.

    B. A religious leader.
    Incorrect.
    Although John Goddard had a religious zeal about achieving his goals, he wasn't a religious leader.

    C. A remarkably accomplished adventurer, driven to achieve difficult, esoteric goals.
    Correct.
    Bingo! You win the pretty stuffed animal.

    D. A well known CEO in the theme park business.
    Incorrect.
    Though, if Goddard ever had his own theme park it would likely be a very interesting place.

2. Why is a dream or a vision without a plan just a wish?

    A. Because dreams or visions provide hope for the future.
    Incorrect.
    This may be true to a point, but it misses the main gist of the question.

    B. Plans rob us of the innocence of simple wishes and are not to be desired.
    Incorrect.

On the contrary, plans can help our wishes come true.

C. Plans put "legs" on dreams and wishes and move them towards becoming reality.
Correct.
Plans provide the infrastructure necessary to achieve a dream or vision.

D. Plans are too structured, too businesslike and ruin the underlying spirit of dreams and visions.
Incorrect.
Certainly plans need to be structured. That's what turns intangibles dreams into tangible reality.

3. What does the acronym, S.M.A.R.T., stand for?

A. Structured, Maximum, Allowable, Results, and Tenacious.
Incorrect.
Come on now, I know you're SMARTer than that!

B. Specific, Measurable, Action-oriented, Realistic (or attainable), and Time-bound.
Correct.
Exactly right!

C. It means that people who write goals are SMART. Period.
Incorrect
People may be smart to do it, but that's not what it stands for.

D. Some Managers Are Really Tough.
Incorrect.
Some truly are. However, it seems, in this case, the question was tougher.

4. Level of effort appears to have a lot to do with perceived probability of success. When is a person's motivation to achieve at the highest level?

   A. People are optimally motivated to achieve when they see their chances at approximately 50/50.
      Correct.
      This perception allows a fair, yet formidable personal challenge.

   B. When they go after the "low hanging fruit."
      Incorrect.
      Low hanging fruit provides little challenge to even try. Move to the back of the orchard!

   C. When they see their chances as one in ten.
      Incorrect.
      Sorry, this usually is demotivating. They see defeat as almost predestined.

   D. When they are entrepreneurial and can do their "own thing."
      Incorrect.
      Entrepreneurs are often highly motivated people. However, they too are affected by the model in question as are others.

5. How do constraints differ from restraints?

   A. Restraints are factors that cannot be changed. Constraints can be.
      Incorrect.
      You may have been reading with a mirror.

   B. Constraints are induced by managers above, while restraints come from the people below.
      Incorrect.
      Please step to the back of the line.

C. Constraints are factors that cannot be changed. Restraints can be with some effort (sometimes lots of effort).
Correct.
Good show. This is the right answer.

D. Constraints are issues that arise from the government, while restraints emanate from the business community.
Incorrect.
No, this just won't do. Go back and read page 120.

FREQUENTLY ASKED QUESTIONS

Q: Why are some people so good at setting and achieving goals while others appear to miss the boat?

A: Setting a goal for some people is like making a New Year's resolution. Their initial motivation is good, but then it seems to fall apart. The underlying reason is that for anyone to be motivated to achieve a goal there are three factors required: (1) presence of the need to achieve; (2) frequency of the need; and (3) strength of the need.

Most people who set out in vain to accomplish a particular goal have the presence, perhaps some reoccurring frequency, but the strength of the need is highly suspect.

Q: How can I become more goal-oriented?

A: There is no magic wand that you can wave to make this happen. Yet, if you realize that people who are goal-oriented achieve more than those who are not, you have taken a step in the right direction. Next, there are some simple tactics that might help.

If possible, keep a picture of your goal where you can readily see it. A friend of mine wanted a sail boat for many years. He taped a picture of his desired boat to the front of his refrigerator. The constant reminder kept him motivated to save his money and eventually he bought the boat.

Set up milestones along the way. This records your progress and cues you that you're getting there, even if completion is a long way off. Share your goal with others so they can support your efforts, especially when things are bogged down. Expect that there will be some problems, surprises, and setbacks. This is just the way it is. Rarely does anything move without some type of friction.

LESSON 7

TAKING STOCK OF YOU

CHAPTER 1 — INTRODUCTION

> *"We can be knowledgeable with other men's knowledge, but we cannot be wise with other men's wisdom."*
> —*Michel de Montaigne (1533-1592)*

In former lessons we discussed three of the four dimensions of Bennis's Model of Leadership. These were: (1) The Management of Trust; (2) The Management of Attention; and (3) The Management of Meaning. The stage is now set for us to tackle one of the most absorbing challenges you'll ever encounter—the Management of Yourself.

However, you might suggest that this is not a big matter. After all, you've been living with yourself for as long as you can remember. This often is precisely the problem. We may be so close to *the action* we cannot be objective in our assessment of ourselves. We may have a sense of who we are that's way off base.

For example, a client of mine once asked me to do a search for an Operations Manager in a medical device manufacturing company. I was interviewing a potential candidate and I asked him how other people misinterpreted his personality. He replied that frequently other people saw him as cold and aloof. But, he quickly added, he was really warm and caring. What do you think about his answer? What does it tell you about him?

Eleanor Roosevelt once said, "I think somehow, we learn who we really are and then live with that decision." The implications of her statement are wide ranging. Unfortunately, not everyone is introspective enough to know themselves. Those who do may understand who they are, but might never honestly accept themselves. The ideal outcome is for a person to know and willingly accept who they are. Then they can chart development activities that build on their strengths and shore up any weaknesses identified.

Which category do you suppose our Operations Manager candidate above fell into? Did you think he was unaware of the impact he had on other people? If you did, you were right. He was a man who was cold and distant. That was the way people experienced him, not as warm and "fuzzy." Obviously, he didn't get the job. Leaders must be in touch with who they are and how they affect other people.

THE OBJECTIVE OF OUR LESSON

I believe wisdom comes from experience tempered by personal reflection, which then hopefully leads to in-depth understanding. The genesis of wisdom arises from a keen acknowledgment of who you really are and the impact you have on others. If you have not reached this point in your own evolution, then this is an area you'll want to continue to work on.

Our objective in this lesson is to provide you with the tools to assess some of your strengths and weaknesses and begin to plan for your further development. We'll also give you a chance to look at your current job and determine any changes required for your continued growth.

CHAPTER 2 — SKILLS SETS REQUIRED AT DIFFERENT MANAGEMENT LEVELS

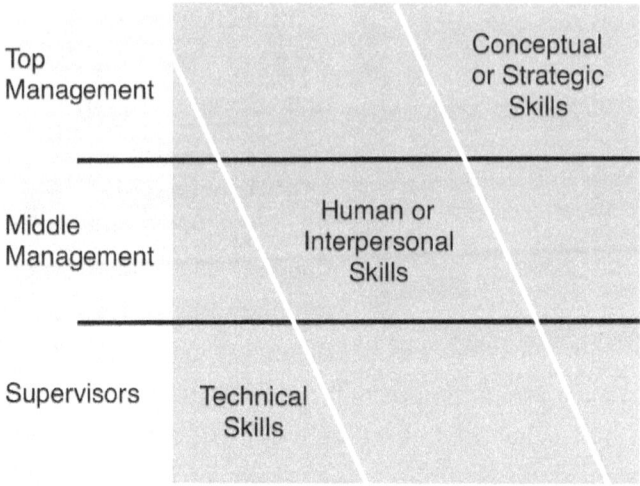

First off, let's take a look at the three major skill sets needed at various levels of an organization. There are really only three legitimate levels of management, although organizations may have far more *layers of management.* This is because organizations sometimes have multiple layers within one level. For example, at the middle management level there might be unit managers, project managers, regional managers, functional directors, etc. At the supervisor level, there could be supervisors, team leaders, leads, foreman, etc.

You'll notice that the three primary skill sets required are technical skills, human or interpersonal skills (sometimes called "Emotional Intelligence"), and conceptual or strategic skills. Technical skills are mandatory at the supervisory level because supervisors are training people, troubleshooting problems, evaluating performance, and sometimes filling in as individual contributors. Without technical know-how, supervisors couldn't do their job or have any kind of credibility with their direct reports—or peers.

When senior managers above want technical information or assistance, they lean heavily on supervisors. So, the higher you move in the management hierarchy, the more you <u>must</u> become a generalist instead of a specialist. Your view must broaden across functional silos so that you're more of a strategist in your thinking and actions.

As a matter of fact, top management should spend no less than thirty percent of their time on strategic issues. This translates into becoming more sensitive to emerging trends, designing forecasts and scenarios, and helping to position the organization for the future. Such ability is absolutely indispensable in the high tech arena. You don't need to be a member of Mensa to foresee what lies ahead for an organization that's eternally blindsided by their competition. If this is the case for your organization, you likely have square pegs in round holes.

A recent trend among chief executives is their desire for managers at all levels to become more strategic in their outlook. Thus, supervisors, who traditionally were almost exclusively tactical, now have to consider longer-term concerns. Middle managers are discovering that instead of crafting one year operating plans, they are expected to prepare two year "road maps."

DERAILING FACTORS

As you look at the model above, what do you notice about the human or interpersonal skill set? There are several things that should immediately stand out. Initially, the skills are a constant no matter what the level of management. Furthermore, this skill set represents the largest of all three needs for managers.

Human or interpersonal skills encompass a number of activities, such as building trust, listening to others, showing you care, resolving conflicts, communicating openly, dispensing kudos, etc. It boils down to the knack of getting along with other people. Research done at both the Center For Creative Leadership and Harvard's Graduate School of Business concluded that most managers who fail do so because they can't get along with other people. The biggest offense within this category was outright arrogance.

This specific behavior will undermine your relationships faster than you can utter, "I am in love with myself!" A similar *perceived attitude* didn't work for Marie Antoinette over two hundred years ago either. At the beginning of the French Revolution she was told that the people had no bread to eat. According to Jean Jacques Rousseau, in his book <u>Confessions</u>, she infamously retorted, "Let them eat cake." She was promptly sent to the guillotine on October 16, 1793.

Incidentally, as an epilogue to this story, Marie Antoinette may not have been what she appeared to be. Many modern historians characterize her actually as more gentle, caring, and thoughtful, if not a bit excessive in her spending habits. However, the perception of the masses was that she was arrogant and spiteful. Unfortunately, she paid the ultimate price for those public <u>misperceptions</u>.

In Lesson 4, I first mentioned derailment. I explained it as being passed over for promotion and finding yourself plateaued, or being demoted, or possibly even terminated. Plainly, none of these three options work in your favor. Yet, derailment can act as an impetus for positive behavioral change when it's treated in a mature, constructive manner. Even so, much of the outcome still hinges off of the attitude of the individual involved.

Over the years, I've coached many managers who were in serious jeopardy of derailment. The primary factor that determined whether the outcome was successful or unsuccessful was the manager's strong desire for change. When they didn't seem to care, or discounted the seriousness of the situation, or didn't grasp the magnitude of how their behavior affected others, failure was imminent.

Any way you slice it, *derailment is a career altering experience.* Those managers who learn from it what's critical can change for the better. Those who don't learn what they need to do will usually wash out of the organization. It may take some time for this to occur, but it will happen sooner or later.

How do you measure up in each of these three skill-set areas? Which one is your strongest skill set? How do you know that's true? How do your strengths in these three areas correlate with your immediate job challenges? Where do you need extra help or development?

CHAPTER 3 — ENHANCING YOUR SELF-KNOWLEDGE

In another of his classic books, <u>On Becoming A Leader</u>, Warren Bennis discusses four aspects of self-knowledge. These are: (1) Listening to your inner self; (2) Accepting responsibility for what you are; (3) Learning at a deeper level; and (4) Reflecting on your experience. I would like to examine each of these in some detail, but I will partially depart from Bennis's path. I believe that deeper learning can only triumph through personal reflection. Accordingly, I will combine these two aspects of self-knowledge into one that reflects that personal conviction.

LISTENING TO YOUR INNER SELF

I recall an experience I had a number of years ago when I went to a local mall to purchase a new suit—before corporate casual became the standard for dress. I tried on a suit that I felt didn't bring out my best photogenic qualities. Nonetheless, the salesman was so slick he convinced me that this suit made me look like Sean Connery. Since I happened to be a big fan of James Bond, it was a done deal. All that was missing was the Aston-Martin.

When I picked up the altered suit a week later, I instantly knew I had made a terrible mistake. To this day, I never liked the suit and rarely wore it. I finally donated it to the local thrift store. Nonetheless, to his everlasting credit, I still greatly admire Sean Connery. The moral of the story is listen carefully to your inner self. I never made that mistake again.

We've all been there and often act against our better judgment to our later regret and dismay. This intuitive inner voice is saying important things to you. Ordinarily we disregard it because it may not be empirically defensible. Yet we know that the most effective leaders follow their instincts as much as they rely on factual data. Our intuitive senses pick up subtle cues, nuances, and subtleties from many different places and synthesize them into an integrated view. *Paying attention to your "gut level feelings" is a very wise thing to do.*

ACCEPTING RESPONSIBILITY FOR WHAT YOU ARE

About twenty years ago I founded my first consulting company with two partners. Both of them were a bit older and more experienced than I was. The company was successful and profitable from the very start. Nevertheless, I couldn't help feeling that I needed additional corporate experience in two key areas: (1) International consulting assignments and (2) Growing a large staff of professionals.

This inner need haunted me until I finally decided to act on it. A job offer subsequently came along which presented international opportunities with a top Fortune 500 Engineering company. I mulled over the invitation for a few days and then accepted it. My partners bought out my position in the company and I moved back into a bustling corporate environment.

Three years later, I accepted another position with a dominant "player" on a fast growth track in the Real Estate Industry. I grew a national staff from 22 to 50 training professionals (and 350 support staff) over a four-year period. Once I knew that I had obtained the experience I wanted, I ventured forth again and founded another company in 1987. I still have that organization today.

So what's this all add up to for you? *Be true to yourself.* As Socrates said, "The only good is knowledge and the only evil is ignorance." Know what you are and what you need to be better. Don't blame others for your shortcomings—accept them. If you have a weakness (we all do), make a positive change. That is, learn something you didn't know before; or gain compulsory experience; or practice crucial coping mechanisms so you can handle your weakness better.

To do this, you'll need feedback from others—from mentors, coaches, and people who act as sounding boards for you. Also, don't forget that some of the most vital feedback comes from 360 degree assessment. These are ratings by people at all organizational levels. That would include your boss, you—your opinion does count—your peers, your direct reports, and possibly outside vendors, suppliers, strategic partners, or customers. This venue is much more comprehensive and accurate than the typical boss-generated performance appraisal. The boss is lucky to see 10% of what you do.

Still, never snub what the boss writes on your performance appraisal. You may not agree with it, but it has serious implications for you. Failure to take to heart what the boss says can ultimately lead to your derailment.

LEARNING AT A DEEPER LEVEL THROUGH PERSONAL REFLECTION

In his book, <u>The Power of Now</u>, Eckhart Tolle talks about how regularly people on their deathbed come to realize what's truly important in their life. He points out that seldom do they wish they had spent more time in the office. This reorganization of their priorities is the onset of personal wisdom, yet it arrives too late. They pass away before they can put this self-knowledge to use.

How pitiful such an outcome is. Wouldn't it be wonderful to have the realization and to live using it, instead of relinquishing it in death? Tolle says that it is possible, but not easy. Only by doing a lot of thoughtful soul-searching, reflecting at a much deeper level of meaning, and acting on what you believe to be *the truth* can you gain in this indispensable phase of self-knowledge.

For example, I have found that far too many managers have lost any semblance of life balance. They ordinarily work an extraordinary amount of hours, are joined to the office with every wireless communication device

available, and travel incessantly. They are pressured, stressed, and jet-lagged. How effective can anyone be when *their batteries* have literally run dry? The truth is not very effective at all, but they likely do not see it at the time.

As Bennis points out, learning at a deeper level transcends absorbing information or mastering your job. It's what led Toyota to move their Lexus design team to California in 1985 rather than design the car in Japan. They believed the California lifestyle would influence the car's design resulting in freer flowing lines. How clever they were to understand this. Yet, this created its own set of problems—as is often the case.

No auto manufacturer then, including Toyota, knew how to bend steel to create the smooth, rounded angles proposed for the Lexus. Toyota had to learn revolutionary manufacturing techniques to make their prized design come to life. And, indeed they learned their lesson well. Okay, what's the message here? *Look beyond what you see, reflect on your own experiences, catch the big picture, and understand what's really important.*

CHAPTER 4 — ANALYZING YOUR JOB

For the majority of this lesson we've delved into the skills necessary at various levels of management. We continued an earlier discussion about derailing factors. We also highlighted three major aspects of enhancing your self-knowledge. Now, it's fitting to concentrate on the make-up of your present job. We'll examine it from the perspective of the kinds of tasks you generally perform and the related implications to your career. These are alluded to in the Task Grid below.

As you check out the Task Grid, you'll see that there are two continuums: (1) The horizontal axis is labeled "Delay Tolerance," and (2) The vertical axis is called, "Demand Probability." When Tolerance For Delay is low, your deadlines are very tight. When it's high, you have the freedom for changing the deadline.

THE TASK GRID

	LOW DELAY TOLERANCE	HIGH DELAY TOLERANCE
HIGH DEMAND PROBABILITY	ROUTINE (TASK TYPE I) Highly predictable in demand, absolute in requiring performance by a deadline.	PROJECT (TASK TYPE IV) The demand is predictable and usually the performer assists in determining it. The performance deadline is prearranged.
LOW DEMAND PROBABILITY	TRLOUBLESHOOTING (TASK TYPE II) Unpredictable in demand and the response must be immediate.	NEGOTIABLE (TASK TYPE III) Unpredictable in demand, but The performance deadline is negotiable.

Probability of Demand is a measure of how often something occurs. When it's high, it happens frequently. When it's low, it's intermittent or seldom happens.

Most jobs consist of a variety of tasks. Some of these tasks are routine, like running the payroll, or getting out mass mailings, or writing regular reports. Routine tasks occur repeatedly and have rigid deadlines. Other tasks are troubleshooting types, such as handling a customer's complaint or determining why an R&D team of scientists can't collaborate. These types of tasks have low Probability of Demand, but like routine tasks, their deadlines are firm.

Another kind of task is negotiable and these allow a tad more latitude. Dealing with a special request cost study or making a presentation to an internal management group would be a task of this type. They don't arise often and their deadlines are usually flexible. Finally, projects are the fourth type of task and they come in a large variety of shapes and sizes. Implementing a new data base system, updating a software training program, or developing a new marketing strategy for a disruptive technology are all examples of project-type tasks.

PROJECTS AND YOUR VISIBILITY

Projects perpetually turn up in the high-tech arena. Because their Probability of Demand is quite high, you might say it's almost a way of life in high tech organizations. Furthermore, the higher you advance in management, the more your work will become project-based. Rarely do you witness senior managers dallying with routine, tactical types of work. Although deadlines with projects are generally prearranged, there may be some room for adjustment.

As you examine your own job, how much of each type of task do you perform? Consider what percentage of your job is routine? Or troubleshooting? Or negotiables? Or projects? The rule of thumb is the more routine your job, the less visibility you will have in your organization. Why? Because you will be buried in minutiae on a daily basis. What you do will customarily be taken for granted until something goes radically wrong. Then, you can bet you'll be noticed, but for all the wrong reasons.

By the same token, the more you work on projects, the more you'll be seen by members of senior management. Why do you think this is? Because projects often have strategic value and directly contribute to the goals of top executives. Think about it and what it indicates for your career growth.

Let's transition for a moment to the work of Rensis Likert (1903-1981), the preeminent management theorist who invented the six-point Likert response scale for measuring attitudes. Likert also originated the concept of the "Linking Pin." This concept below exemplifies the fact that you're a member of two working groups — the one you directly supervise and the one that reports to your boss. By the way, "Direct Reports" in the model signifies *Direct Report— the person(s) who report directly to you.* I much prefer that moniker than subordinate, which has some negative connotations.

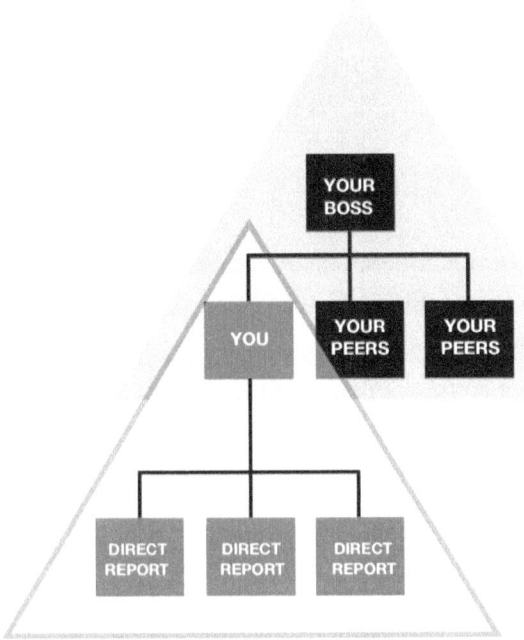

Likert pointed out that albeit managers belong to two distinct groups, they mainly think of themselves in only one—the group they supervise. Why is this the case? It's a result of the composition of their job. They're performing too much routine work, likely hanging on to a multitude of tasks they ought to delegate, and continually "bailing out" their direct reports. You might argue correctly that leaders need to take care of their followers. You're right in principle, but some leaders make their people dependent on them rather than help them grow towards independence.

They also do this at the expense of "looking up" for projects that exist at higher levels. When you free yourself from routine, you create opportunities for yourself. You're more likely to have time for important projects which help develop specific skills and simultaneously furnish greater visibility. This correlates with the likelihood of receiving added promotional considerations.

Therefore, look closely at your job and gauge (ball park if you must) the task percentages. What can you delegate? What projects can you volunteer for? What positions do you envision for yourself in the future? What skills will you need for these positions that you don't currently have? What actions do you need to take right now to gain exposure to those critical skills?

CHAPTER 5 — CONCLUSION

We have no doubt covered a substantial amount of ground in this lesson that should aid you with the Management of Self dimension. This also completes our commentary on the Leadership Competency Model of Warren Bennis first introduced in Lesson Four.

You should now have a better understanding of the major skill sets necessary at various management levels. Your heightened awareness of how derailing factors can get in the way of your success will hopefully help you avoid them. Arrogant behaviors undermine relationships faster than just about any other behavioral impropriety. Getting along with other people is essential if you're going to be an effective leader.

Gaining maximum self-awareness is a large part of your individual improvement. We discussed the value of intuitiveness, accepting responsibility for what you are, and learning at a deeper level. Wisdom only comes from reflecting on your experiences and seeing the bigger picture. Discerning what's really important and acting on it is putting this critical self-knowledge to work for you.

We also weighed the value of different types of tasks and their implications to your career development. Frequently, when managers are spending the bulk of their time on routine tasks they can short circuit their career. They are not a viable linking pin to higher management. Their focus is on what's below, i.e., on their own functional needs which may have limited strategic value to those above.

Superior visibility is an inherent part of project work. It's important to assess how your job is divided among the various task groups and decide what changes will be necessary to further your advancement.

LESSON SEVEN ASSIGNMENT

A large part of the Management of Self competency is being able to answer important questions about yourself, your career, and your future. Try to address each of these areas below as best you can.

Career Planning and Self-Assessment Questions

1. What are my strengths in my current position?
   a. _____
   b. _____
   c. _____

2. What are my developmental needs—weaknesses—in my current position? What are my biggest challenges and where are the crucial gaps in my skills?
   a. _____
   b. _____
   c. _____

3. What developmental activities would be most useful to me now?
   a. _____
   b. _____
   c. _____

4. What is my desired next job assignment?
   _____
   _____
   _____

5. What competencies will I need to build to be ready for this assignment?

   _____
   _____
   _____

6. What developmental activities would be most helpful to me in building these?

   _____
   _____
   _____

LESSON SEVEN MULTIPLE-CHOICE QUIZ
(Answers on the Following Pages)

1. What are the three major skill sets required at various management levels?

    A. Trust, caring, and listening.
    B. Technical Skills, Human or Interpersonal Skills, and Conceptual or Strategic Skills.
    C. Self-awareness, humility, and sensitivity.
    D. Technical Skills, Learning Skills, and Conceptual or Strategic Skills.

2. The prime factor in helping a manager recover from potential derailment is...

    A. The manager's strong desire for change.
    B. A transfer to another part of the organization.
    C. A heart-to-heart talk with their boss.
    D. A well deserved sabbatical.

3. Why do managers frequently disregard their own inner voice or intuitive instincts?

    A. Because they want a high tech approach to a high-tech challenge.
    B. They're too busy with the demands of the external world to pay attention.
    C. Many managers in high tech organizations don't have these so-called instincts to begin with.
    D. Because they're not empirically defensible.

4. Which type of task, according to our discussion of the Task Grid, gives you the most desired visibility and why?

A. Troubleshooting Tasks because they might precipitate an emergency situation.
B. Routine Tasks because when things go wrong, everyone is looking.
C. Project Tasks because they often have strategic benefit.
D. Negotiable Tasks because your adeptness in presenting your position may be noticed.

5. What is a Linking Pin?

A. A titanium pin used in major hip replacement surgery.
B. A manager who is primarily linked to his boss's group through strategically anchored project work.
C. A manager who especially looks to take care of the needs of his or her direct reports.
D. A manager who acts as a liaison between project teams.

LESSON SEVEN MULTIPLE-CHOICE QUIZ
(Answers)

1. What are the three major skill sets required at various management levels?

    A. Trust, caring, and listening.
    Incorrect.
    Unquestionably important, but not what I wanted to hear.

    B. Technical Skills, Human or Interpersonal Skills, and Conceptual or Strategic Skills.
    Correct.
    Yes, this is it!

    C. Self-awareness, humility, and sensitivity.
    Incorrect.
    All very important, but you're on the wrong page.

    D. Technical Skills, Learning Skills, and Conceptual or Strategic Skills.
    Incorrect.
    Close, but that's only good in horseshoes.

2. The prime factor in helping a manager recover from potential derailment is...

    A. The manager's strong desire for change.
    Correct.
    Good...I am very pleased with you. Did you feel that pat on your back?

    B. A transfer to another part of the organization.
    Incorrect.

This, unfortunately, happens too often. It only shifts the problem to someone else.

C. A heart-to-heart talk with their boss.
Incorrect.
Sounds nice, but I've seen these go nowhere without the answer I'm seeking.

D. A well deserved sabbatical.
Incorrect.
All it does is postpone the inevitable confronting of the problem.

3. Why do managers frequently disregard their own inner voice or intuitive instincts?

A. Because they want a high tech approach to a high-tech challenge.
Incorrect.
The underlying cognitive processes that we call intuitiveness may be very high-tech biologically.

B. They're too busy with the demands of the external world to pay attention.
Incorrect.
I'm sure there's an element of truth in there, but this isn't the central reason.

C. Many managers in high tech organizations don't have these so-called instincts to begin with.
Incorrect
Almost everyone has these instincts, some are simply more developed than others.

D. Because they're not empirically defensible.
Correct.
I had a *hunch* you'd get this right.

4. Which type of task, according to our discussion of the Task Grid, gives you the most desired visibility and why?

    A. Troubleshooting Tasks because they might precipitate an emergency situation.
    Incorrect.
    It could usher in an emergency situation, but that's usually the exception.

    B. Routine Tasks because when things go wrong, everyone is looking.
    Incorrect.
    This is not the kind of visibility you want, unless you're a masochist.

    C. Project Tasks because they often have strategic benefit.
    Correct.
    Absolutely, positively right.

    D. Negotiable Tasks because your adeptness in presenting your position may be noticed.
    Incorrect.
    You probably will be presenting your position to only your boss.

5. What is a Linking Pin?

    A. A titanium pin used in major hip replacement surgery.
    Incorrect.
    This is a very un-hip answer.

B. A manager who is primarily linked to his boss's group through strategically anchored project work.
Correct.
Good job! I've just promoted you to Lesson 8.

C. A manager who especially looks to take care of the needs of his or her direct reports.
Incorrect.
I regret to inform you…this is the antithesis of the Linking Pin.

D. A manager who acts as a liaison between project teams.
Incorrect.
No. Move back two spaces and do not pass "Go."

LESSON SEVEN FREQUENTLY ASKED QUESTIONS

Q: Can a manager who has very limited interpersonal skills succeed as a leader?

A: That's like asking, "Can an ostrich fly?" Sure, if they purchase an airline ticket! Interpersonal skills are <u>absolutely</u> essential for leadership effectiveness. Certainly someone can manage a function with no direct reports. But they still have to depend on others at their own level and above for their success. If they cannot get along with other people, they will not win any points with others and will not receive their cooperation.

Q: How can someone who is typically not introspective become more self-aware?

A: Unless they're the Evil Queen with the infamous Magic Mirror (from Snow White), better to query others. They should consider asking for ongoing feedback from people they work with. Seeking out a mentor, asking for coaching from their boss, and using peers as sounding boards all make good sense. Additionally, 360 degree feedback, which includes opinions from direct reports, is exceptionally valuable. Human resource professionals frequently have assessments and other tools that can augment this information.

Q: Why is arrogance so pernicious to a manager's effectiveness?

A: No one likes arrogance, especially people who have to live with it day in and day out. Arrogant behavior is like acid to others, it eats away at them. It's one of the deadly cardinal sins of leadership.

LESSON 8

WHAT THE YOUNG TECHNICAL PROFESSIONAL WANTS FROM THEIR BOSS

CHAPTER 1 — INTRODUCTION

> *"Today, promotions reward leadership ability and are mandates to serve the troops rather than be served. The manager who (it's practically unthinkable) would say, 'You have to do what I say because I'm the boss' rather than, 'How can I help you get the result?' is a dinosaur."*
>
> —Marilyn Moats Kennedy, Editor,
> Kennedy's Career Strategist

Even though I started my career over twenty-seven years ago, I've always been in many ways a Gen Xer at heart. I suppose that's one of the reasons I enjoy working with managers and leaders in helping them see things from a different, more effective perspective. Marilyn Moats Kennedy reinforces my view above. Dinosaurs may have been powerful in their own day, but the working environment today is not Jurassic Park, and their time has passed.

Hewlett-Packard discovered many years ago what the most significant factors were in distinguishing their best project managers from mediocre ones. It was their ability to motivate, coach, support, and lead their team members. As a consequence, they structured training programs to help their managers improve in these salient areas. *(See Lesson 4, Chapter 4).*

Technical professionals spend an enormous amount of time mastering their chosen field. They have a specialized knowledge base that adds exceptional value to an organization. They certainly cannot be considered or treated as a liability. Knowledge workers, especially, are prominent assets who are not easily replaced.

Most importantly, technical professionals have a tendency to identify far more with their field than they do with their company. If you ask an ordinary professional what they do for a living, they'll typically tell you, "I'm an electrical engineer," or "I'm a molecular biologist." They won't say, as you would likely hear from someone who is not highly educated, "I work at General Motors."

Thus, technical professionals are a "special breed" with different needs. Leaders who don't understand this are bound to make terrible mistakes that will be costly to both themselves and their organizations. As we plunge into the new millennium, greater numbers of managers will find themselves supervising bright, highly educated technical professionals from around the globe. They will need a battery of skills giving them the wherewithal to respond properly in achieving important goals.

THE OBJECTIVE OF OUR LESSON

Therefore, the objective of this lesson will be to focus on the special needs of technical professionals and what might underlie some of these idiosyncrasies. We'll couple this with how managers will need to lead this diverse group of younger people now and in the years ahead. This vital discussion should add depth to your repertoire of these skills. Future lessons will probe even further into some of the most essential capabilities you'll want to sharpen as you become the kind of leader others admire.

CHAPTER 2 — INTERPERSONAL SKILLS AND "BEDSIDE MANNER"

It's rare to find a doctor who has neat, legible penmanship. In fact, it almost seems like becoming a sloppy writer is a rite of passage for the majority of physicians. The same analogy could reasonably be made regarding most technical professionals and their adeptness with interpersonal skills. Sadly, the bulk of them simply do not shine in the interpersonal skill arena.

Imagine a scenario where a doctor walks into the waiting area adjacent to the hospital's emergency room and asks, "Is the widow Jones here?" A woman anxiously replies, "I'm Mrs. Jones. I brought my husband into the emergency room earlier, but I'm not a widow." Whereupon the doctor unequivocally states, "You are now!"

What would you think if you had witnessed such an exchange? Would you have been shocked? Perhaps you even snickered a bit. The vignette is so extreme it appears silly. Yet, it should point out that a doctor's bedside manner is imperative, and that dictum applies equally well to technical professionals. How often have you heard technical employees criticize their managers because of poor interpersonal skills? It happens so frequently that it's almost expected, but never welcomed.

In terms of career progression, where do most managers of technical professionals come from? Look at your own background or those of your peers. If you're like the usual *garden variety manager*, you rose up through the ranks. So, it's very likely you're a technical professional yourself. How are your interpersonal skills stacking up?

INTERPERSONAL SKILLS ARE SKIMPY

Think back a moment to our last lesson and mull over the skills necessary at various management levels. You should recall that not getting along with other people was the major cause of manager derailment. Unfortunately, as Bernard L. Rosenbaum points out in an article published in the Journal of Training & Development, "Technical leaders who come from technological backgrounds have abilities, personalities, and interests that are oriented more toward things than people."

The result of this is that technical managers usually do well managing the technical aspects of the job, but stumble when it comes to managing people. For example, one of my students was sharing a meeting she was having with her boss that was representative of his usual behavior. She works as a technical writer in a software development company and he's in charge of technical support. She can never capture his attention as his eyes wander everywhere except where she's sitting. In spite of her constant complaining to him about this frustrating mannerism, nothing changes. The outcome is that she avoids him whenever possible and thinks he's a very incompetent leader. What do you think?

One of the inherent problems faced by most technical professionals had to do with their education. Generally, it was so complex, there was little room left for learning people skills. If any course work was dedicated to it, it's probably safe to assume it was cursory at best. Therefore, this whole interpersonal skill set area has gone begging for development.

MANAGING VERSUS COACHING

As Hewlett-Packard learned, their superior project managers were excellent at coaching their direct reports. Like other successful technical managers, they listened, asked questions, facilitated, orchestrated activities, and provided administrative support. Because technical professionals are primarily self directed, they don't need, nor do they want, close supervision. They prefer to be coached and encouraged. As Bill Gates aptly said, "What I do best is share my enthusiasm."

One of the more significant challenges technical managers must brave is maintaining the delicate balance among their staff between interpersonal competition and collegial support. Technical professionals usually relish collegiality as an important factor in their discipline. However, occasionally competitive pressures can override this, ushering in a climate of self-centered ungraciousness. Under these conditions, communication deteriorates and people break into factions and become secretive.

Communicating openly with staff members and listening attentively can go a long way in preventing this. In our next lesson, we'll examine the communication process more closely and furnish you with some practical tools and techniques. In the meantime, be sensitive to your own group—particularly how well they're working together as a team, and how satisfactorily you keep them *in the loop.*

Oren Harari, in a Management Review article, said that the manager's role needs to change from that of *people organizer* to *knowledge accelerator.* Harari contended that the manager must establish an intelligent work force that is an extension of management. He pointed out, "In the new organizational structure, there must be a sense of sharing and interdependence and managers must be adept in building communications links between areas of the company."

I consulted with an IT group several years ago where there were a number of uncooperative IT units that rarely shared information. The backlog of uncompleted projects was enormous and top management was quite unhappy with the function's overall performance. The Vice President of IT was a quiet, reserved man who spent most of his time alone in his office. He showed little interest in people and no inclination to intervene in any internal conflicts.

After about six months of intense work with his group, it became crystal clear that he didn't have the basic skills necessary to lead IT. He was eventually let go and a new person had to be recruited from the outside because he developed no bench strength within his group.

An unhappy ending for someone who should have stayed with a technical career track rather than a management career track.

Sometimes we spot a top performing individual contributor who opts for a management position when it's not in anyone's best interest. They're initially drawn into it by the power, prestige, and money. Nonetheless, they're ill suited for management. What you wind up with is the loss of a good professional contributor and the gain of a poor or mediocre manager.

CHAPTER 3 — THE PLIGHT OF THE PERFECTIONIST

Back in Lesson 5, I introduced you to the work of Jim Collins and his intense, five-year study that resulted in his concept of Level 5 Leadership. As you can see from the model on the next page, to be a Level 5 Leader, you must also excel at levels 1-4. So briefly, what are they?

Level 1 Leaders are competent in the basic knowledge and skills of their field. They have good work habits and are productive in getting things done. Level 2 Leaders are good team players who enjoy working with others. They have desirable interpersonal skills and are active contributors. Level 3 Leaders are capable managers who are able to organize people and resources necessary to achieve formal objectives. Finally, the Level 4 Leader is able to elevate commitment from others, articulate a clear and compelling vision, and maintain high performance standards.

Incidentally, for a review of our earlier discussion of Level 5 Leadership, go back to Lesson 5, Chapter 3. As you look at all of these lofty descriptions, you probably feel that there are only a few managers like this who are *able to leap tall building with a single bound.* Is this real, or does one have to literally immigrate from the distant planet Krypton? Oh, it's real all right, but not as widespread as we certainly would like.

Although Collins found only 11 companies out of 1435 that had authentic Level 5 Leadership at the top, that doesn't mean it didn't exist elsewhere. Also, you don't have to be flawless in everything you do. We'll talk more about that below. So, the bottom line for you is that Level 5 Leadership is rare, but it's something worth going after—no doubt about it. Take a moment to study the model below.

LEVEL 5	**LEVEL 5 EXECUTIVE** Builds enduring greatness through a paradoxical blend of personal humility and professional will.
LEVEL 4	**EFFECTIVE LEADER** Catalyzes commitment to and vigorous pursuit of a clear and compelling vision, stimulating higher performance standards.
LEVEL 3	**COMPETENT MANAGER** Organizes people and resources toward the effective and efficient pursuit of pre-determined objectives.
LEVEL 2	**CONTRIBUTING TEAM MEMBER** Contributes individual capabilities to the achievement of group objectives and works effectively with others in a group setting.
LEVEL 1	**HIGHLY CAPABLE INDIVIDUAL** Makes productive contributions through talent, knowledge, skills, and good work habits.

This thinking has guided us throughout our course and will continue in the lessons ahead. I want you to be the best you can be as a technical leader. I'm sure you do too, or we wouldn't be having this conversation, would we? Accordingly, let's look at another skill you can hone that will likely help you become a first-class manager and leader. This has to do with your delegation skills or what is principally called empowerment. There is good news and bad news here.

PERFECTION AT A COST

Many technical professionals are perfectionists at heart—they fully believe no one can do it as good they can. The good news is they do an incredibly beautiful job. The bad news is they regularly don't develop others and they don't allow them the autonomy they crave. Further, they're a slave to their own compulsiveness.

Let me give you an example of what I mean. Our gated yard at home has an abundance of topiary which requires extensive, periodic trimming. Being a card-carrying, compulsive perfectionist for years, I preferred doing the yard myself. I honestly believed no one could match my dexterity with a precision hedge trimmer. Yet, if the truth be known, I always hated doing this chore.

Maybe you're asking, so why did I do it? Basically, I couldn't let go! The only thing I really enjoyed about this drudgery was viewing it when I was done. I shamelessly admired my good work. Still, one day my wife coerced me into hiring Victor, a local gardener, to do the work instead. You could easily see that Victor loved his gardening and, to my astonishment, was genuinely better at it than me. What a startling revelation!

Although I was dismayed that Victor's work eclipsed mine, I simultaneously became unshackled. I was liberated from a task that I shouldn't have been doing in the first place. I now comfortably confess that I never liked doing any of it. I ascertained I now had the best of four worlds: I didn't have to do what I disliked, I could spend my time on more productive pursuits, I could still get the original job done, and I could stick with my penchant to admire the topiary when it was neatly shaped. What an epiphany! My only regret is that I wished I had delegated the task years earlier.

Can you identify with any of this? You might say that you can identify with most of it, but unlike my example, you love the technical aspects of your work. That's fine. Then what you'll gain is the best of three worlds instead of four. Not a bad trade off.

THRIVING ON CHALLENGE AND ACHIEVEMENT

I'm sure you know that technical professionals want autonomy to do the job *their way*. They're achievement-oriented and obtain untold self satisfaction from their work. Let me repeat this. Technical professionals *thrive* on achievement. When their skills are underutilized, they become apathetic, alienated, and they might emotionally burn out. The tougher the challenge, the more that they have to apply their knowledge and skills to solving difficult problems, the more eager and happier they are.

A boss who hovers, who over-controls, or who stifles their creativity extinguishes the flame of motivation. As Albert Einstein said, "Imagination is more important than knowledge, for while knowledge points to all there is, imagination points to all there will be." This is so important, I've written a whole lesson on it. Lesson 10, "Learning To Let Go and Develop Others," will be dedicated to this entire skill set.

CHAPTER 4 — ORCHESTRATING YOUR PEOPLE'S DEVELOPMENT

Not only do leaders develop technical professionals through challenging assignments and autonomy, but by other processes as well. However, whenever I do 360 degree feedback on managers, I usually see that this total area of developing employees is weak. Yet, one of the greatest fears technical professionals have is losing their edge or becoming obsolete. Consequently, a manager's weakness here goes right to the heart of their technical staff's biggest fear. Plainly, this needs to be avoided.

Remember, technical professionals are loyal first to their field and secondly to their employer. Leaders who help them grow their expertise sustain their allegiance to the Organization. Notwithstanding their recent problems, Lucent Technologies provides every employee with 15 days of training each year. They know that this commitment to their employee's development encourages them to stay with the company.

As important as training is, it's simply not enough. The best technical leaders are coaches who act as a sounding board, supportive *critic,* resource, mentor, advisor, etc. The old idea of directing—that is, issuing orders or commands—doesn't fit in the new millennium. A coach has an unpretentious interest in helping his or her people develop their talents.

THE FOUR FUNCTIONS OF A COACH

Dennis Kinlaw suggested four functions of the leader coach, as reported by Patricia M. Buhler, in an article in <u>Supervision</u>. The functions are counseling, mentoring, tutoring, and confronting. When counseling, the leader helps the employee learn more about themselves and how they feel about what they do. This requires asking pertinent questions, actively listening, and sustaining a dialogue.

The second function is that of mentor. Mentors are role models who share experiences, offer suggestions and advice, help people avoid organizational "land-mines," and fashion career development activities. Acting as a mentor is a powerful force in assisting technical professionals and often accelerates their career growth. Plus, it's enormously satisfying to watch someone blossom.

Years ago, I was asked to mentor a young graduate from the same university I attended. She also received a degree in the exact field as mine. I met with her to see if this was something I wanted to do. She was bright, talented, and exhibited many of the qualities I would want in a training professional. I willingly agreed to become her mentor shortly thereafter.

Within nine months, I introduced her to a client of mine in the banking industry. He immediately offered her a career position in their Training Department. A year later, the bank was acquired by a larger national company and many of the staff were out placed, including her. She asked me at that point in her career what she ought to do. I suggested she move back home with her mother and pursue a Masters Degree in the field—which she did.

Two years later, armed with the Masters Degree, she landed a high paying position in the health care industry. Within eighteen months, she was promoted to manager of the department at about $100K. She stayed on for about two years in that position.

Today she is an independent consultant, a college instructor, and a leadership coach. I've observed this career path with considerable pride and enjoy the small—but meaningful—part I've played in her splendid success. The same opportunities await you and your staff if you spend the necessary time to mentor them.

Tutoring is the third function Kinlaw identified. When managers play the tutor role they help their people refine their technical prowess. They might teach them how to do something differently. Or perhaps they ask provocative questions or play the Devil's Advocate, getting their staff member to *see things from a different perspective*. Maybe they suggest a course, a book, or a learning activity to bolster the individual's expertise. All of these ideal actions are part of the tutoring role a manager might engage in.

Finally, the coach needs to confront the technical professional when performance is not up to par. This requires at least moderate proficiency with the following simple four step model:

1. Expressing your sincere concern
2. Understanding the whole situation
3. Reinforcing the correct performance
4. Discussing alternatives with them and deciding on an approach that solves the problem

The thing I like best about this model is that it is simple and easy to recall. Next time you have to confront a staff member's job performance, give it a try to see how it works out.

CHAPTER 5 — CONCLUSION

As in all of our lessons, we've covered quite a bit of territory for you—a leader of technical professionals. While businesses and industries progressively become more specialized, while technology grows more ubiquitous, and while we continue to sow the seeds of creativity, our need for technical professionals will proliferate. Our society and our very way of life depends on our ability to innovate. Yet, managing the innovations and leading the innovators is a monumentally important calling.

Technical professionals invest a substantial amount of their time and energy learning their fields. Peter Drucker calls them knowledge workers, and as such they provide a competitive advantage—an asset—to the organizations in which they work. No right-minded manager today could even think of their staff as a liability. Not for a nanosecond.

Leading technical professionals entails that you possess insightful understanding and an array of skills necessary to do the job. Since most technical managers have been promoted from within the technical ranks, they often lack some of the fundamental, prerequisite skills. This is often noted relating to interpersonal conduct. Many technical people are just not oriented in this direction, nor have they taken much course work here either.

Technical professionals thrive on challenge and achievement. They identify more with their field than they do their company. There's a preference to do things their own way, and they favor a manager who provides high levels of autonomy. The thing they fear the most is becoming obsolete or irrelevant, so they want ongoing coaching from their leaders.

Dennis Kinlaw pointed out four functions within coaching behaviors. They are counseling, mentoring, tutoring, and confronting. Together, these form a powerful structure for leading technical professionals and shaping their overall performance.

IRV GAMAL, M.A.

LESSON EIGHT ASSIGNMENT

Think of a manager you personally know or have observed, perhaps at your current organization, whom you especially admire. Answer the following questions about them to the best of your ability.

1. How would you characterize their interpersonal skills or "bedside manner?" What do you particularly like and what don't you like?

   _____
   _____
   _____
   _____

2. Do they actively coach their people? What do they do best in the coaching process (i.e., counsel, mentor, tutor, or confront)?

   _____
   _____
   _____
   _____

3. How effective are they in giving their people challenging assignments and the freedom to perform their job?

   _____
   _____
   _____
   _____

4. Look back at the Lesson 7 assignment and compare your strengths and development to these above. What can you feel good about, and where do you want to place more effort to grow?

   _____
   _____
   _____
   _____

LESSON EIGHT MULTIPLE-CHOICE QUIZ
(Answers on the Following Pages)

1. Why do technical professionals identify more with their field than with their organization?

    A. Their company may have them working on unchallenging projects.
    B. They are likely new to the organization and haven't assimilated.
    C. Because of the propensity of companies to continuously downsize.
    D. Because they have made a substantial investment of time, money, and effort in learning their field.

2. What was the distinguishing characteristic Hewlett-Packard discovered about their best project managers?

    A. They completed projects on time and under budget.
    B. They were excellent at coaching their direct reports.
    C. Most had advanced degrees from M.I.T.
    D. They all had been with the company for over ten years.

3. Which president is the ideal embodiment of what Jim Collins calls Level 5 Leadership?

    A. Bill Clinton.
    B. Theodore Roosevelt.
    C. Abraham Lincoln.
    D. Richard Nixon.

4. 4. When technical professionals are underutilized, they…

    A. Become apathetic, alienated, and could burn out.

B. Stop paying their union dues.
   C. Start whining and complaining.
   D. Generally ask for a sabbatical.

5. What are the four functions of the leader coach according to Kinlaw?

   A. Sensing, asking, probing, and clarifying.
   B. Counseling, mentoring, tutoring, and confronting.
   C. Guide, control, structure, and define boundaries.
   D. Support, encourage, recognize, and discipline.

LESSON EIGHT MULTIPLE-CHOICE QUIZ
(Answers)

1. Why do technical professionals identify more with their field than with their organization?

    A. Their company may have them working on unchallenging projects.
    Incorrect.
    This could be the case. However, it's not correct.

    B. They are likely new to the organization and haven't assimilated.
    Incorrect.
    I'm afraid you haven't assimilated the necessary information.

    C. Because of the propensity of companies to continuously downsize.
    Incorrect.
    Gong. Try again.

    D. Because they have made a substantial investment of time, money, and effort in learning their field.
    Correct.
    Good show! This is the right answer.

2. What was the distinguishing characteristic Hewlett-Packard discovered about their best project managers?

    A. They completed projects on time and under budget.
    Incorrect.
    No doubt this is operationally important; however it's also incorrect.

B. They were excellent at coaching their direct reports.
Correct.
Way to go!

C. Most had advanced degrees from M.I.T.
Incorrect.
Nothing against M.I.T., but this is a M.I.S.S.

D. They all had been with the company for over ten years.
Incorrect.
HP's a great company, but this isn't a great answer. Sorry.

3. Which president is the ideal embodiment of what Jim Collins calls Level 5 Leadership?

A. Bill Clinton.
Incorrect.
Although you're off base, I'm sure Bill thinks you're right.

B. Theodore Roosevelt.
Incorrect.
Teddy's brashness was way too big for Level 5.

C. Abraham Lincoln.
Correct
You make Honest Abe proud. Probably our greatest president and a true Level 5 Leader.

D. Richard Nixon.
Incorrect.
Tricky Dicky just doesn't measure up.

4. When technical professionals are underutilized, they...

A. Become apathetic, alienated, and could burn out.
Correct.

LEADERSHIP SKILLS FOR MANAGING TECHNICAL PROFESSIONALS

Right on the money.

B. Stop paying their union dues.
Incorrect.
You're not paying your dues in this lesson. Go back to Chapter 3.

C. Start whining and complaining.
Incorrect.
I'm really upset. I just don't know what to think about your answer. What's the matter with you? Can we talk?

D. Generally ask for a sabbatical.
Incorrect.
If they're underutilized, perhaps they already are on one.

5. What are the four functions of the leader coach according to Dennis Kinlaw?

   A. Sensing, asking, probing, and clarifying.
   Incorrect.
   Go sit in the corner with the cone-shaped hat.

   B. Counseling, mentoring, tutoring, and confronting.
   Correct.
   You're on your way to being valedictorian.

   C. Guide, control, structure, and define boundaries.
   Incorrect.
   Houston, we've got a problem.

   D. Support, encourage, recognize, and discipline.
   Incorrect.
   These are actions, not functions. Stay after class.

LESSON EIGHT FREQUENTLY ASKED QUESTIONS

Q: Why do technical managers often feel uncomfortable with their interpersonal skills and political agility?

A: This is certainly an area where they usually do not shine. As technical professionals they designed systems that either worked or didn't. Often, technical outcomes are far more clear-cut than are "people outcomes." The satellite successfully goes into orbit or it winds up as an addition to the the offshore reef. On the other hand, human interaction and politics are convoluted, cryptic, and questionable. As a result, technical managers feel vulnerable here and may withdraw when they sense heightened exposure.

Q: If technical professionals identify more with their field than their company, how do you create more company loyalty?

A: The greatest fear technical professionals have is becoming obsolete, like yesterday's newspaper. Companies that invest in their people by helping them maintain their up-to-date knowledge base and retain their professional edge, foster closer emotional ties with the organization.

LESSON 9

BECOMING A BETTER COMMUNICATOR

CHAPTER 1 — INTRODUCTION

> *We know that communication is a problem, but the company is not going to discuss it."*
>
> —*AT&T Long Lines Division*

A while back, a contest was held on the Internet for the best real-life examples of what was termed "Dilbert-Style Management." This was devilishly inspired by the famous cartoon strip that appears in so many papers across the nation. The example above was presumably submitted by an employee with AT&T Long Lines Division and made the final *short list*. All the submissions were supposed to be true and accurate. I'm assuming this was the case here.

Can you even imagine a manager saying such an outlandish thing? There were many similar examples I could share with you from this contest. For example, a manager from the Electric Boat Company said, "Email is not to be used to pass on information or data. It should only be used for company business."

I can only wonder what company business is about. How do apparently smart, experienced people wind up making such foolish statements? The reasons are many. Deplorably, communication problems abound within organizations, not only about what managers say to their employees, but also with their individual style and especially their day-to-day practices.

We know from previous lessons that technical professionals fall somewhat *short* in the interpersonal skills area. They might have quirks or habits that undermine their ability to motivate or direct others. Or they may altogether avoid one-on-one and group meetings that could help people bond with them and the organization. If profits are the lifeblood of an organization, then communication is the underlying infrastructure that holds it all together.

Prior to September 11, an AON Consulting survey reported that 65% of 1,800 workers queried planned to stay with their employers for only a few years. This was a five-year low and it was corroborated by another study of 2,795 workers across the country. The second analysis was done by Minneapolis-based Walker Information. In the original study, AON found only 45% of respondents would stay long-term if offered a similar job at higher pay. Following the World Trade Center tragedy, 54% wouldn't leave their current employer <u>even if they were offered higher pay</u>. People now want more predictability in their lives and are willing to give their commitment—if they perceive their commitment is deserved.

Frederick Reichheld, a Bain & Co. consultant who specializes in the effects of worker commitment, discovered some provocative facts. Reichheld learned that a nominal 5% increase in employee retention can lead to profit increases of 25% or more. This is a startling figure! International Truck and Engine (formerly called Navistar) dramatically increased employee morale and earnings by initiating regular contact between corporate executives and front line people. Seems so basic, doesn't it?

Communication is one of the most fundamental of human needs. Babies, who are not actively held and touched by their parents or care givers, lose weight, eventually become ill, and frequently die. We never outgrow this need to feel connected to other people. In survey after survey, we find that *the feeling of being in on things* is usually within the top three needs indicated by employees. What exactly does that particular <u>feeling</u> mean? Essentially, it conveys that you're in the fold, you're aware of what's going on, and you're not inclined to be surprised or broadsided by any unexpected news. The underlying message received is that management thinks you are important.

THE OBJECTIVE OF OUR LESSON

The best leaders and the most admired companies in the world know this well. In Lesson 4, we talked about some straightforward, credible communicators like Harry Truman, Donald Rumsfeld, and Rudy Guiliani. Each of these men are recognized leaders who have been or are considered exceptionally trustworthy.

In this lesson we'll scrutinize three primary areas related to sharpening your communication skills that will strengthen your credibility. We'll look at listening techniques that you can apply in one-on-one sessions, suggestions for conveying negative information, and guidelines for reinforcing positive behavior. That's our game plan, so if you're ready, let's move ahead to the next chapter.

CHAPTER 2 — LISTENING TECHNIQUES FOR ONE-ON-ONE COMMUNICATION

The higher you are promoted in an organization, the more your job becomes one of communicating with others. Many years ago, Dr. Paul Rankin of Ohio State University studied communication patterns of managers and discovered that at the upper levels they spent approximately 80%-90% of their time communicating. Rankin classified communications into four specific categories: writing, reading, speaking, and listening.

The listening process occurs on three progressively more meaningful levels: hearing, comprehending, and understanding. Unfortunately, as behavioral scientists point out, the average person hears only about 25% of what is said under the best of circumstances and remembers as little as 10%. Those are fairly shocking figures. If you add in the typical communication blocks we usually encounter, the figures might even be lower. Many people never get beyond level one— hearing—let alone the other types.

Listening is an active rather than a passive process. Often, people view themselves as "empty goblets" ready to be filled up. They think that by being passively involved in the communication process, they can hear, comprehend, understand, <u>and remember</u>. It seldom—if ever—works that way.

Time, or more accurately, the absence of it, contributes to poor listening habits. Listening requires that we give people a block of time so they can express their ideas and feelings. People want our undivided attention when they are communicating with us. If we show impatience, or constantly look around, or check our watch, we project to them that they are unimportant. That immediate turnoff dismantles any positive communication from that point on.

There are many reasons why listening is not as easy as it first appears. To begin with, most of us have the capacity to process 500-800 words per minute, yet the average person speaks at about 250 words per minute in typical everyday conversations. The average lecturer, on the other hand, speaks at about 135-150 words per minute. All of these disparities in the rate of words spoken and the ability to process information leads us to let our minds wander elsewhere. Consequently, we miss something and the message gets distorted or ignored.

ACTIVE LISTENING IS YOUR BEST ANSWER

The cure for all of this is to become an active listener. Since you may need to reverse years of poor behavioral habits, becoming an active listener may require appreciable energy. There are three basic skills required of active listeners, beginning with *(1) attention skills:* These are those things you do to put the person speaking at ease.

Maintaining eye contact, eliminating opportunities for distractions, and concentrating on both the verbal and nonverbal messages, are examples of attention skills.

Let's take just a moment to talk about nonverbal communications. First, what would be considered nonverbal? Gestures, facial expressions, posture, spatial distancing, eye contact, and tone of voice are all nonverbal in nature. You're probably asking, if that's the case, what's left that's verbal? The verbal element is only the words you use. That's it, everything else is nonverbal. So, what it comes down to is that human communication is predominantly a nonverbal process.

Second, the irony of this is that many people, especially technical professionals, have a tendency to overlook the nonverbal side of communications. Yet, as much as 93% of the impact of a message is carried through the nonverbal channel. Thus, it doesn't make a whole lot of sense to ignore this critical factor, does it?

(2) Following Skills: These are the skills we use to encourage conversation to continue; to show we get the point the other person is making. Nodding your head, saying "uh-huh," "I see," and "go on," are following techniques. Asking appropriate questions to bring out a point, or allowing silence without jumping in are also examples. These techniques let the speaker know you are with him or her, and helps them get to the point.

Now you might be proclaiming that these things are fundamentally common sense. However, common sense is an oxymoron, like jumbo shrimp or awfully nice. It's not common. In the spirit of what I asserted above, many of these things are overlooked, violated, or relegated to the *Who Am I Kidding* category of things "I consistently do—but really don't." Get it? I hope you really do!

(3) Responding Skills: This is where we determine if we received and interpreted the message as the speaker intended it. An example would be, "If I understand you correctly, you mean..." Or, "You seem really interested in the new quality process, Mary." Like attention skills, responding skills are basically a form of feedback, but these specifically acknowledge the sender's message.

USING PARAPHRASING AND REFLECTION

There are two broad categories of responding skills: *paraphrasing and reflection.* Paraphrasing deals with the content of the message. By putting the message into your <u>own words</u>, you show the other person you heard, comprehend, and understand. You could paraphrase in the following manner, "You are not completely certain what those terms mean?" This tells your direct report that you heard what they said and <u>do understand</u>. It's much better than saying something like, "Why not?" or "Don't worry about it, you'll figure it out." Paraphrasing is then good, positive feedback to your direct report, and in this case, paves the way for additional communication.

Reflection is responding to the feelings of the other person. Suppose an employee says, "Haven't we received that damn change request yet?" The answer may be "no," and you could say that, but you'd be neglecting another very important part of the message. That important part is the emotional or feeling portion. A better response would be, "George, you seem to be really upset over the change request."

When should you use paraphrasing or reflection to verify or clarify the messages of other people? When you are unsure of a message, either from a content or feeling standpoint. Although this is true, it's only part of the answer. You can also do it when you feel sure you understand the message, however, you want to verify <u>your understanding</u>.

To verify, you can restate your understanding by saying things like: "In other words..." "It sounds like..." "If I understand what you're saying..." "What you mean is..." Acknowledge obvious feelings being expressed with phrases like: "You sound upset. What you're telling me is..." "That's obviously important to you. Let me be sure I understand..."

If the message is unclear: (1) avoid jumping to conclusions before responding. (2) Ask for more information, interpretation or explanation. (3) Use questions or statements like: "I don't understand. Can you tell me more?" "I'm not real clear. What exactly is the problem?" "I'd like to hear more about that before I try to respond." Keep in mind, this is what a straightforward communicator like a Harry Truman or Rudy Guiliani would do.

PUTTING IT ALL TOGETHER

Using these ideas above, here are some suggestions to follow when conducting a one-on-one discussion with your people.

- When your direct report approaches you, stop what you're doing and put your work aside. Eliminate all temptations to do anything else other than giving them your complete attention.
- Bite your tongue! One of the most immediate signals that you're not listening is when you cut off other people in midstream. Allow them the latitude to finish their thoughts <u>before</u> you speak.
- Be friendly, smile, and lean forward to show you're engaged in the conversation. A simple smile can have a calming effect that contributes to a more comfortable climate. By leaning forward you demonstrate a high level of interest in what they're saying.
- Ask questions, nod your head, or use exclamatory remarks— "Uh-huh," "Very interesting," "Go on," etc., that encourages them to continue. This shows you are committed to tracking with them in resolving whatever issue they're sharing.
- Use paraphrasing or reflection to verify and clarify the message and your understanding of it. This confirms that you have been listening and helps you to sort through the complexity of the issues with them.

CHAPTER 3 — COMMUNICATING- NEGATIVE INFORMATION

Most of us are well acquainted with "You-Messages," although the term, itself, may not *ring a bell*. When you look back on your life, it's likely you grew up with a blaming finger pointed in your direction. Why? Because that's the way most kids experienced childhood. Our parents said things like, "You left your room a mess!" or "You didn't eat your broccoli!" Of course, we all quickly went into absolute denial. We became defensive, angry, and sulked. Sound familiar?

We know from experience that blaming messages don't work. Yet we still use them. It's because many of us assumed there was no other way to communicate negative information. For the most part, we blamed others for their transgressions, then we blamed them again when they didn't own up to them. That's called a double whammy.

So how can you communicate information that people really don't want to hear, but would be willing to possibly accept? We do it through what's called "I-Messages." I-Messages are one of the most useful techniques for expressing concern without finger-pointing or condemnation. Listen to the following statements: (1) "Julie, you've been making too many errors in your paperwork." (2) "Jason, You've been spending too much time in the office lately." Or (3) "Bob, you don't follow through on what you say you will."

FINGER POINTING AND DEFENSIVENESS

These are not I-Messages, but You-Messages. If you were the receiver of any of these messages, how would you feel? You would probably feel defensive, resistant, and resentful. You might also feel guilty and that you've been "put down." People naturally don't like to receive You-Messages. These statements fail to positively influence others because they allow no room for voluntary change. They blame people and reinforce a "you-versus-me" mentality.

Look at the difference between the preceding statements and the following I-Messages: (1) "Julie, when I see you having difficulty with your paperwork, I get worried and think that our client service will suffer." (2) "Jason, I get anxious when I see you in the office most of the time because it seems that our field support is being neglected." Or (3) "Bob, I'm concerned about these incomplete financial statements. The things which you have committed to do are still left undone."

Clear and accurate I-Messages like these reflect the feelings of the person with the problem. Being open, honest, and direct with people is central to effective communication. This is also basic to an I-Message. The components of an I-Message include the following: (1) A description of the *unacceptable behavior or condition,* (2) A description of the *sender's honest feelings,* and (3) A description of the *specific effect of the behavior on the sender* (or the *consequences of the behavior).*

Let's look at an example of this communication technique and see how the components fit together. "When I saw a copy of the new contract, I was very disappointed (feeling) in the wording (unacceptable condition). I feel it's going to affect our relationship with this new customer (effect)."

By learning to use appropriate I-Messages in interpersonal communications, you'll accomplish several things. Not only will you take responsibility for your own feelings about the problem, but you'll also allow others the freedom to volunteer to address the problem and feel good about themselves.

A FOUR-STEP APPROACH

Shifting from active listening to using I-Messages demonstrates an understanding and acceptance of the other person's problem and a desire to pave the way for possible change. When you couple this with three other principles, it looks like the four steps you see below. Incidentally, this is the same model I introduced in Lesson 8, with a slight modification to include your I-Message.

- Use I-Messages to express your sincere concern
- Understand the whole story
- Reinforce the correct performance

- Discuss alternatives with them and decide on an approach which solves the problem

Clear and open communication is a prerequisite to problem-solving. That's why it's important to begin the process by carefully and thoroughly explaining what's on your mind. Use "I messages" like...

"I've anxiously observed the backlog going up."
"I'm concerned about..."
"I have a problem with..."

Avoid opening with a question or anything that may sound like a judgment or accusation. Questions like... "Can't you keep up with the work?" or "Where were you when Jim was looking for you?" only serve to increase defensiveness and anxiety. Be tactful, but be <u>direct</u>. If you are too subtle, you may create misunderstanding and doubt.

Once you've expressed your I-Message, immediately follow up with a question that invites explanation. For example...

"What happened?"
"What led to it being done that way?"
"Tell me about it."

You must understand the problem thoroughly to solve it constructively. Listen carefully, ask clarifying questions, and confirm your understanding even though you may not agree with what the person did in that situation. Use phrases like...

"What you're saying is..."
"The reason you..."

Genuine listening is a vital ingredient of both motivation and problem-solving. Often, you may discover that behind poor performance were the best of intentions. If so, it's important to reinforce the good parts of the performance so that you can focus problem solving only on the error or misjudgment. Otherwise, the person is likely to assume both the reason <u>and</u> the actions were inappropriate or incorrect.

For example, suppose a report contained several errors because your direct report thought it was more important to complete the report by a given deadline. Reinforcing the person's concern for timeliness will help preserve this quality while seeking solutions to the problem of accuracy.

Having expressed your I-Message, listened in order to understand the whole story, and focused on the issue by reinforcing good performance, you can now discuss alternative ways to handle the situation the next time it occurs. This is the fourth step in the process for giving negative feedback (sometimes known as constructive criticism). It's important because it takes the pressure off past performance and looks constructively toward the future.

There are two ways to approach this step of the process. If you want to draw out the other person's ideas, or if you can't think of any other alternatives of your own, ask them for possible solutions. If you have a suggestion yourself, or if there is only one course of action open, make your suggestion. Don't try to "lead" the other person to a solution you've already thought of by asking a series of questions. People are likely to become resentful of such a manipulative technique.

Here's how it might sound. *"It was a tight deadline, and I appreciate the extra effort you took to get the report out on time. What can be done to reduce the number of errors and still get the work out on time?"*

Accurate, timely, and genuine feedback on performance is one of the cornerstones of a positive motivational climate. Praise and recognition become more meaningful when it is specific, reinforces personal qualities, and emphasizes payoffs. Even negative feedback is seen as supportive when you follow a process of open two-way communication and constructive problem-solving.

CHAPTER 4 — GUIDELINES FOR POSITIVE REINFORCEMENT

Historically, managers understood little about the value of praise and recognition (positive feedback). They assumed that if people were performing as expected, that's what they got paid to do. Wages served not only as compensation, but also as an indicator that work was satisfactory. In the past, managers used punishment (negative feedback) almost exclusively. Try that today and you're liable to find yourself in an unemployment line.

Probably the most important lesson for management from the behavioral sciences is the role of positive reinforcement. It appears to be a much more powerful motivator than negative reinforcement. While continuous negative reinforcement may result in a short-term lapse of an undesirable behavior, it usually won't inspire good performance. In fact, it may produce strange, unpredictable, even undesirable behavioral change.

A PAYCHECK IS NOT ENOUGH

Unfortunately, it appears many managers still do not provide enough feedback to employees about their work. Full appreciation of work done ranked very high in a survey of over 40,000 employees conducted by the U.S. Chamber of Commerce. Supervisors guessed the employees would rank it eighth. After researching what they called "high performing U.S. companies," Tom Peters and Bob Waterman, reported in their classic, best selling book *In Search of Excellence*, "Our general observation is that most managers know... little about the value of positive reinforcement. Many either appear not to value it at all or consider it beneath them (or) undignified."

"The evidence from the excellent companies strongly suggests that managers who feel this way are doing themselves, their employees, their companies, and their shareholders a great disservice.

The excellent companies seem not only to know the value of positive reinforcement, but how to manage it as well."

In many instances, managers feel uncomfortable giving feedback because they don't know how to say what they really mean. They can't seem to find the right words to express how they genuinely feel. Often it comes out "Yeah, er, nice job. Thanks." Despite how it's said, such brevity is unlikely to convey the true meaning or intent of the manager.

There are three ways you can add strength and meaning to positive feedback. They are: (1) be specific, (2) reinforce a personal quality, and (3) emphasize the payoffs. You can use one or more of these elements in any order to add content to your positive feedback. The choice depends on the circumstances, how you truly feel about the performance, and your personal style.

By being specific, you add depth to what might otherwise appear to be an offhand remark. For example, if you're giving positive feedback to someone about a report he or she has just written, you might say something like...

"I particularly like the way it's organized step-by-step through the problem."

"It was written in a nice, easy-to-read style."

"The section on features and benefits was really clear and hard-hitting."

By being specific, you leave a lasting impression that you really meant what you were saying.

Often there are underlying factors that stimulate a person's good performance. A few of these intangible factors are...patience, perseverance, attention to detail, tactfulness, thoroughness, and hundreds of other qualities that are woven into the very fabric of an individual's personality. If you value these personal qualities and you want people to continue doing them, you need to reinforce them through positive feedback. Some examples of reinforcing a personal quality are...

"I'm glad you took the initiative."
"You were firm, but fair."
"That's a very creative approach."

Many people, particularly those who are results-oriented, like to know what they're doing has purpose or value. A third method, then, for adding substance to positive feedback is to emphasize the payoffs. Tell the person how you, the organization, or a customer or client has benefited or will benefit from their performance. Here are some examples.

"They called the order in right after you left."
"You really helped me out of a tight spot."
"That means we'll be able to design more units of that type."

When you put all three together, it might sound something like this:

"I'm glad you were sensitive to the possible misunderstanding and called them back to double check. It could have been an embarrassing and expensive situation."

Choose whatever words are comfortable and appropriate. But when you give positive feedback, *be specific, reinforce a personal quality, and/or emphasize payoffs.*

CHAPTER 5 — CONCLUSION

Communication underlies everything you do as a manager. As I said in the very beginning of this lesson, it is the infrastructure that holds organizations together. It is the "glue" that bonds people to one another. If you can't communicate with someone in either a business or personal setting, that relationship is doomed to failure.

Often technical professionals underestimate the importance of this crucial interpersonal skill. Typically, this is because their strengths lie elsewhere. Yet, as Frederick Reichheld pointed out, a 5% increase in employee retention can lead to profit increases of 25% or more. Dramatic returns like these cannot be overlooked by anyone in a leadership position. To do so is nothing less than abdication of a foremost obligation to your organization, your employees, and your stockholders.

Listening is one of the most pertinent communication skill. The very act of listening signifies that the person being listened to is important. When we ignore someone, the converse is also true. We imply that they are not important. When people believe they are special, they often begin to act accordingly and their performance improves.

Occasionally, we have to deliver less than favorable information to people. Most managers resort to You-Messages because that's all they have ever experienced. Finger pointing and blaming leads to defensiveness, denial, and a heightening of tensions. Rarely will you find a positive outcome to a blame-centered conversation. A better way to convey negative information is to use I-Messages. I-Messages have three parts: (1) A description of the *unacceptable behavior or condition,* (2) A description of the *sender's honest feelings,* and (3) A description of the *specific effect of the behavior on the sender* (or the *consequences of the behavior).*

On the other hand, when employees do a good job they should be positively reinforced. After all, as a manager, you'd like to see more of the good behaviors. But, saying "good job" is simply not enough. That doesn't tell the employee what they need to know to repeat it. What specific part of the task did the manager like the best? The three criteria I introduced to augment your positive feedback are: (1) Be specific, (2) Reinforce a personal quality, and (3) Emphasize the payoffs. Any, or all, of these criteria added to your comments will make your positive reinforcement a potent tool for managing performance.

IRV GAMAL, M.A.

LESSON NINE ASSIGNMENT

Now that you've been introduced to I-Messages, I'd like to give you an opportunity to practice writing them. This will help you to internalize the three key elements of what an I-Message is. Do you remember what those three elements are? (Below, you can check on what the answer to that is).

See how you would change the following You-Messages into I-Messages:

1. "Helen, you put in seven hours of unauthorized overtime this week. You know you must get my approval for this in advance."

   _____
   _____
   _____

2. "Paul, this is the third time you've called in sick in two weeks. Don't you care about how this adds to our work load on the project?"

   _____
   _____
   _____

3. "This report's unacceptable, Maureen. Your work has gotten just too sloppy."

   _____
   _____
   _____

The components of an I-Message include the following: (1) A description of the unacceptable behavior or condition, (2) A description of the sender's honest feelings, and (3) A description of the specific effect of the behavior on the sender (or the consequences of that behavior). Often, when people are learning to use I-Messages, they forget about the last criteria. Did you do that? If you did, note it and make an extra effort to include it next time.

Let's look at an example of how I converted number one into an I-Message. "Helen, <u>I'm unhappy</u> about your <u>seven hours of unauthorized overtime</u>. You need my prior authorization because this <u>impacts our billable-time budget</u>." I've underlined the three key parts of the I-message. You'll notice in this example, the feelings came first, the unacceptable behavior second, and the consequences third. That's okay as long as all three components are included.

LESSON NINE MULTIPLE-CHOICE QUIZ
(Answers on the Following Pages)

1. Since September 11, 2001, less people nationwide are willing to leave their current employer. Why is this so?

   A. It's an offshoot of the patriot fervor that swept the country.
   B. They want more predictability in their lives.
   C. The recession has made job hopping a tougher tactic.
   D. Outplacement funding has diminished and more people have to change jobs without this support, which they're unwilling to do.

2. Listening occurs on three progressively more meaningful levels. What are they?

   A. Verbal, nonverbal, and intuitive.
   B. One-on-one, small group, and large crowds.
   C. Hearing, comprehending, and understanding.
   D. Acting, thinking, and feeling.

3. One of the biggest barriers to effective listening is...

   A. The disparity between the capacity to process information and the rate at which most people generally speak.
   B. Cell phones, beepers, and other electronic devices.
   C. The graying of the population and their related hearing loss.
   D. Open area office design, that is, the cubicle layout that's so prevalent today.

4. I-Messages are a way of communicating negative information without the usual defensive repercussions. Why don't more managers use them?

A. Because they'd rather use We-Messages, which imply teamwork.
B. I-Messages make you sound weak and ineffective.
C. Most people grew up with You-Messages and are oblivious to other ways of doing it.
D. Most managers believe I-Messages sound self-centered and egoistic.

5. Why do so many managers feel uncomfortable giving positive feedback to their employees?

   A. Often they're having a bad day and it doesn't fit their current attitude.
   B. They rarely see positive performance that warrants it.
   C. They might appear too "touchy-feely."
   D. They don't know how to say what they really mean.

IRV GAMAL, M.A.

LESSON NINE MULTIPLE-CHOICE QUIZ
(Answers)

Quiz (Answers

1. Since September 11, 2001, less people nationwide are willing to leave their current employer. Why is this so?

    A. It's an offshoot of the patriot fervor that swept the country.
    Incorrect.
    I regret that you have but one right answer to give for this question—and this isn't it.

    B. They want more predictability in their lives.
    Correct.
    Yes…you've now given me peace of mind.

    C. The recession has made job hopping a tougher tactic.
    Incorrect.
    Recessions have a propensity to do that. However, this is not the right answer.

    D. Outplacement funding has diminished and more people have to change jobs without this support, which they're unwilling to do.
    Incorrect.
    Good guess, but guess what? You're wrong.

2. Listening occurs on three progressively more meaningful levels. What are they?

    A. Verbal, nonverbal, and intuitive.
    Incorrect.

Sorry, one demerit to go. Something tells me you weren't tracking.

- B. One-on-one, small group, and large crowds.
  Incorrect.
  I hope you didn't surely think this was right.

- C. Hearing, comprehending, and understanding.
  Correct.
  You've hit the mother lode. That's right!

- D. Acting, thinking, and feeling.
  Incorrect.
  Oops, way off. Do you think you need to sharpen your inner listening skills a bit?

3. One of the biggest barriers to effective listening is...

   - A. The disparity between the capacity to process information and the rate at which most people generally speak.
     Correct.
     You haven't won the Nobel prize, but you've won my noble admiration!

   - B. Cell phones, beepers, and other electronic devices.
     Incorrect.
     Interesting answer, yet not on the right frequency.

   - C. The graying of the population and their related hearing loss.
     Incorrect
     What'd you say? Oh, yes I see, 'er hear. No, this answer is wrong.

   - D. Open area office design, that is, the cubicle layout that's so prevalent today.
     Incorrect.

Cubicles don't provide privacy, and that's all the more reason for improved listening behaviors. Go back three spaces.

4. I-Messages are a way of communicating negative information without the usual defensive repercussions. Why don't more managers use them?

   A. Because they'd rather use We-Messages, which imply teamwork.
   Incorrect.
   I'm rather concerned about your answer.

   B. I-Messages make you sound weak and ineffective.
   Incorrect.
   Only if you use them when you're in the fetal position.

   C. Most people grew up with You-Messages and are oblivious to other ways of doing it.
   Correct.
   Yes…yes…yes!

   D. Most managers believe I-Messages sound self-centered and egoistic.
   Incorrect.
   This is the other side of "A" above. It's still incorrect.

5. Why do so many managers feel uncomfortable giving positive feedback to their employees?

   A. Often they're having a bad day and it doesn't fit their current attitude.
   Incorrect.
   Bad hair days are no excuse for bad behaviors.

   B. They rarely see positive performance that warrants it.
   Incorrect.

Perhaps they need to examine their feedback habits to determine if that's having a negative affect on performance.

C. They might appear too "touchy-feely."
Incorrect.
I wouldn't worry too much about this happening.

D. They don't know how to say what they really mean.
Correct.
It's as simple as this. Say what you mean and mean what you say.

LESSON NINE FREQUENTLY ASKED QUESTIONS

Q: Why do managers have such difficulty listening to others?

A: This is not only true of managers, it's true of people in general. It's the biggest complaint that wives seem to have against their husbands. (I know this firsthand!) It's often the biggest complaint that customers have with companies. Listening takes work, but it looks so easy on the surface. It's a real dichotomy that creates many communication breakdowns and subsequent emotional turmoil.

Q: Aren't I-Messages just another cute, but cumbersome and contrived communication tool?

A: Anything that's new often seems ill-fitting and somewhat cumbersome. How long does it take to break in a new pair of Levis? Perhaps six months or longer. How does it feel while you're getting used to them? For a while, they kind of rub you the wrong way, but then they feel naturally comfortable. The same logic applies to any kind of interpersonal or cognitive model. I-Messages are meant to be helpful—and they are—but if you think they're cute too, hey, who am I to argue!

Q: Why do people always have to be told they're valued and appreciated. Doesn't it get a bit repetitive?

A: Sure it's repetitive, but so is eating. I don't know about you, but I think some types of repetitive things are good. People never tire of hearing that they're appreciated. What they get tired of is hearing it said insincerely or repeatedly being taken for granted.

LESSON 10

LEARNING TO LET GO AND DEVELOP OTHERS

CHAPTER 1 — INTRODUCTION

> *"The unfortunate thing about this world is that good habits are so much easier to give up than bad ones."*
>
> —*Somerset Maugham*

In Lesson 3, we mentioned President Jimmy Carter and his administration's failure to get things moving again in the country. Carter was the consummate engineer by trade, a man so detail-oriented, that when he moved into a leadership role, he simply couldn't let go of his earlier habits. A story is told that as President, he actually oversaw the scheduling of the White House tennis courts. Whether this is true or not, the anecdote is quite telling of how others perceived his leadership eccentricities.

Carter couldn't separate the wheat from the chaff; that is, he didn't know his priorities. He acted more like a manager than a leader. Furthermore, he never understood the principle of leverage as it's applied to leadership.

Leverage suggests that as a leader you are able to expand your influence and affect on others. For example, when you do individual contributor work that you could possibly delegate to someone else, there is no leverage. One hour of input equals one hour of output. On the other hand, let's assume you spend one hour of leadership time showing a direct report how to perform a task. Afterwards they work for eight hours without further direction. You now have a leverage ratio of 1:8.

Now imagine you did that with eight staff members together and they each worked for eight hours. Your leverage is now 1:64. In other words, you obtained 64 hours of individual contributor productivity or output from only one hour of leadership direction. That's what I mean by the *principle of leverage.*

When you try to do it all by yourself, you're not acting in the role of a leader. Remember, leaders have followers. Once you accept the title of leader, you need to relinquish old, worn out habits that hinder your effectiveness. You can no longer just comfortably depend on yourself for your success. You must depend on others for it, and this fact may not be comfortable for you.

THE OBJECTIVE OF OUR LESSON

Leadership requires *learning to let go and develop others.* When you cling to the familiar responsibilities you had before becoming a leader, you deprive the technical professionals, who report to you, of the challenges they so desperately need. Morale will sink faster than the Titanic and you'll wind up working twice as hard.

Therefore, in this lesson we'll address the delegation process, and its other form called empowerment. I will share proven techniques and sound practices that will help you become a more effective leader with a vibrant, committed team of professionals.

CHAPTER 2 — THE UNDERLYING REASONS MANAGERS DON'T DELEGATE

Someone once said that there is not a right way to do the wrong thing. Managers who don't delegate usually express a myriad of *practical reasons* why they can't delegate. Still, no matter how you "slice it," limiting what and how you delegate is the wrong thing. In Lesson 8, we touched on a few causes for this lack of delegation—such as being a perfectionist, or truly enjoying the technical aspects of your job. We didn't however, get into all the excuses you hear for holding on to too much of the work. Nor did we attend to the real, underlying reasons managers have for doing this.

Now, it's time for this discussion. But, before we get to that, let me ask you a few pertinent questions. Do you often find yourself bringing work home with you? Do you sometimes feel like a stranger in your own home? Are you thinking about work-related projects when you're supposed to be having quality time with your family? Are you feeling guilty about having to sneak into the office on the weekend to tie up a few loose ends? If you answered yes to two or more of these questions, then the ensuing discussion will be even more meaningful for you.

Frequently, technical managers say they can't delegate for the following common justifications:

- *"It would take me longer to explain, than do it" attitude.*
- *I'm unwilling to spend any more precious time guiding or counseling my people.*
- *My employees are not trained to carry out delegated tasks.*
- *Our plans, policies, procedures or goals are not clearly established and understood.*
- *I lack some confidence in my direct report's ability.*
- *I feel a bit uncomfortable allowing my people to make what could be a major mistake.*

Left unsaid by these managers, are some of the following underlying—maybe even buried - reasons:

- I don't trust my people.
- I fear a loss of control.

- Okay, I'm a perfectionist, unwilling to "let go." Yet, that also means I'm the only one who can do the task <u>the right way</u>. *(Since I've dealt with this issue previously in Lesson 8, I won't take unnecessary time to reiterate it here).*
- I'm insecure or inexperienced.
- I'm impatient and results—not people—oriented.

The two most significant motives for failing to delegate are the manager's lack of trust and their fear of losing control. Plainly speaking, far too many technical managers don't trust their people to get the job done right. They may equate delegation with how they would feel teaching an adolescent—perhaps their own teenage children—to drive. What a frightful thought that is!

Have you ever had *the trauma* of teaching a young person to drive a car? If you can, fantasize for a moment that you're in your prized automobile with a teenager sitting impetuously behind the wheel. You notice that although the traffic is moderately heavy, it's moving along quite briskly. You want to have them merge into this unending flow of traffic without incident. How would you react to all of this? Would you feel better if you had dual controls in front of you? Perhaps a lot better?

What does having the dual controls do for you? Basically, it puts you back in control, doesn't it? You can now do things the way you want to. You may think of yourself more like a pilot and copilot, as opposed to a driver and co-driver. Woefully, you know co-drivers don't really exist; therefore, you're either a driver or you're a passenger.

DELEGATION SHOULDN'T BE LOSING CONTROL

Some managers perceive delegation as not even being in the car as a passenger. They see assigning responsibility for a project or a task as similar to a parent handing their teenager the keys to the family car. Mom or dad wants to allow them some freedom to drive the car, but concurrently hold them accountable for any resulting damage. Beyond that, the parents may also want to make the decisions as to where their teenager will go, with whom, what time they should be home, etc.

In other words, they are unwilling to extend the authority to make decisions about how their teenager uses the car. Or, maybe they do it and then have second thoughts as their anxiety grows. They cannot entirely let go because they don't trust them and they fear losing control. It's the same old issue that won't go away. When managers don't allow their people any freedom or autonomy, they stifle their direct reports' initiative and send a clear, unmistakable message that they don't trust them.

Believe me, people pick up on this very quickly and resent it. Managers who hover, who keep awkwardly asking questions, who circumvent their direct reports, who pull some authority back, all ultimately undermine their people's confidence in themselves, their performance, and their morale. Of course, all of this weakens the manager's effectiveness as a leader as well. It's not a pretty picture.

Realistically, when you delegate or empower others, you do lose a fair amount of control. Nevertheless, it should not be <u>absolute</u>; there are standards that have to be met, deadlines imposed or negotiated, and progress checks along the way. Furthermore, if they are qualified to handle it, why stand in their way? What it comes down to is this: Far too many managers are inclined to delegate responsibility, maintain accountability, and <u>withhold</u> authority to carry out the job. It's like asking someone to prepare dinner, but then not allowing them in the kitchen.

BUT I DON'T HAVE TIME TO DELEGATE!

Well, why would you? Ever think about which came first, the chicken or the egg? Managers habitually complain that they can't delegate because it would take longer to explain it than to do it themselves. This excuse is closely allied to an unwillingness to spend any more time guiding or counseling their people. With either point of view, is it then surprising that their people might not be able to handle it? It shouldn't be.

Whether we're talking about delegation or empowerment, they each take time. Empowerment—another form of delegation—is pushing decision making down to the lowest organization level where those decisions can be made most effectively. Both help managers build for the future by <u>investing</u> in their people today. This always takes time —which is frequently in short supply. Managers who give in to the temptation to try to do it all themselves satisfy short-term needs at the expense of long-term advantages. They personally don't grow and their people stagnate. In the end, they'll never have the time to delegate.

When people sense they aren't trusted, they start to question why their manager feels that way. They ask themselves, "What did I do wrong?" "Did I step on someone's toes?" "Am I not doing the job?" Slowly, their anxiety and frustration levels amplify as they search for answers. Instead of two people growing in their individual abilities, all that has occurred is a transfer of negative emotion—the distrust from the manager erodes the self-esteem and job satisfaction of the bewildered direct report.

Managers need to know the heavy price everyone pays when this happens. The moral of this story is to give responsibility to those you can trust—at least somewhat—and then provide proportional authority in order to carry it out. Finally, everyone must be held accountable. Your direct reports should be aware of their accountability for completing any assignment. If they don't believe they are, their efforts will be diminished by the perceived unimportance of the job. Never forget though, at the end of the day, you—the manager—are the one accountable for the work of <u>all</u> your people.

CHAPTER 3 — GUIDELINES FOR DELEGATING

There is a Golden Rule of Delegation that roughly states, *"Anytime you perform a task that someone else can do, or can be trained to do, you do that task at the expense of another, perhaps higher level task, that only you can do."* If you're not doing that latter task, it's probably not getting done at all. You might not realize it now, but that task may be essential to your future success. It would be a terrible shame to neglect it.

We know that one of the finest ways to convey your trust and respect[1] is to give another person challenging work and the freedom to perform it as they see fit. Once you do this, you are free to do those higher level tasks that stretch and develop you further as a leader. So, if you're tracking with me on this, let's look at how you can jump-start this entire effort.

First off, always choose capable people to assist you and explain fully and clearly the task to be done. Start with a general overview of the job and then proceed to the individual details. Everyone has a preferred style for processing information. Some employees perform better with written instructions, others do well with a verbal disclosure. If you're not sure—which you probably won't be—back up all verbal instructions with an email that summarizes your conversation.

DELEGATION IS MORE LIKE A RHEOSTAT

Give your direct report the appropriate amount of authority and responsibility to carry out the task. This is very important. The wise manager is always discriminating about the degrees of freedom he or she provides to employees. For each direct report, consider the area of responsibility and their competence to carry it out. Then, communicate clearly the degree of freedom the person may exercise for each assigned task. For most people, this will vary considerably from task to task. Customarily, the better someone gets at performing on-the-job, the more freedom they should be allowed by their manager.

Many managers view delegation in a polarized context, like an on/off switch. That is, I delegate or I don't! In reality, delegation is more like a rheostat, with multiple levels of freedom they could choose from, depending on their level of trust. These are outlined below starting with the highest level of freedom and trust. *Control Over Timing* indicates who initiates the action, and *Control Over Content* depicts who controls what is done.

---

[1] Trust plus respect equals confidence. The more you trust and respect an individual, the more confidence you have in their performance.

Degrees of Freedom To Act	Control over Timing	Control over Content
1. Act and report routinely	Report	Report
2. Act and report immediately	Report	Report
3. Seek approval before acting	Report	Report
4. Seek direction before acting	Report	Manager
5. Wait until told what to do	Manager	Manager

Freedom also carries with it initiative. At Level One, the direct report has the highest level of personal freedom and must also demonstrate the highest level of self-initiative. At Level Five, there is no self-initiative required. People wait until they're told what to do. This is called close supervision and perpetuates dependency among employees. It also mandates that the manager works long hours to get the work out. After all, everyone depends on the boss for direction. Isn't it time for this to change?

YOUR FIRST MEETING

Once you've decided what to delegate and the probable level of freedom, it's time to meet with your direct report. Your initial interaction is at the heart of the delegation process. It determines, more than anything else, the outcome of a delegated function. There are three key areas in the process: (1) Interpersonal—explaining how you'll work together; (2) Informational—sharing expectations and the structure of the task; and (3) Decisional—defining standards, reporting requirements, processes, and the level of freedom.

The key aspects of your first meeting with them can be summed up in this fashion:

Interpersonal
- Establish clear, open channels of communication
- Create a climate of trust and respect; reinforce your belief in their ability

- Discuss the employee's hopes and concerns
- Develop a mutual commitment to the task at hand
- Be <u>reasonable</u> in what you want

Informational
- Describe the project fully (big picture first, then the details)
- Outline the expected outcomes (the "deliverables")
- Define task parameters and resources available (5M's—See Lesson 3, Chapter 2)
- Obtain feedback from the direct report

<u>Decisional</u>
- Decide on the degree of delegated responsibility, authority (level of freedom, who they have authority over, etc.), and accountability
- Agree on the method of work (the process)
- Agree on the nature, means, and timing of reporting back
- Agree on standards of performance (MSP's—See Lesson 6, Chapter 4)
- Ensure that the direct report has accepted (or rejected) the work

FOLLOWING THROUGH

More often than not, changes occur that will affect how a direct report carries out a delegated task. Their responsiveness to this depends, to a large extent, on their access to important information. If you hoard information, or in any way keep a lid on it, people cannot be conscientious in addressing changing demands. Many times managers don't think their people are quick enough in making necessary adjustments. The problem has more to do with access to information than anything else.

There must be regular exchanges of information between you and all staff members. This doesn't mean a sharing just between you and them, but an open verbal dialogue among <u>all</u> players. This can be supplemented by use of the company's Intranet, faxes, emails, one-on-ones, staff meetings, progress reviews, etc. Ask yourself this question for starters: Do your direct reports know what your goals are for the year? How can they effectively support your efforts if they don't know your priorities?

Expecting results from the direct report you've delegated to in your first meeting is certainly legitimate. However, doing that without following through with support, information, and resources is unreasonable.

Here are some quick rules of thumb for your follow-through:

Interpersonal
- Encourage independence and allow the freedom agreed upon
- Support their initiative, responsibility, and creativity
- Be available to them and respond to voice mail or e-mail within 24 hours
- Compliment their efforts and reward good results
- Share your honest feelings and show interest in them
- Be open to suggestions for changing the task, process, etc.
- Accept some mistakes as inevitable

Informational
- Share all pertinent information and updates
- Gather information at predetermined times (do NOT hover!)
- Provide honest feedback on their performance
- Ask for their ideas and opinions

Decisional
- Assess results and compare to your expectations
- Correct mistakes, deficiencies, etc., when necessary
- Decide on needed modifications
- Evaluate performance at preset milestones
- Plan for their future

CHAPTER 4 — WHAT SHOULD YOU BE DELEGATING?

To become an effective delegator, you must have your own job well in hand. This means that occasionally you need to:

- Review your duties and responsibilities as a technical manager. How have they changed? What new things do you have to learn? How do they affect your unit or function? What are the new challenges? What old practices need to be stopped?
- Reaffirm the primary objectives of your group. Have there been any changes that affect priorities or that need to be communicated to your direct reports?
- Highlight the key result areas. What are the make-or-break factors in your assignment? What are the areas in which specific results are essential?
- Re-examine your workload to identify those few tasks only you can do.

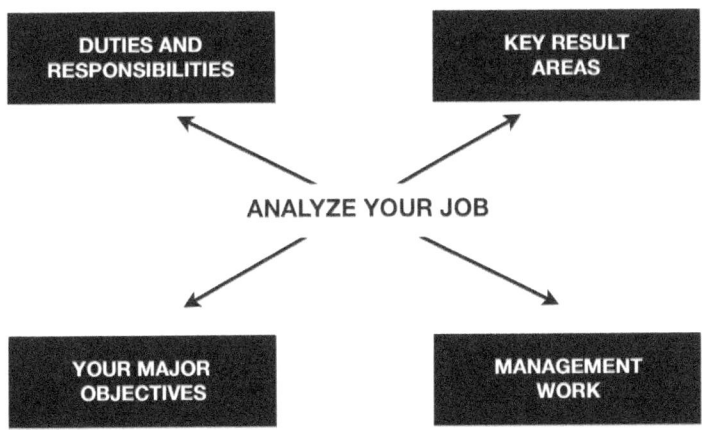

Remember that you are a manager, not an individual contributor. It's your job to utilize your technical professional staff effectively to accomplish organizational goals. You must sort out the important from the unimportant and advance on a priority basis. Don't fall into the *Jimmy Carter trap!* The more you develop your people, and the more you delegate to them, the more they can help you identify key result areas and meet pivotal objectives.

Let go of tasks that rightfully belong to your people. That includes troubleshooting and problem solving in their areas of responsibility. Be sure they are properly trained and help them when they flounder. And, by all means, give them a chance to do the job for which they were originally hired or promoted.

Managers usually delegate to give themselves more time to do complex and difficult management-related tasks, to improve productivity, or to develop their direct reports. Some of the types of work you should consider delegating are listed below:

- *Decisions you make most frequently.* Minor decisions and repetitive activities often consume a major portion of the day. Most, if not all, of these can be delegated by teaching employees the policies and procedures that apply. They probably already know the details better than you!
- *Functions that are in your technical or functional specialty.* These are usually operating tasks rather than management functions. You can teach others to do them. In fact, your challenge as a manager is to motivate others to produce better results than you ever did as an individual performer. Part of the time you save can be used to learn about other functions you supervise so that you can manage them better.
- *Tasks and projects for which you are least qualified.* It's almost certain that some of your employees are better qualified and can do parts of the job better than you. Let them.
- *Functions you dislike.* Having to perform functions you dislike is distasteful. It is common for people to put those activities off or do them poorly because they're coping. Examine the likes and dislikes of your staff as well as their talents. You will nearly always find someone who likes the job and can do it well. Provide training if that employee needs it.

- *Work that will provide experience for employees.* This makes growth in the present job a reality and helps keep employees challenged and motivated.
- *Assignments that will add variety to routine work.* A change of pace is usually welcome and is often a good motivator for a direct report whose job is becoming dull.
- *Activities that will make a position more complete.* As employees become more proficient, they often have time to spare. Add complementary duties and responsibilities to give their positions more substance.
- *Tasks that will increase the number of people who can perform critical assignments.* Maximize the strength of the group by giving people the experience needed to back one another up during emergencies or periods of unusually heavy work loads.
- *Opportunities to use and reinforce creative talents.* Employees are not creative in a stifling environment. Stimulate them with difficult problems and projects, and reward creative solutions.
- *Assignments that will provide direct exposure to related functions in other departments.* Employees who perform related functions often learn from each other and come up with better ways to do the work.
- *Tasks that will bring high-potential individuals in contact with more senior management.* This is a positive way for upper-level managers to develop an appreciation for the quality staff being developed within the organization.

CHAPTER 5 — CONCLUSION

The very act of delegating enables a leader like yourself to exercise leverage. As a result, you can expand your sphere of influence, impact, and act more like a Linking Pin (for a thorough discussion of this concept see Lesson 7, Chapter 4). However, letting go of the things that have made you successful up to this point in your career is not easy. If it was, we wouldn't even find it necessary to have this discussion.

So, the fact of the matter is that delegation skills are often a chink in the armor of technical leaders. There are many seemingly plausible explanations tendered for why this is so. Nonetheless, most of them are more fluff than anything else. The real underlying reasons have more to do with issues of trust, respect, confidence, control, compulsiveness, and insecurity.

We've addressed many of these hard-to-admit feelings and have hopefully demonstrated that delegation isn't an "either-or proposition." Delegation can be a finely tuned process that is gauged to perceived levels of trust and competency. As the report's trust and competency grows, their levels of freedom and authority can be ratcheted up accordingly by the leader.

The delegation process, itself, must be structured appropriately with boundaries, expectations, and standards agreed to beforehand. This keeps the leader in the communication loop and sustains limited, but important, controls. It also requires ongoing follow-through until the task or project is finally completed.

All of this is not possible until the leader decides what it is they would like to delegate. I have given eleven examples of different kinds of tasks that would be helpful to both leaders and their direct reports. You'll likely benefit by mulling over this list and evaluating the pros and cons of each in judging your own people. Then make a commitment to move forward using at least three of them within the next week.

LESSON TEN ASSIGNMENT

As you think about options for developing your direct reports, examine the list below. Consider things that you might delegate or assign to them that could accelerate their development. Successful development plans should have the following aspects:

- Limited focus with no more than three or four areas for development
- Joint responsibility for the process of implementation of the plan
- A variety of activities for development
- Well-defined areas of skill and knowledge to be developed
- Resources made available to the individual
- Specific time frames for accomplishment
- Check those activities that could be considered developmental for a direct report:
- Increased responsibility in substance of current job tasks—more complex tasks, larger projects, or higher visibility work.
- Increased responsibility in scope of current job—working with larger numbers of employees and teams, cross-functional groups and/or other locations.
- Working with mergers, acquisitions, or new divisions that are growing to improve business results.
- Increased responsibility in depth of current job—coordinating, managing, or evaluating the work of others.
- Facilitating conflict resolution between two employees or teams.
- Course work—formal and informal training, internal and external.
- Self-development—books, tapes, videos, CD-ROM, etc.
- Special projects • Task forces • Chairing a committee • Teaching others • Job rotation • Planning special events • Interviewing subject matter experts • Mentoring others

• Coaching others • Leading improvement teams • Lateral transfers • Attending conferences, trade shows, or special meetings • Temporary promotion • Completing a feedback profile • Developing a training manual • Implementing a change

As you review those things that you checked off, which would be most meaningful to your direct report? I suggest you also speak with them to obtain their thoughts. Then make a final decision and implement it within the next several weeks.

LEADERSHIP SKILLS FOR MANAGING TECHNICAL PROFESSIONALS

LESSON TEN MULTIPLE-CHOICE QUIZ
(Answers on the Following Pages)

1. The two most significant reasons preventing technical managers from delegating are…

   A. A lack of time and their own insecurity.
   B. Inexperienced staff and limited administrative controls.
   C. Their lack of trust and fear of losing control.
   D. Impatience and an unwillingness to invest more time guiding or counseling their people.

2. Empowerment is…

   A. A term used in the energy industry to connote a power surge.
   B. Giving people the resources they need to perform the job.
   C. A "laissez-faire style" of management resulting in an inattentive working climate.
   D. Pushing decision making down to the lowest organization level where those decisions can be made most effectively.

3. The highest level of employee initiative is required when one of your people acts and routinely reports. Why is this so?

   A. They have control over both their timing and the content of what they do.
   B. They're likely to be a high potential employee.
   C. Their visibility in the organization dictates nothing less.
   D. It's mandated by a Memorandum of Understanding (MOU).

4. Three key areas of the delegation process are…

   A. Your workload, available staff, and deadlines.
   B. Interpersonal, Informational, and Decisional.

213

C. Top, moderate, and low priorities.
D. Life balance, personal effectiveness, and staff development.

5. Occasionally direct reports seem unresponsive to changing conditions that impact a delegated task. One of the primary reasons for this is…

   A. The unavailability of necessary information.
   B. An unacceptably heavy travel schedule.
   C. Their inability to manage multiple priorities.
   D. A disconnected boss who's unaware of their actual performance.

LEADERSHIP SKILLS FOR MANAGING TECHNICAL PROFESSIONALS

LESSON TEN MULTIPLE-CHOICE QUIZ
(Answers)

1. The two most significant reasons preventing technical managers from delegating are...

   A. A lack of time and their own insecurity.
   Incorrect.
   Come on now, I know you can do better.

   B. Inexperienced staff and limited administrative controls.
   Incorrect.
   Mayday...Mayday!

   C. Their lack of trust and fear of losing control.
   Correct.
   Can you see my smile in your mind?

   D. Impatience and an unwillingness to invest more time guiding or counseling their people.
   Incorrect.
   Sorry, this answer is not quite on target, although in many cases it's true.

2. Empowerment is...

   A. A term used in the energy industry to connote a power surge.
   Incorrect
   Your urge to merge this concept with a surge has me on the verge!

   B. Giving people the resources they need to perform the job.
   Incorrect
   Very resourceful answer. Unfortunately, it's wrong.

215

C. A "laissez-faire style" of management resulting in an inattentive working climate.
Incorrect
Try again.

D. Pushing decision making down to the lowest organization level where those decisions can be made most effectively.
Correct
The Gipper would be very happy with you, and I am too!

3. The highest level of employee initiative is required when one of your people acts and routinely reports. Why is this so?

   A. They have control over both their timing and the content of what they do.
   Correct
   Right in the cross hairs!

   B. They're likely to be a high potential employee.
   Incorrect
   Maybe, maybe not. Go back three spaces and think.

   C. Their visibility in the organization dictates nothing less.
   Incorrect
   This isn't an issue of visibility. Can you see that?

   D. It's mandated by a Memorandum of Understanding (MOU).
   Incorrect
   Start bailing! You're sinking here.

4. Three key areas of the delegation process are…

   A. Your workload, available staff, and deadlines.
   Incorrect
   Oh my gosh, you bit the wrong hook.

B. Interpersonal, Informational, and Decisional.
   Correct.
   And the winning ticket is…yours!

C. Top, moderate, and low priorities.
   Incorrect
   Perhaps you need more greens in your diet?

D. Life balance, personal effectiveness, and staff development.
   Incorrect
   Certainly these are all important, but they're not the key areas.

5. Occasionally direct reports seem unresponsive to changing conditions that impact a delegated task. One of the primary reasons for this is…

   A. The unavailability of necessary information.
      Correct
      Bosses who keep a lid on information hinder their staff's adaptability.

   B. An unacceptably heavy travel schedule.
      Incorrect
      You're beginning to lag behind.

   C. Their inability to manage multiple priorities.
      Incorrect
      Get a cup of coffee and guess again!

   D. A disconnected boss who's unaware of their actual performance.
      Incorrect
      Strike three! You know what that means.

IRV GAMAL, M.A.

LESSON TEN FREQUENTLY ASKED QUESTIONS

Q: Why are so many technical professionals perfectionists?

A: Good question. Why are so many Penguins found at the South Pole and not in Hawaii? Why do the bulk of politicians have such huge egos and a lust for power? I've been to Hawaii eleven times over the years and I've yet to see a Penguin applying sunscreen on Waikiki Beach. Most of the politicians I've studied over the years seem to relish power and I haven't come across any lately taking a vow of poverty. So what gives?

It's all about being drawn to those things that complement how you're hard wired. Technical professionals thrive on details and want to be right about what they do. They're methodical, systematic, and exacting. Thank goodness! If they weren't such perfectionists, most of the things that they designed and then were manufactured would quickly fall apart. Ouch!

Q: I've heard of the concept, "Completed Staff Work." What is it?

A: Completed Staff Work was a principle or doctrine used by the military. It received some acclaim because of its successful use by General Dwight D. Eisenhower when he was Supreme Allied Commander in charge of the European Theater of Operations during World War II.

The doctrine, according to the Provost Marshal General (circa 1942), essentially stipulates that a direct report thoroughly study a problem and then present one or more recommendations to their immediate supervisor. The recommended solutions are to be detailed enough for their boss to make a sound decision and for them to implement it—if it's accepted.

The whole idea behind this canon was to get direct reports to stop dumping problems in their boss's lap without thinking them through. The practice helped avoid upwards delegation and kept problems at the appropriate level where they could best be dealt with. Plus, it won World War II in Europe!

LESSON 11

LEADING ORGANIZATIONAL CHANGE

CHAPTER 1 — INTRODUCTION

> *"Change is inevitable, except from a vending machine."*
> —*Anonymous*

> *"It ought to be remembered that there is nothing more difficult to take in hand, more perilous to conduct or more uncertain in its success, than to take the lead in a new order of things. Because the innovator has for enemies all those who have done well under the old conditions and lukewarm defenders among those who may do well under the new."*
> —*Machiavelli, "The Prince"*

To many company insiders, IBM used to mean "I've been moved!" because of their ingrained culture of frequently relocating their people. Every year approximately 20% of the American population packs up their belongings and moves elsewhere. That's an impressive figure if you truly consider the implications. Moving means leaving behind relatives, friends, schools, your favorite market or hardware store, service providers (doctors, barbers, tailors, mechanics, etc.). Then you have to re-establish all of these core and ancillary connections in your life when you settle into a new community.

I recently had a conversation with a neighbor whose husband just accepted a partnership position in Dallas with his firm. They have dwelled all their lives in Southern California, so this is a monumental change for them. She explained their decision as a big adventure—a great career opportunity for her husband and an exciting place to live for the family. However, they're both hedging their bets. They will lease their home in California and buy another in the Dallas area. They simply don't want to sever all of their significant roots.

Behavioral scientists have said that the average person in the world will die within 50 miles of the location of their birth. For most people change is not easily accepted. In fact, about 93% of the population will resist change. This resistance will manifest itself along a linear continuum from active, destructive resistance all the way to passive resistance. When people are passively resistant, they feign cooperation, but never follow through with the necessary actions.

In spite of this emotional muddle, the pace of change within organizations has dramatically accelerated over the past decade and that will continue. There are many underlying factors that led to this such as globalization, advancing technology, demographic patterns, the Internet, Free Trade Agreements, etc. The trends clearly indicate that change is inevitable and a fact of organizational life. Yet, as Machiavelli wrote many years ago, it is a difficult undertaking to manage and lead change efforts. Too often, because of a lack of understanding, attempts at change falter or fail with serious repercussions for the organization.

THE OBJECTIVE OF OUR LESSON

One of the premier measurements of leadership success is the ability to produce dramatic and useful change. When leaders are unable to deliver this particular outcome, the hold on their job is seriously weakened. Therefore, this capacity must be sharpened through a comprehensive understanding of the change process itself.

In this lesson, I'll unravel the confusion surrounding the predictable phases of change and how employees generally react to them. I'll share the fundamental reasons people have for not embracing change and what leaders like yourself can do about it. The focal point for furthering your mastery of the change process will be a hardy model that will *stick to your ribs*. In addition to outlining change in a coherent manner, the model will also point out compelling actions for you to take—and why.

CHAPTER 2 — WHY DO PEOPLE RESIST CHANGE?

How many times have you heard about couples who were married for a lifetime marked by reciprocal or unilateral abuse? Perhaps one or both were alcoholics, substance abusers, or dysfunctional human beings who took out their frustrations and anger on each other. Why, we might ask, did they stay together in their mutual misery? The answer is typically their greater fear of the unknown.

Fear of the unknown is a powerful magnet to maintain the status quo. If things are bad, at least we know how bad they are. If we leave or try to make a major change, our situation may become even worse. Heaven help us! Perhaps you've known someone who stayed in a job they hated, but wouldn't leave no matter what. The status quo is like gravity. It has a powerful pull to stay put and adapt. Breaking away is comparable to a rocket blasting off at Cape Canaveral. It has to reach a certain escape velocity to free itself from the gravitational field of the Earth.

ORGANIZATIONAL FEARS AND HABITS

Organizations sometimes have the same primitive fears as people. Remember the Avon Lady? Avon had thousands of female representatives ringing door bells across America several decades ago. Because of the extraordinary influx of women into the working environment during the last twenty-five years, few of them were home to answer that door bell. Furthermore, Avon was using slogans, packaging, and marketing approaches dating back to 1953. Nonetheless, they still persisted in doing things the archaic way since it conformed to their basic business model. In the last few years, their talented new CEO, Andrea Jung, has finally made significant changes that have resurrected the organization from imminent disaster.

Organizations, in many ways, emulate the behavior of individuals. Sometimes they stick to outmoded practices that inhibit their growth because of a fear of failure. IBM continued to market their large main frame computers even though customers were moving into smaller, networked personal computers. Why? Very likely they were afraid of losing the wide profit margins they made selling the big main frames. This shortsightedness resulted in a substantial loss of market share to competitors like Compaq (now merged with Hewlett-Packard) and Dell.

A number of years ago, a close colleague of mine asked me if I knew how the standard four foot eight and-a-half inch gauge (width) of a railroad track came about? I thought about it and hastily suggested that perhaps the early inventors of the railroad may have settled on it as a compromise. Frankly, I had no idea. He related a very interesting story from folklore that explains a lot about people and organizations.

During the time of the Roman Empire, the Romans built thousands of chariots that served as an important means of transportation. These chariots traversed the plentiful roads and trails throughout the entire Mediterranean region. Some of these routes were even built by the Greeks prior to the Romans. Eventually the chariots wore deep ruts into the roadways and so practical travelers would try to keep the wheels of the chariot in these ruts. Otherwise, the chariot would bounce in and out of the depressions making their journey very uncomfortable and sometimes hazardous.

Over the years, many wagons and carts were built with their axles the same width as a chariot's so they too could ride in these ruts. This became somewhat of a standard practice throughout Europe and the

Middle East. By the time railroads were invented in the early 1800's, the width of an axle was a fairly established measurement adapted in various countries. Of course, there were exceptions, like the five foot width in Russia, or Spain's five foot six inch gauge.

Also, many railroad purists insist that the gauge actually came from George Stephenson (who adapted the gauge for the Stockton and Darlington Railway in 1821). However, what they overlook is that Stephenson, an admirer of ancient Rome, was previously employed at the Northumbrian Coal Fields located close to Hadrian's Wall. The gauge of the mine's railways were four foot eight and-a-half inches. You can draw your own conclusions. So, the long-winded answer to the foregoing question is that the gauge of most railroad tracks is probably the same as a 2,000 year old Roman Chariot.

Old habits die very slowly, don't they? A friend of mine has an attractive, late model motorhome. When I first rode in it, I noticed his rearview mirror mounted on the inside of the windshield—as you'd expect to see in any automobile. However, in a motorhome, you can't see out the back looking in a rearview mirror. You only see into the living areas of the motorhome. So, why the rearview mirror? Why do you think it's there?

It's there because drivers anticipate it will be there. Most drivers would be very anxious if they didn't see a rearview mirror in front of them. All cars have them. Trucks have them. Even vans have them. Consequently, it follows that motorhomes should have them as well—even though they are operationally useless. They serve only an emotional purpose. It's an old habit that doesn't easily disappear.

THE PATH OF LEAST RESISTANCE

How many times have we heard someone say, "But we've been doing it this way for years!" I'll be the first to admit there is value in tradition, but we need to be careful about where we apply that axiom. If tradition compromises innovation, competitive advantage, leadership edge or anything else affecting our long-term viability, or our organization's, it's not good. Look at what happened to Avon. It occurs every day within many organizations.

People too often take the path of least resistance when it comes to change. Doing things differently generally means extra work and effort for them. At first thought, it might seem more advantageous to let things stay the way there are. It's easier and requires far less work. But this is misleading and disadvantageous in the long run. Of course, *things that don't change stay the same.*

Imagine what it would be like standing in the supermarket's checkout line if they didn't have scanners. What if their clerks didn't want to learn the new scanner process years ago? Ponder what your job might be like if you didn't use a computer. How would that affect your productivity, quality, or professional satisfaction? What if you refused to learn to use a computer or the various types of software required? How marketable would you be in your field?

Let's sum up below some of the most common reasons why people and organizations don't readily embrace change. We'll also add a few more to our list that we haven't directly discussed, although they may have been implied. For instance, people may become angry if they feel changes are threatening to their security. As a technical leader, you will find it necessary at one time or another to work through all of these with your people. Our next chapter will help prepare you more thoroughly for this responsibility.

- Fear of the unknown
- Fear of failure
- Insecurity or anxiety
- Breaking old habits (leaving your comfort zone)
- Extra work or effort
- Learning curves
- Anger

CHAPTER 3 — A MODEL OF THE CHANGE PROCESS

By the time we reach adulthood, most of us have experienced quite a bit of change in our lives. Some of it is <u>good</u> and some of it is <u>not so good</u>, but <u>all of it</u> causes us some stress. In reality, if you analyzed any of the reasons listed above for resisting change, you'd come to realize they all instigate some degree of stress. On a Social Readjustment Rating Scale, the following events are given stress values as follows (higher numbers equal greater stress):

Stress Value	Event
• 100	Death of a spouse
• 73	Divorce
• 53	Death of a close family member
• 50	Getting married
• 47	Terminated from work
• 38	Change in financial status
• 29	Change in work responsibilities
• 28	Outstanding personal achievement

Isn't it interesting that even good changes cause stress for people? Most managers fail to grasp that elementary principle. So, we can reliably conclude that all changes cause some stress. The key is how do you manage and lead people through it all. To do that effectively, we must visualize what the change process looks like. With that in mind, I want to share a Change Model with you below.

Notice that the vertical axis is associated with productivity and attitudes of people. The horizontal axis depicts the passage of time. You'll also observe numbers 1-4, which I'll explain in detail. Number 1 represents events and activities that occur <u>before</u> the change. This embodies everything that leads up to the eventual *Point of Implementation*. It is the ending of the way things used to be. Number 2 represents events and activities that occur directly following the change. As you can see, the productivity and attitudes of people plunge into the *Valley of Despair*. This sounds pretty terrible. After all, despair is a sense of <u>hopelessness</u>. Yet this is what people begin to feel as they experience all the negative aftereffects of the change.

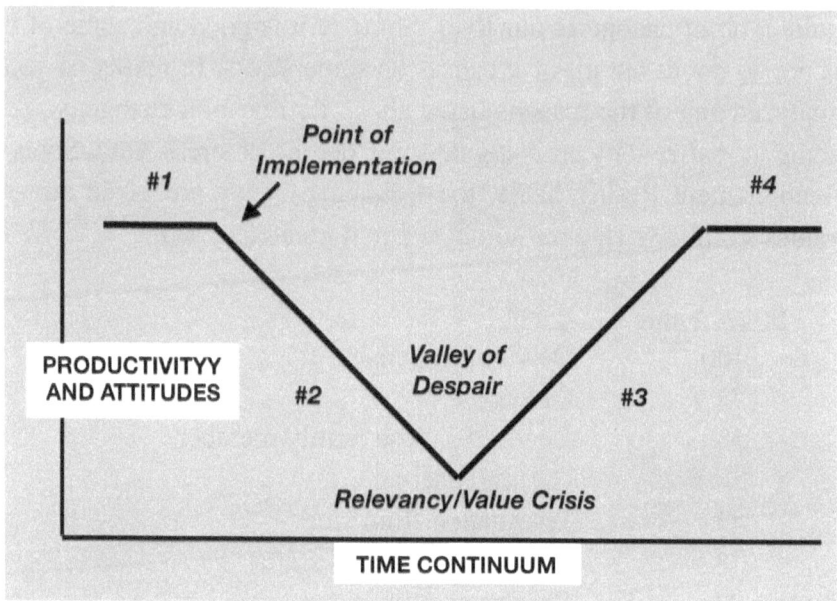

Number 3 represents the upside when things actually begin to improve and people start pulling together. Number 4 is the achievement of the goal. It becomes a *new beginning* for the group or organization.

The interesting thing about the whole change process is that managers present it to their people as if there were an invisible bridge that extended across *The Valley* from number 1 to number 4. As an illustration, they might say to their people, "We're merging divisions to reduce costs, streamline operations, and achieve economies of scale." It makes it sound so easy, as if we will journey from where we are today at "1" to where we want to be at "4." Wouldn't that be wonderful! However, that happens about 5% of the time. The rest of the time—95%—it's a linear plunge into the Valley of Despair.

SIGNS AND SYMPTOMS OF EACH STAGE

During the first stage, people are generally in <u>denial</u> about the impending change. Even if you've talked about it countless times, they still shrug it off with concealed disbelief. Their outright motivation is highly suspect and frequently it tends to be very selective. At this juncture, *they usually don't know what they don't know.*

Once the change is executed, they arrive at the Point of Implementation where stark reality quickly sets in. This locus is analogous to the *event horizon* of a galactic black hole. The force of gravity at the event horizon is so monumental, there's literally no possibility of escape. The same logic applies here, but it's precipitated by cynical emotion rather than gravity. The prevailing sentiment here is one of <u>resistance</u>.

In this phase, anxiety and insecurity are ubiquitous. People also grieve for what they perceive has been lost. There's frustration and dissatisfaction with the need to do things differently. These feelings magnify as the situation deteriorates, leading up to the *Relevancy/Value Crisis* at the bottom of the Valley of Despair. During this crisis, people accuse their leaders of bringing on this terrible predicament. They'll heap blame on you for being mislead. Can you recall, from your own experience, a situation where you promoted a change by being unnecessarily optimistic? What did your people say to you and what was the eventual outcome?

At the bottom of *The Valley,* people question the relevancy and value of the change. They often urge a retreat to the way things were. Leaders who give in to this unremitting pressure, even if it's the right thing to do, will lose some credibility. The next time they attempt to initiate any type of change, they'll find the going gets even tougher. This doesn't seem fair, but that's the toll people exact from their leaders for making 180 degree turns.

If you persevere through the Relevancy/Value Crisis, slowly things generally begin to improve. Instead of always fighting fires, you will now find a little time to do some fire prevention. You will discover that your direct reports are more willing to <u>explore</u> fresh ways of thinking and working. There's often a burst of creativity and collaboration here that facilitates teamwork.

Hopefully you can take advantage of the renewed goodwill and move your group along to stage 4—the achievement of the goal. This is the summit where you can celebrate the litany of emotion, events, and achievement. It's here that you'll obtain real, honest <u>commitment</u> from your team. Despite this victory, there are some dangers lurking in the shadows that could undermine what you have collectively attained.

Have you ever seen a champion athlete, who won a prized event, later become flabby and out of shape? In a subsequent contest, their poor condition is conspicuously apparent and results in a humiliating defeat. Complacency can naturally set in anywhere and with anyone, draining away all prior efforts. You can prevent this through a process I call *institutionalization,* a big word with a very important purpose. I'll discuss this, along with a number of other critical actions you'll need to take in the next chapter.

CHAPTER 4 — THE SPECIFICS OF LEADING ORGANIZATIONAL CHANGE

When managers are first exposed to the Change Model and gain an understanding of its stages, a pertinent question often arises. They ask, how can we get through the Valley of Despair more rapidly? This is a worthy concern and one that deserves our immediate attention. How quickly a group moves through the phases of change depends, to a large degree, on what the leader does before implementation in stage 1.

Because people are at various levels of readiness to change, much of their attitude depends on how any change is presented to them. Therefore, a leader must do four explicit things. First, inform people as early as you possibly can. Second, involve them in planning and other critical incidents. Third, encourage them by sharing the benefits of the change; and fourth, assure them that things will ultimately be okay. It's advisable to also let them know that you'll all likely hit some bumps along the way. It won't necessarily be smooth sailing!

Throughout any kind of change process, openness of communication is an absolute prerequisite. Leaders must share information early on and keep at it. Remember, during stage 1, people are in denial, so expect cursory motivation and lukewarm defenders—as Machiavelli would have put it.

Involving your direct reports in planning and other aspects of the change helps foster ownership. It puts their "fingerprint" on the process and broadcasts a conviction that the change is not being imposed from above. Encouraging them by emphasizing the personal benefits of the change, recognizes the selfishness that's an inherent part of our human psyche. Assuring them that we'll get through this, alleviates some of their insecurity and associated anxiety. No one wants to admit it's there, but nevertheless, it's there—and often in spades.

HOW TO DEAL WITH THE DOWNSIDE OF THE VALLEY

Once your people have set up *housekeeping in The Valley,* you will need to be eternally vigilant. You'll surely see poor performance and there's a strong likelihood you'll be counseling many of your people. Whether you like it or not, maximum leadership control is frequently required to keep everyone on track. I have found that the minute you take the pressure off of people, they instinctively go back to the old way of doing things. I know you want to avoid that at all costs.

Also, necessary resources will become scarcer than they normally are and they must be carefully monitored by your team. Be certain that each person has the training they need, when they need it. I call that, "just-in-time training." If they receive it too far in advance, they'll have a tendency to forget too many details.

Allow a time for grieving about the past. It's normal for people to first look at what they have to give up, what they will lose, rather than what they'll gain. Recognize that they have this sense of loss. Yet, be careful of the *Relevancy/Value Crisis.* You need to strike a very delicate balance there. Don't condone your direct reports wallowing in self pity, or compulsively placing blame on you for their unhappy circumstances. Accept whatever "licks" you have coming, yet stand tall and have the courage to continue to move ahead with the change. Lead by example.

THE UPSIDE OF THE VALLEY AND ULTIMATE ACHIEVEMENT

Once things begin to get a little better, there's always the temptation to ease up and hand out *weekend passes to the troops.* This is not a good idea! Instead, maintain appropriate levels of responsibility, authority, and accountability with each of your direct reports. Find some one-on-one time to coach or encourage your people and simultaneously recognize and reward good performance. "Atta-boys" and "Atta-girls" are a sincere expression that conveys the attitude that people are not taken for granted. You may also want to build in some appealing incentives for meeting specific performance targets.

Another thought to keep in mind is that sometimes the leader might perceive things are getting better, when—in actuality—their direct reports aren't experiencing that at all. This scenario becomes a disconnect between the leader and his or her followers, and can compromise group cohesiveness. How can you avert this? By being a good listener and preserving an open door policy. *(This is a good time to review Listening Skills in Lesson 9).*

Let's assume you've done everything right and your team has finally reached the fourth phase, or goal achievement. You now want to *institutionalize* this accomplishment. I introduced this term earlier in Chapter 3. What it means is to weave the change into the very fabric of organizational life.

In other words, we do things like hold people accountable for reporting on the change. Or, we reward people in a manner befitting how well they have mastered the change. Or, we may create some traditions surrounding the change. Or, we dovetail other salient practices with the change. Better yet, we do all of these things as part of an overall leadership strategy that helps lock in the change.

Institutionalizing change deters the change from drifting away to Never-Never Land. Haven't you witnessed organizations implementing one program after another only to see them evaporate over time? I call that the *program of the month club approach to leadership*. It's a big waste of time, resources, effort, and it brazenly robs the spirit of people in the organization. If you carefully follow the steps I've outlined in this lesson, you'll do a skillful, and hopefully fulfilling, job of leading people through all the intricacies of the change process. Furthermore, they'll emerge at the other end, intact and ready for whatever challenges may lie beyond.

CHAPTER 5 — CONCLUSION

It's remarkable how insightful Machiavelli was about change. With all the changes we observe in organizations in this new millennium, some things appear not to change. One of them is the basic nature of human beings. On the whole, people resist change and the kind of resistance that crystallizes will vary depending upon the individual. Some people will aggressively resist, while others will be quite passive. They'll say the right things to the boss, but then they generally fail to deliver "the goods."

The underlying core reasons for not subscribing to change has a lot to do with fear, insecurity, and extra work or effort. People quickly get comfortable with their personal habits and have a genuine distaste for anything that disrupts them. Even good changes, like receiving a promotion or getting married, can result in some level of personal stress. It's crucial for leaders to understand this basic principle, along with others regarding change.

One fact of organizational life is that change *is* the natural state of things. It can also be delineated as a four phase process that occurs almost 95% of the time. Therefore, it behooves leaders to become familiar with this change model and the accompanying behaviors that apply to leading people through each phase.

The cardinal emotions in each of the four phases are denial, resistance, exploration, and commitment, respectively. By focusing on these pivotal emotional states with reciprocal behaviors, leaders are able to make indispensable progress. When they forget the basics of each phase, they can easily fall into traps that exacerbate the entire situation.

A significant distinction of being a leader is to produce dramatic and useful organizational change. This lesson will help you make that expectation a day-to-day reality.

LESSON ELEVEN ASSIGNMENT - ISSUES AROUND CHANGE

The purpose of this activity is to give you an opportunity to think about a recent change, how it affected you and your team, and what you would now do differently. Contemplate a recent challenging or dramatic change and its affect and answer the questions below.

1. Recent Change: Describe a recent change in the organization or unit you lead. This might be any related business experience affecting where or how you work, or who you work with.

   _____
   _____
   _____

2. Feelings: How did you and your direct reports initially feel about the change? How did you and the others feel afterwards?

   _____
   _____
   _____

3. Outcome of This Change: What was the final outcome of this change (either positive, negative, or both) on you and your people?

   _____
   _____
   _____

4. Motivation: How did you keep yourself and your people going or motivated during the change?

   _____
   _____
   _____

5. In Retrospect: Looking back, and with knowledge of the change model in this lesson, what would you do differently?

_____
_____
_____

LESSON ELEVEN MULTIPLE-CHOICE QUIZ
(Answers on the Following Pages)

1. Behavioral scientists say that the average person in the world will die within 50 miles of where they were born. Why is this so?

   A. They probably had difficulty obtaining a visa or passport.
   B. Moving is a change, and 93% of the population will resist it.
   C. They married someone local and set down roots.
   D. They might have difficulty adapting to different weather patterns.

2. Two of the most common reasons for resisting change are...

   A. Not understanding the change and not buying into it.
   B. Not trusting the organization and not respecting the boss.
   C. Fear of the unknown and fear of failure.
   D. Personal disorganization and impatience.

3. Why do even good changes cause some personal stress?

   A. Because it means doing things differently and that takes extra energy.
   B. Only major good changes cause personal stress.
   C. Because it's just another task to add to the list of "To Do's."
   D. Because good changes almost always have rigid, short deadlines.

4. The Relevancy/Value Crisis...

   A. Is what senior management wrestles with prior to deciding on an organizational change.
   B. Has to do with the financial return on a pending change.
   C. Is part of the debriefing and analysis following phase 4.

D. Is at the bottom of the Valley of Despair, where many leaders give up.

5. What do we mean by the term institutionalization?

    A. Weaving changes into the very fabric of the organization.
    B. Adopting outmoded bureaucratic policies.
    C. The maturing of an organization with more defined leader roles.
    D. When an organization becomes rigid and inflexible.

LESSON ELEVEN MULTIPLE-CHOICE QUIZ
(Answers)

1. Behavioral scientists say that the average person in the world will die within 50 miles of where they were born. Why is this so?

   A. They probably had difficulty obtaining a visa or passport.
      Incorrect.
      There's a need for change here—and it's your answer.

   B. Moving is a change, and 93% of the population will resist it.
      Correct.
      Good start! (I'm really moved.)

   C. They married someone local and set down roots.
      Incorrect.
      Nope, put down your bouquet (or boutonniere) and try again.

   D. They might have difficulty adapting to different weather patterns.
      Incorrect.
      Seasons are not the reasons.

2. Two of the most common reasons for resisting change are...

   A. Not understanding the change and not buying into it.
      Incorrect
      Although these certainly add to the difficulty, they are not primary causes.

   B. Not trusting the organization and not respecting the boss.
      Incorrect
      Again, these will worsen the controversies for the leader, but these aren't the core issues.

C. Fear of the unknown and fear of failure.
Correct
Fear not! You're absolutely right.

D. Personal disorganization and impatience.
Incorrect
Nope. Go to the back of the line—and do not pass "Go."

3. Why do even good changes cause some personal stress?

A. Because it means doing things differently and that takes extra energy.
Correct
Yes, and I'm enlivened by your astuteness.

B. Only major good changes cause personal stress.
Incorrect
Just about every change—good or bad— causes personal stress.

C. Because it's just another task to add to the list of "To Do's."
Incorrect
Negative; read chapter 3 again.

D. Because good changes almost always have rigid, short deadlines.
Incorrect
Not necessarily so.

4. The Relevancy/Value Crisis...

A. Is what senior management wrestles with prior to deciding on an organizational change.
Incorrect

Good guess, but you're off the mark and need to change your answer.

B. Has to do with the financial return on a pending change.
Incorrect
My apologies, this answer just doesn't pencil out.

C. Is part of the debriefing and analysis following phase 4.
Incorrect
Good try, but try again.

D. Is at the bottom of the Valley of Despair, where many leaders give up.
Correct
Where shall I send your medal?

5. What do we mean by the term institutionalization?

A. Weaving changes into the very fabric of the organization.
Correct
My admiration is looming.

B. Adopting outmoded bureaucratic policies.
Incorrect
No dessert for you tonight!

C. The maturing of an organization with more defined leader roles.
Incorrect
Somewhere we have a short circuit.

D. When an organization becomes rigid and inflexible.
Incorrect
Nope. Your account is overdrawn and maybe arthritic.

IRV GAMAL, M.A.

LESSON ELEVEN FREQUENTLY ASKED QUESTIONS

Q: What part of the change model seems to be the most difficult for leaders to deal with?

A: Good question. Of course, all portions of the change model present their own challenges. However, from my vantage point, I believe that leaders drop the ball mostly in phase four, "New Beginnings"—when the goal has been achieved. Why? Because they have hit their target and now get distracted with other things that take precedence.

Moreover, they don't institutionalize their achievement and it then becomes fair game for the program of the month club. Before you know it, people are back to what they did before and no one seems to care. As I said in the lesson, this robs people of their spirit or vitality and is terribly demoralizing.

Q: What can you do with a boss who closely guards information about impending changes?

A: Bosses, like anyone else, are motivated by certain things. Closely guarding information is frequently a way of exercising control and power. Bosses who hoard information may be somewhat insecure or just thoughtless. When you have received information from the boss, let him or her know afterwards how helpful that information was. Explain how it enabled you to do your job better and what that meant to the overall change.

Show him or her how effective that behavior was and contrast it, if you can, with another manager (perhaps a competitive peer of theirs[2]) who kept things to himself or herself. Cite how that created problems for their people, and eventually the manager. Hopefully, all of this will get them to re-examine their motives, behaviors, and the related outcomes.

---

[2] Be careful of the person you select. Given your individual situation, you might want to talk about a manager in a PREVIOUS organization and the consequences of their behavior for everyone, including themselves.

LESSON 12

BUILDING A HIGH-PERFORMANCE ENVIRONMENT

CHAPTER 1 — INTRODUCTION

> *"No man is an island, entire of itself; every man is a piece of the continent, a part of the main."*
>
> —*John Donne (1573?-1631)*

One of the perplexities of organizational life is that it often requires a certain degree of what's called *rugged individualism* to rise up within the ranks. If we blend in too much with others, we don't get noticed by top managers. Then—magically—we're supposed become a dedicated team player within our peer group as well as to foster teamwork among our direct reports.

To add to this challenge, technical professionals can be fiercely competitive although they do value collegiality. *(See Lesson 8 for a definitive review of the characteristics of technical professionals).* Yet, no leader can expect to create a high performance environment without relying heavily on teams. In a recent Business Week article, John

Chambers, CEO of Cisco Systems noted, "I learned a long time ago that a team will always defeat an individual. And, if you have a team of superstars, then you have a chance to create a dynasty."

USC's Center For Effective Organizations points out that in 1996, 78% of all organizations had some self-directed teams. This compares to only 28% in 1978, an increase of 278% in just 18 years. Furthermore, this statistic only applies to self-directed teams and doesn't cite other types of teams which may have assigned leadership obligations.

Over the last two decades, organizations have adopted an abundance of internal improvement initiatives such as TQM, Business Process Re-Engineering, ISO 9000, U.S. Malcolm Baldrige National Award criteria, etc. The vast majority of these systematic practices or requirements are dependent on widespread team efforts. Some companies, in their rush to achieve results, push ahead prematurely without establishing bona fide teams. Instead, what they wind up with are actually groups disguised as teams—and, pitifully, they can't tell the difference.

Of course, the differences are profound and perhaps only later acknowledged when the desired results are never produced. All too often organizations mistakenly think they have authentic teamwork when all they have are groups of people working side by side. Oddly enough, when you consider the differences between the two, they are indeed striking. Teamwork exists when *there's emotional ties to the work and among the members of the team. There's support, trust, commitment, a common vision and mission, etc.* On the other hand, *group work is just being together with others in the same proximity.*

Many years ago, I worked as a member of a brilliant professional group of internal Organizational Development Consultants in an engineering firm. Each of us had a speciality area where we excelled and which seemed to complement the skill-sets of our peers. We accomplished monumental feats for our company and, as a result, we were well respected within the organization. To this day, over twenty years later, we still maintain business relationships and periodically socialize as well.

There is no doubt in my mind we were a team, and not a group. We genuinely had an affinity for each other and, although we were strong individualists, we pulled together in the same direction. Our casual get-togethers are analogous to an alumni club. In fact, I would speculate that the ties that bind us are even more robust than if they were reinforced officially by the organization's culture. However, that doesn't thwart the power of formalized structure. As a case in point, in Lesson 2, we observed that Disneyland had a formal Alumni Association and I invited you to consider whether you would be a member if your organization had a similar group. The implications are important because it expresses something about the level of teamwork you honestly perceive.

The bottom line is this: When people feel a fundamental bond to their associates, there are higher levels of commitment, loyalty, affection, and emotional connections that are difficult to sever. All of these *ingredients* help to perpetuate a climate of elevated energy, focus, and productivity that culminate in *high performance achievements.*

THE OBJECTIVE OF OUR LESSON

Therefore, in this lesson, I'll assist you in building such a high performance environment by stimulating and sustaining vigorous levels of teamwork within the people you lead. We'll delve into eliminating any vestiges of group work by understanding the team development process. I'll share relevant personal experiences, consider issues that can undermine teamwork, and what you can do to overcome them. Essentially, I will underscore that you never settle with anything less than creating a team of technical professionals resolved to achieving challenging organizational goals.

Of course, if you reflect on it, each one of our lessons have been fashioned to create this special kind of working climate. It's my wish, however, that this lesson will serve as the capstone for our entire course on Leadership Skills For Managing Technical Professionals.

CHAPTER 2 — THE TEAM DEVELOPMENT PROCESS

As John Donne said, no man is an island. We all need other people in our lives and we require healthy emotional links with those in our family and with our inner circle of friends. About forty years ago, Abraham Maslow, the Harvard Behavioral Psychologist, identified social needs as one of man's universal affective necessities. Without those supportive ties in our life, we sink into isolation, loneliness, and depression. Thus, having meaningful relationships nourishes our emotional well-being.

When you weigh how much time you spend at work, as compared with other portions of your life, does it seem that work occupies a significant segment of your existence? These days most people work an average of approximately 47 hours a week. You might be working considerably more and yearn for only 47 hours as a bit of a break.

Whatever the case may be, your working life consumes a major amount of your time. Since you only have so much time to apportion, chances are you will not have as much discretionary time for family and friends as you'd ideally desire. Therefore, obtaining some emotional nourishment at work through your relationships becomes even more compelling.

This doesn't mean that family isn't your first priority, which it ought to be. It signifies that there's innate value in establishing relationships at work that transcend business issues alone. With this as a foundation for the potency of teamwork's contribution, let's focus on the team development process.

THE PHASES OF TEAM DEVELOPMENT

Working as an effective team, like most human endeavors, involves a cycle of development and growth in which people have an opportunity to acclimate themselves, test their limits, and then become highly productive contributors. Trying to work as a team without an understanding of how teams develop can create problems. It can be likened to trying to raise a child without any concept of the child development process. Our expectations may be inappropriate for the child's stage of development.

This can deteriorate into a situation which creates frustration on the parents' side and a sense of failure on the child's. Understanding the stages of a child's development enables us to better cope with the child as he or she moves through the stages of growth.

Teams, like individuals, evolve in a fairly predictable manner. To illustrate, they typically go through four phases of development: *Forming, Storming, Norming, and Performing.*

Phase I: Forming (Orientation)
- Getting acquainted
- Communicating goals
- Establishing operational guidelines
- Seeking a place in the group

Phase II: Storming (Conflict)
- Experiencing conflicting expectations
- Expressing differing opinions and having various capabilities
- Fearing some kind of loss and/or failure
- Competing for resources, time, position (status), etc.
- Struggling for power
- Mistrusting and manipulating others

Phase III: Norming (Cohesion)
- Realizing a new sense of identity
- Finding enthusiasm for the task
- Being sensitive to the needs of others
- Sharing ideas, information, and resources

Phase IV: Performing (Interdependence—the result)
- High degree of commitment
- High degree of effectiveness
- Productive problem solving
- High morale
- Highly creative approaches
- Intensely loyal

A CLOSER LOOK AT DEVELOPMENT PHASES AND ISSUES

<u>Phase One</u>. Teams invariably begin as nothing more than a collection or group of people who have been brought together to achieve some objective. The process of uniting these individuals to form an effective team begins with the *Forming Stage* of team development. Here people become acquainted, communicate the goals of the team, and establish basic operational ground rules, such as when to meet, how decisions will be made, and who does what. It is also during this phase that individuals seek to establish a place for themselves in the group. *(See model below).*

Key Issues of this Phase:
- Goals of the team
- Roles of the members
- Procedures (ground rules they'll follow)

PHASE IV	PHASE I
PERFORMING Empowering Open and trusting Flexible Confident Resourceful Close and supportive Interdependent Team pride Defer to team needs Much work is completed	**FORMING** Polite, impersonal Getting to know each other Watchful, guarded Cautious participation Optimism or nervousness Grouping No trust yet Uncommitted members Unclear roles Minimal work is completed
NORMING Involving Cooperative Communication Appreciation & Trust Building Focused Purposed well defined Procedures established Constructive confrontation Sense of team cohesiveness Feedback given and received Confide, share problems Moderate work is completed	**STORMING** Jockeying for position Increased tension Trying out new ideas Conflict is unresolved Confronting people Defensiveness, resisting Unsuccessful problem solving Polarization of group members Anxiety abounds Feeling of being "stuck" Opting out Minimal work is completed
PHASE III	PHASE II

Phase Two. This is the rocky shoal against which most teams invariably crash. Here, individuals selfishly begin to compete for attention and influence. Self-interest often supersedes both the interest of the team and the organization, resulting in subsequent power struggles. Issues, such as power, authority, and resources, must be settled during this phase before the team can function properly.

Key Issues of this Phase:
- Interpersonal issues
- Hidden agendas

Phase Three. The team that reaches this phase has successfully passed through the prior phases. They have obtained a new sense of identity and enthusiasm for their task. They are more sensitive to the needs of their team members and are willing to reveal ideas, information, and resources in the interest of achieving the team's objectives. Task considerations of the team are now beginning to override personal ambitions and concerns.

Key Issues of this Phase:
- Interpersonal effectiveness
- Task focus

Phase Four. The final phase of development is the *Performing Stage*. Team members have resolved structural and interpersonal issues at this phase and can work together with a high degree of commitment and effectiveness. All their efforts are directed toward productive problem solving and achieving the objectives of the team. Team members exhibit high morale, high creativity and productivity, and are intensely loyal to other team members.

Key Issues of this Phase:
- Interpersonal loyalty
- Creative problem solving

Nearly seventy-five percent of the time when I'm consulting with an organization with the aim of improving teamwork, the major issues revolve around goals, roles, or procedures. What this indicates to me is that many times organizations have difficulty getting beyond Phase One of team development. By thoroughly understanding this growth process, you'll be able to progress well beyond this initial level.

CHAPTER 3 — A TEAM DEVELOPMENT EXPERIENCE

The most effective teams are those closely linked to the strategic goals of an organization. Those sweeping goals become the reference point or beacon for all of their activities and helps firmly anchor their vision and mission. Let me recount a personal experience with you about how a parallel type of scenario unfolded. Many years ago, I was with a company that was rapidly expanding through acquisitions and new office openings across the United States. One of our corporate managers discovered we were losing over $17 million a year because of nonproductive new offices. They presented this alarming disclosure to top management who enlisted my help to turn it around.

I was given an absolute mandate so it was necessary to move fast. I knew I could only solve the complexity of problems with a senior group of managers drawn from various locations across the country. This introduced both advantages and disadvantages into our development process. On the plus side, we gained multiple perspectives, regional variations on our company's culture, and people who knew local issues affecting new offices. On the negative side, we inherited strangers who didn't know each other, regional variations on our company's culture (they can concurrently be positive and negative), and strong individualists with their own hidden agendas.

Because we had to swiftly become a performing team, I had to somehow find a way to move everything into warp-drive. I decided to launch our initiative with a three-day retreat in the picturesque mountains of Southern California. The first day would be accentuated by a Ropes—Outward Bound abbreviated—type of experience that would be videotaped. The second and third days would be dedicated to planning and implementation issues.

I chose a Ropes Experience because it would trigger deep emotional imprinting during our time together. That is, the very nature of Ropes—the activities and presumed risks—create a profusion of anxiety, fear, and exhilaration. This, in turn, compresses the time required to learn about each other and would move us full-tilt through Phase One into Phase Two and beyond. When people viewed the video the first evening, they laughed, cried, hugged, swore, clapped, whooped, etc. The parade of emotions witnessed that day fully cemented our group into a team by the end of our retreat.

As you might expect, the good feelings, closeness, and focus of the team easily diminished when the individual members returned to their regional offices. I knew this would possibly happen because the nature of people is to manage those things that are in front of their noses. At the tail end of our retreat, we scheduled a number of follow-up meetings to be hosted by alternate team members around the country. These meetings would be progress reviews to hold members accountable for their project goals, reinforce our team's commitment, and to handle special problems that would surely arise. We also built in social time to have some fun together.

We were developing an intense national training program for all new office managers to attend. The program would have to teach them the skills, provide the information, and supply critical resources necessary for them to succeed. All of this entailed a literal mountain of work to be completed within a short period. To give *presence to the project and to the team,* we designated a name for our project, designed a logo, handed out team sweatshirts, and other labeled paraphernalia. We had a defined vision, mission, and a detailed action plan. Everyone had their marching orders, budgets, and deadlines. Individual project goals were incorporated into each team members annual performance appraisal to close the loop on accountability.

Our meetings were very spirited events with a structured agenda and specific, delineated outcomes. Everyone had a copy of the agenda beforehand and knew what to review, what to bring, and what would be discussed. We maximized every second of our time because we didn't have a choice. Even our social time had a purpose—to continue the bonding of the team.

On a few occasions, I had to jump in and resolve interpersonal conflicts among members. These were very accomplished senior managers with big egos that occasionally needed soothing and corralling. I saw that as part of my job being the team leader. Sometimes, members were pulled away into other ventures and I found it necessary to gently remind their bosses of the importance of our work. In one instance, I remember a recalcitrant boss who simply wouldn't back off. I *diplomatically* urged him to call our company's CEO to explain why he was shanghaiing my team member for his own pet project. Needless to say, he immediately had a noble change of heart.

THE EPILOGUE

You might be wondering what the culmination of all this team energy was? We rolled out a six-day training program in record time—and exactly on schedule. It was radically different from anything seen previously in the company. As a matter of fact, attendees, at first, didn't quite know what to make of it. People were sworn to secrecy about the particulars of the program, but were free to talk about how they felt afterwards. Word of the program spread like wildfire across the nation and everyone wanted to be nominated to attend.

The comprehensive training was enormously successful and, within a year, curtailed most of the losses propagated by new offices. Some offices were bad choices to begin with and had to be closed.

Nonetheless, the program exceeded everyone's expectations and continued to be presented for many years within the organization. The original team later received national recognition for their outstanding contribution to the organization.

CHAPTER 4 — OVERCOMING OBSTACLES TO TEAM DEVELOPMENT

Any group has the potential to become a team. This applies to the people you supervise, a cross-functional group, problem-solving groups, ad-hoc committees, etc. In the example I recounted with you above, I would never have achieved the goals without a solid team of people behind me. The same is true of yourself. Group work will only carry you so far. If you are determined to achieve your own career ambitions, you will have to build a team of supporters. Just as I had no choice about some facets of the training project, you have no choice about this fact of organizational life.

Below, I'll catalog some of the most typical obstacles that can get in your way of effectively building a team. I'll also list out some possible ways of dealing with each one.

Obstacle	**Possible Ways To Improve**
<u>Problems With Goals</u>	
• *Unclear*	Outline goals in written form and have your people confirm their understanding.

Obstacle	Possible Ways To Improve
• *Unachievable*	Obtain feedback from the team on the achievability of goals. (Give some examples of relevant success stories).
• *Unrealistic*	Carefully monitor your progress toward the goal and, if necessary, re-evaluate.
• *Inconsistent with personal philosophy*	Talk one-on-one with the person to discover the resistance and show them—if possible—how to achieve their personal goals without undermining the team goal. Point out the benefits of this to them.

Problems with Roles

• *Undefined*	Analyze the team's objectives to learn what needs to be done and the skills required.
• *Overlapping*	Clearly define functional responsibilities in written form and distribute to the team.
• *Inappropriate*	Be selective about the members of the team. Readjust assignments if people cannot deliver.
• *Not linked to ability*	Move people so they can work from their strengths. Provide extra training if necessary.

Obstacle	Possible Ways To Improve

Problems with Procedures and Systems

- *Inadequate* — Be willing to change your procedures or provide support in working around them.

- *Too complex* — Simplify or interpret them so they are understood. Provide training.

- *Archaic/outdated* — Look for better ways to achieve your results.

- *Not documented* — Put them in writing so everyone's working from the same page. (Documentation has power!)

- *Not agreed upon* — Facilitate a forum for ironing out differences of opinion. Encourage compromise.

Problems with Interpersonal Issues

- *Inadequate communication skills* — Demonstrate the importance of good communication skills. Provide relevant training in the communication process.

- *No understanding of interpersonal style differences* — Train in conflict resolution, style differences, and use personal assessment process.

Obstacle	Possible Ways To Improve
Problems with Hidden Agendas	
• *Fear of loss or failure*	Meet privately with team members to discuss their personal objectives.
• *Territory or control*	Help them look for ways to achieve their personal objectives.
• *Competitiveness or self-interest*	Openly discuss with the team the potential for hidden agendas that could hinder team achievement. Talk generally about each type of agenda and their destructive potential. When they arise, handle them discreetly in private.

Allow me to elaborate on some of these dysfunctional hidden agendas. <u>Fear of loss and/or failure</u>. The losses we fear can be almost anything—resources, status, money, responsibility, influence, power, or position. Fear of loss almost invariably demonstrates itself in resistance to change.

<u>Territorial behavior</u>. Protecting our territory is a fundamental human drive. We protect our jobs because they keep roofs over our heads and feed and clothe our families. Over-protecting our territory is indicated by the inability to tolerate change. The individual who over-protects, feels threatened, at risk, and will resist change almost on principle.

<u>Control</u>. Unrestrained control indicates a lack of confidence or trust in the ability of others to make *the right* decision, or produce a specific result. Extreme control often indicates an inflated self-image which requires control and power to fuel it.

<u>Excess Competition</u>. A limited amount of internal competition can be valuable to a team. It spurs people on to greater levels of performance and makes work more exciting and fun. Superfluous

competition creates a different type of work environment—and it is *not fun*. Excess competition is usually demonstrated by an insatiable need for approval and an oversized need to be right. Someone else has to lose something, either status, power, or resources, for the prodigiously competitive (zero sum) person to feel good about himself or herself.

Self-interest. Self-interest refers to the inability to do anything above our own personal interest. Our success is measured by the personal rewards we achieve, such as career advancement, gaining more authority and responsibility, and being rewarded financially for the effort. It is a "What's in it for me?" mentality versus an approach which asks instead, "What service can I provide?" or "How can I contribute to the well-being of others?"

Certainly there are other factors to keep in mind as you strive to build a team. For example, optimal team size is 7-9 people. Yet, we cannot—nor is it my intention—to cover everything that could possibly stand in your way. What you have here is a distillation of the most prominent obstacles and how to judiciously move through them. The rest is up to you.

CHAPTER 5 — CONCLUSION

Organizational life for a manager is sometimes analogous to walking on a balancing beam. On the one hand, you need to be an accomplished individual performer, and on the other, a committed team player. Not only that, but you need to build a team with those people you supervise and with other groups you lead. The challenges you face in accomplishing all of this are impressive.

Teams are now an integral part of most organizations and as such they're here to stay. They are often central to internal initiatives geared to improving some aspect of quality, service, or achieving a coveted industry standard. Managers who are able to move beyond mediocre group work to establish genuine teamwork frequently achieve remarkable results. This subsequently opens doors to unforeseen opportunities and normally accelerates their own career advancement.

Technical professionals are readily drawn to work in high performance environments where they become active contributors. Their penchant for competitiveness, though, can easily undermine any trace of collegiality or teamwork. Therefore, managers who want to exercise leadership need to reign in this idiosyncrasy and foster consistent team behaviors. That requires a sound understanding of many things, including the phases of the team development process. We characterized those phases as: Forming, Storming, Norming, and Performing.

I shared with you an actual team development experience where I *compressed* the time required for moving through some of these stages. This was planned out of necessity, but could be replicated in almost any given situation. There were bumps along the path and it was necessary to intermittently jump into uncomfortable situations. As the team leader, that's an expected obligation you cannot delegate. Our ultimate success was a direct result of the high levels of talent, commitment, and focus we had as a team.

Unfortunately, even when you pull off most things correctly, obstacles will arise that could undo plentiful good work. When this occurs, you'll need to take action immediately and follow some generally accepted guidelines. These steps should move you further ahead, and in most instances, alleviate the majority of problems the team will encounter.

IN RETROSPECT

Congratulations! We've likely been together for some time now and you've admirably stayed the course. Frankly, I'm very pleased. As you look back over the breadth of the program in this book, you'll likely glimpse that you've studied a considerable amount of material—ideas, principles, anecdotes, models, research, etc. Leadership Skills For Managing Technical Professionals is a special type of self-study course. It was designed and written especially for you, the professional manager who wants to perform better as a leader. It's my earnest hope that I've been able to play a small, but meaningful, part in helping you to achieve this very worthy goal. Now go forth and make me proud.

LEADERSHIP SKILLS FOR MANAGING TECHNICAL PROFESSIONALS

LESSON TWELVE ASSIGNMENT — TEAMWORK QUESTIONNAIRE

The purpose of this questionnaire is to give you an opportunity to think about your people's awareness of and commitment to effective teamwork. Circle the points for each statement that (in your opinion) best describes your situation (with "10" being high). Answer candidly and honestly. This questionnaire will provide you with a reliable appraisal of your current situation, and an important "benchmark" for measuring your improvements over the coming year.

1. Goals. To what extent are organizational goals carefully developed and clearly communicated to staff members?

   1   2   3   4   5   6   7   8   9   10

2. Roles. To what extent are roles formally defined and communicated to staff members?

   1   2   3   4   5   6   7   8   9   10

3. Procedures. To what extent are ground rules for your team plainly understood?

   1   2   3   4   5   6   7   8   9   10

4. Interpersonal Issues. To what extent are interpersonal issues overcome and not allowed to impair the team's productivity?

   1   2   3   4   5   6   7   8   9   10

5. Hidden Agendas. To what extent are hidden agendas exposed and addressed in your team?

   1   2   3   4   5   6   7   8   9   10

6. Cohesion. To what extent does your team operate as a cohesive unit that strives to achieve a common goal?

   1   2   3   4   5   6   7   8   9   10

7. Loyalty. To what extent does your team exhibit loyalty to other team members?

    1   2   3   4   5   6   7   8   9   10

8. Communication. To what extent are channels of communication open? To what extent do team members communicate freely?

    1   2   3   4   5   6   7   8   9   10

9. Safe Environment. To what extent do team members feel that they operate in a safe environment where they do not hesitate to express their beliefs and ideas?

    1   2   3   4   5   6   7   8   9   10

LESSON TWELVE MULTIPLE-CHOICE QUIZ
(Answers on the Following Pages)

1. What's the fundamental difference between a group and a team?

   A. A group is made up of the people you supervise at work and a team is what you observe in professional sports.
   B. Team's have leaders and groups don't.
   C. Members of a team are committed to their goal and to each other. People working in proximity to one another are simply a group.
   D. A group is temporary and a team is far more permanent.

2. The four phases of team development are...

   A. Getting acquainted, communicating goals, establishing guidelines, and finding a place in the group.
   B. Individual contributor, audience or crowd, group work, and team work.
   C. Creating a vision, defining your mission, action planning, and implementation.
   D. Forming, Storming, Norming, and Performing.

3. How can you hold people accountable for team goals?

   A. Hold periodic review meetings and make them part of their annual performance appraisal process.
   B. Make personal appeals that have an emotional flavor to them.
   C. Dangle a "carrot" as an incentive.
   D. Show them what's in for them, i.e., the benefits.

4. About seventy-five percent of the time, team problems center around what three issues?

A. Commitment, implementation, and accountability.
B. Goals, roles, and procedures.
C. Vague mission, poor meetings, and interpersonal conflict.
D. An axe to grind, hidden agendas, and oversize egos.

5. What are two things you can do to handle a team member's hidden agenda?

    A. Expose it in a staff meeting and call them on it.
    B. Send them an email making them aware you know and explain how it disrupts the team.
    C. Share your concerns with other team members and seek a volunteer to confront them.
    D. Meet with them <u>privately</u> and explore ways to help them achieve their personal goals.

LEADERSHIP SKILLS FOR MANAGING TECHNICAL PROFESSIONALS

LESSON TWELVE MULTIPLE-CHOICE QUIZ
(Answers)

1. What's the fundamental difference between a group and a team?

   A. A group is made up of the people you supervise at work and a team is what you observe in professional sports.
   Incorrect
   You're out! Sorry, but you can create a team anywhere.

   B. Team's have leaders and groups don't.
   Incorrect.
   Both can have leaders.

   C. Members of a team are committed to their goal and to each other. People working in proximity to one another are simply a group.
   Correct.
   Right on the money!

   D. A group is temporary and a team is far more permanent.
   Incorrect.
   Both of them can be temporary or permanent.

2. The four phases of team development are…

   A. Getting acquainted, communicating goals, establishing guidelines, and finding a place in the group.
   Incorrect
   This is all about the first phase only.

   B. Individual contributor, audience or crowd, group work, and team work.
   Incorrect
   Pull over, this is reckless thinking!

261

C. Creating a vision, defining your mission, action planning, and implementation.
Incorrect
Certainly part of what a team might do, but not the stages of growth.

D. Forming, Storming, Norming, and Performing.
Correct
Bingo!

3. How can you hold people accountable for team goals?

A. Hold periodic review meetings and make them part of their annual performance appraisal process.
Correct
You get an "A" for being Absolutely right.

B. Make personal appeals that have an emotional flavor to them.
Incorrect
This doesn't work the majority of the time.

C. Dangle a "carrot" as an incentive.
Incorrect
This might provoke some level of personal motivation, but it does nothing for accountability.

D. Show them what's in for them, i.e., the benefits.
Incorrect
This could heighten their motivation, but it contributes little or nothing to accountability.

4. About seventy-five percent of the time, team problems center around what three issues?

A. Commitment, implementation, and accountability.
Incorrect

These three can be formidable issues, but they are not the biggest.

B. Goals, roles, and procedures.
Correct
Another direct hit.

C. Vague mission, poor meetings, and interpersonal conflict.
Incorrect
Nope, this isn't it.

D. An axe to grind, hidden agendas, and oversize egos.
Incorrect
Better review the lesson again.

5. What are two things you can do to handle a team member's hidden agenda?

A. Expose it in a staff meeting and call them on it.
Incorrect
Better have someone walk you to your car after work.

B. Send them an email making them aware you know and explain how it disrupts the team.
Incorrect
Emails are good for many things. This isn't one of them.

C. Share your concerns with other team members and seek a volunteer to confront them.
Incorrect
This is your baby—you can't dump it off on someone else.

D. Meet with them <u>privately</u> and explore ways to help them achieve their personal goals.
Correct
Very good. You're on your way to building excellent teams.

IRV GAMAL, M.A.

LESSON TWELVE FREQUENTLY ASKED QUESTIONS

Q: How can I honestly tell if the group I supervise is a team and not just a group?

A: For starters, why not ask them? Pay attention to the things they say about their peers. Do they genuinely respect and like one another? Do they ever socialize outside of the work environment? Do they willingly share information and support each other emotionally? Are they committed to an overall vision and mission? Will they go the extra mile to help someone within the group who's in need?

All of your answers to these questions will provide valuable information that should indicate the level of teamwork in your group. Additionally, how do their answers match up with your own? What's your take on your team?

Q: Why is it so hard to maintain teamwork when an organization begins to downsize or generally go through some hard times?

A: Often, when people are scared, which is what they are in the situation above, they run for the life boats. Everyone has to fend for themselves! Is this the right thing to do? Of course not. Yet, it's generally what happens.

People begin to feel isolated and alone; that they are experiencing things somewhat differently than others. The truth of the matter is that they are all experiencing similar things. If they're not constantly reminded of this by their leader they don't reach out for one another.

Q: I tend to be more on the quiet side. I'm not the cheerleader type. How do I build a team given my own personality style?

A: Remember Level 5 Leadership? These are the best leaders according to Jim Collins. Level 5 Leaders are not cheerleaders either. They are committed, honest, straightforward, and unpretentious leaders who care about what they're doing and care about their people. There's a quiet strength and confidence in them that attracts others.

Be yourself. You'll do just fine.

APPENDIX

LESSONS 1 - 12 PRE-TEST
(Answers Beginning on Page 281)

Directions: Circle the letter of your preferred answer. When done, determine your score.

1. Generation Xers tend to be somewhat lacking in their interpersonal skills when compared to other generations preceding them. Why is this so?

   A. Gen Xers spent more time interacting with technology in their youth than they did interacting with each other.
   B. Public education did not stress this as an important skill set.
   C. Gen Xers are still in a learning curve regarding these skills. It's still too early to tell.
   D. Gen Xers are so good at mastering technology, it makes their interpersonal skills look weak by comparison. It just isn't so.

2. Generalized statements made about any generation usually pertain to about what percentage of that group?

   A. One standard deviation from the mean, or 68% of the people.
   B. About 80% of the people.
   C. The entire generation.
   D. About 20% of the people.

3. Gen Xers tend to be jaded and leery about trusting organizations with their financial security or career. Why?

   A. Most of them had stay-at-home moms who encouraged them to avoid big organizations.
   B. They distrust anyone over thirty years of age.
   C. They watched lots of TV portraying organizations as big and impersonal.

D. They witnessed the hypocrisy of mass layoffs, lukewarm teamwork, and poor quality of life for their parents.

4. What do we mean by the term *world-class organization?*

   A. A high technology, trendy organization.
   B. A company that has its operations spread around the globe.
   C. An organization that sets the standard for others to follow.
   D. A company that generally makes the news.

5. How can a company absorb lower profits, declining market share, and a depressed stock price and still be considered world class?

   A. Because things in the external world occur which are beyond anyone's control. For example, the "tech wreck" of 2000, September 11, etc. Many excellent companies struggle through bad times and emerge even stronger than before.
   B. The world class title is only loosely applied to both good and mediocre companies.
   C. Once a company receives that designation, it cannot be taken away.
   D. They can continue to perform poorly until someone blows the whistle.

6. Why is it important for companies to give their employees something to believe in and care about?

   A. People are isolated today and need a laudable cause.
   B. People feel they are doing something significant and that makes them feel important.
   C. People believe most organizations are self serving and this won't work.
   D. The pressures of work are more intense and stressful than ever.

7. Many managers would have no difficulty explaining what management is, but hedge when it comes to elaborating on leadership. Why is this so?

   A. For the last 100 years, the emphasis has been on management, and not on leadership.
   B. Management and leadership are essentially the same, so the small differences that do exist are tricky—at best—to explain.
   C. Leadership needs to exist at the top of an organization and management at all other levels. Leadership is for the leaders to explain.
   D. The concept of leadership is so cryptic it defies explanation.

8. Managers who don't provide enough direction for their direct reports may later discover that…

   A. Employees are happier with the lack of structure.
   B. Collectively, their direct reports have risen to the occasion in spite of them.
   C. Most people don't care one way or the other.
   D. Their people become frustrated and anxious about their job performance.

9. What is meant by managing the emotions of an organization?

   A. This is the essence of effective leadership: responding to the predominant emotional needs that exist at any given time.
   B. Offering an Employee Assistance Program for the rank-and-file.
   C. Listening and displaying genuine empathy to employees.
   D. Adults are children grown larger and a boss needs to treat them more as a parent would.

10. One of the rising trends in the country is for technical professionals to seek union representation. What do you believe is the underlying pivotal reason for this?

A. Strong arm tactics by coercive union representatives.
B. Lucrative union health plans and other fancy benefits.
C. The underlying lack of trust in top management.
D. Unions see white collar professionals as a new source of revenue to supplant their thinning ranks.

11. Why is integrity so critical to building trust within an organization?

    A. It's not. Integrity is a situational "thing."
    B. Without integrity, there is no possibility of trust. Without trust, there can be no worthy, long-lasting relationships.
    C. Integrity, by its very nature, plays a secondary role related to trust.
    D. Virtue is back in style, so it's politically correct to say integrity is critical.

12. Why is it important to show *authentic concern* for people?

    A. We live in a "feel good" age where managers are being taught en masse to *make nice to people.*
    B. Human Resource managers have made this an important appraisal characteristic that receives consistent scrutiny.
    C. First off, authentic means it's real. People aren't being manipulated. Secondly, concern means you care. When you show that then people care about what they do.
    D. People expect it and it meets that tepid expectation.

13. Many technical managers feel *like a fish out of water* when it comes to being visionary. Why do they feel this way?

    A. They missed or dropped out of a visioning course in their undergraduate work.
    B. It's not in their current job description.
    C. They believe visioning is analogous with being a psychic like Nostradamus.

D. They compare themselves with great visionaries in the media and apparently come up short.

14. What is a Vision Statement?

   A. It's an ethics code of practice for ophthalmologists.
   B. It's a mission statement written in the future tense.
   C. It's a compelling, powerfully worded, hoped-for state for an organization. A destination to be achieved in unison sometime in the future.
   D. It's a carefully worded document that nobody pays attention to.

15. An example of aligning a Vision Statement in an organization would be…

   A. Straightening the framed Vision Statement on the lobby wall.
   B. Having the top management team share their sentiment for it.
   C. Supporting the Vision Statement through relevant training, coaching, and performance evaluation.
   D. Making sure all margins are even on the final printed copy of the vision statement.

16. In the final analysis, the bottom line for leaders is what?

   A. Maintaining shareholder value.
   B. Achieving results.
   C. Increasing profitability, or in the case of not-for-profit or non-profit organizations, cutting costs.
   D. Creating "brand recognition" for products and services.

17. What was John Goddard's claim to fame?

   A. He was the first to establish international theme parks.
   B. He was an unconventional religious leader.
   C. He achieved a remarkably difficult number of very esoteric goals.
   D. He was a renowned rocket scientist.

18. An individual's level of motivation appears to have a lot to do with how they perceive their probability of success. When do you suppose their motivation to achieve is at the highest level?

    A. When they seek the "low hanging fruit."
    B. When they see their chances at about ten percent.
    C. When they are entrepreneurial and have the freedom to perform as they see fit.
    D. People are optimally motivated to achieve when they consider their chances at approximately 50/50.

19. The most important criteria in helping a manager snap back from possible derailment is...

    A. Their strong personal desire for change.
    B. A confidential, forthright talk with their immediate supervisor.
    C. A carefully considered promotion.
    D. A transfer to another part of the organization.

20. What's the difference between a management layer and a management level?

    A. There are only three layers of management and there can be multiple levels.
    B. A management layer is specifically associated with managers who are assigned in an "acting role."
    C. The three levels of management pertain to officers, middle, and lower management. Multiple layers can exist within each level.
    D. Layers relate to pay grades and levels to stock options.

21. Which type of job task that an individual might perform provides the most organizational visibility and why?

A. Negotiable Tasks because the person's adeptness in presenting a position may be noticed.
B. Project Tasks because they often have strategic value.
C. Routine Tasks because when things go wrong, everyone is probably looking.
D. Troubleshooting Tasks because it might instigate an emergency situation.

22. The greatest weaknesses of technical professionals often lie within which skill set?

    A. Their Conceptual or Strategic Skills because they tend to be focused on the here-and-now.
    B. Their penmanship frequently is hard to decipher because their thoughts race faster than their hands can move.
    C. Their Interpersonal Skills because it's typically not their strength, nor have they had much training in it either.
    D. Their inclination to disregard current fashion or the importance of proper business attire.

23. Technical professionals customarily identify more with their field than with their organization. Why is this so?

    A. They have made an immense investment of time, money, and effort in learning their field.
    B. They may be new to the organization and haven't quite adapted.
    C. The propensity of companies to continuously cut staff.
    D. Their company may have them working on mundane, boring projects.

24. Technical professional thrive mostly on...

    A. Impulsive opportunities to do things differently.
    B. Intuitive synthesis of apparently unrelated items.

C. Opportunities to do stand-up presentations in front of a group.
D. Challenge and achievement.

25. There are three progressively more meaningful levels of listening. What are they?

    A. One-on-one, small group, and large crowds.
    B. Verbal, nonverbal, and intuitive.
    C. Hearing, comprehending, and understanding.
    D. Acting, thinking, and feeling.

26. Nonverbal communication represents a major part of our overall communications. What might be a typical example of non-verbal communications?

    A. Gestures, or tone of voice, or facial expression.
    B. *Reading between the lines* with respect to what someone says.
    C. Gut-level reactions to a given situation.
    D. Past, present, or future tense of the message.

27. Paraphrasing and reflection are two key responding skills that help you to…

    A. Keep the conversation going.
    B. Verify and clarify.
    C. Identify where a project went off track.
    D. Maintain a calm attitude in a difficult situation.

28. The two most prevalent reasons keeping technical managers from delegating are…

    A. Job pressures and an unwillingness to invest more time guiding or counseling their people.
    B. Novice staff and limited administrative controls.
    C. Their lack of trust and fear of losing control.
    D. The scarcity of time and their own impatience.

29. What is the principle of leverage as applied to leadership?

   A. Heavy objects can be moved with ease when a fulcrum is set in the proper place.
   B. Manipulative behaviors can move people to action, but there's a price the leader may pay.
   C. Output has an inverse relationship to input.
   D. You are able to expand your influence and impact on others through effective delegation.

30. An employee's initiative must be at the highest level when he or she acts and routinely reports. Why is this so?

   A. Their visibility in the organization mandates nothing less.
   B. Because they have control over both the timing and the content of what they do.
   C. Very likely they're a high potential employee.
   D. It is established by a Memorandum of Understanding (MOU).

31. Why do even good changes cause people some level of personal stress?

   A. Only <u>major</u> good changes cause personal stress.
   B. It means doing things differently and that takes extra energy.
   C. It's just another responsibility to add to the list of "To Do's."
   D. Good changes almost always have strict, short deadlines.

32. How was the standard gauge of most railroad tracks settled on?

   A. It was established when the transcontinental railroad was built across the United States in the 19th Century.
   B. It was a compromise worked out by the League of Nations after World War I.

C. It's based on 1/10 the distance of the standard length of a railroad boxcar.
D. It's probably based on the axle length of ancient Roman Chariots.

33. When everything is considered, two of the most ubiquitous reasons for resisting change are...

    A. Impatience and personal disorganization.
    B. Not trusting the organization and not respecting the boss.
    C. Not understanding the change, nor buying into it.
    D. Fear of the unknown and fear of failure.

34. What types of internal organizational initiatives almost always require a high commitment to teamwork?

    A. TQM, Business Process Re-Engineering, ISO 9000, etc.
    B. Reduction in force, or consolidating operations.
    C. Improved Human Resources processes such as new performance appraisals, various interviewing formats, etc.
    D. Implementing new executive compensation programs or defined pay grades.

35. What's the most basic difference that defines a group as compared to a team?

    A. A group is a temporary unit and a team is far more permanent.
    B. People working in close proximity to each other are a group. Members of a team are committed to their goal and to one another.
    C. Team's have leaders and groups don't.
    D. A group is made up of the people you supervise at work and a team is what you might observe in the sport's world.

36. The four specific phases of team development are...

   A. Individual contributor, spectators or crowd, group work, and team work.
   B. Getting acquainted, discussing goals, confirming guidelines, and fitting into a group.
   C. Creating a vision, defining your mission, action planning, and implementing the plan.
   D. Forming, Storming, Norming, and Performing.

Now, check your responses on the following pages and come up with a percentage of correct answers.

LESSONS 1 - 12 PRE-TEST
(Answers)

1. Generation Xers tend to be somewhat lacking in their interpersonal skills when compared to other generations preceding them. Why is this so?

   A. Gen Xers spent more time interacting with technology in their youth than they did interacting with each other.
   Correct
   Obviously, this was not the case for previous generations. This is the right answer.

   B. Public education did not stress this as an important skill set.
   Incorrect
   Unfortunately, public education did not stress many things! The correct answer "A."

   C. Gen Xers are still in a learning curve regarding these skills. It's still too early to tell.
   Incorrect
   We're all learning until the day we die. Yet, the youngest Gen Xers can legitimately make this statement. However, the correct answer is still "A."

   D. Gen Xers are so good at mastering technology, it makes their interpersonal skills look weak by comparison. It just isn't so.
   Incorrect
   It is so. The correct answer is "A."

2. Generalized statements made about any generation usually pertain to about what percentage of that group?

A. One standard deviation from the mean, or 68% of the people.
   Incorrect.
   About one standard deviation from the mean, plus the strongest 16%, will usually exhibit the characteristics. The lowest 16% to 20% will not. Your correct answer is "B" or about 80% of the people.

B. About 80% of the people.
   Correct.
   About 20% of the make-up of a generation will customarily be the exception to the rule.

C. The entire generation.
   Incorrect.
   There will always be exceptions to the information. Your correct answer is "B" or about 80% of the people.

D. About 20% of the people.
   Incorrect.
   This indicates that 80% of the generation will be the exception. This is too high a number. Your correct answer is "B" or about 80% of the people.

3. Gen Xers tend to be jaded and leery about trusting organizations with their financial security or career. Why?

   A. Most of them had stay-at-home moms who encouraged them to avoid big organizations.
      Incorrect.
      Most of their moms worked and many Gen Xers were in day care. The correct answer is "D."

   B. They distrust anyone over thirty years of age.
      Incorrect.

This is more of a throwback to the self-indulgent 1960's and the Baby Boomers. The correct answer is "D."

C. They watched lots of TV portraying organizations as big and impersonal.
Incorrect.
Although they did watch quite a bit of TV growing up and this helped imprint some of their values, it didn't create their overall attitude toward organizations. The correct answer is "D."

D. They witnessed the hypocrisy of mass layoffs, lukewarm teamwork, and poor quality of life for their parents.
Correct.
Many of them became disgusted at what they saw as gross violations of words and actions within organizations.

4. What do we mean by the term *world-class organization?*

A. A high technology, trendy organization.
Incorrect.
World class-organizations may be found in any industry, and might—in fact—be very low tech. The correct answer is "C."

B. A company that has its operations spread around the globe.
Incorrect.
Although a world-class organization may operate worldwide, that's not the criteria for being world class. The correct answer is "C."

C. An organization that sets the standard for others to follow.
Correct.
The standard may be in one or a variety of areas, like: customer service, quality, on-time delivery, working climate, etc.

D. A company that generally makes the news.

Incorrect.
Sorry, you may read or hear about them in the news, but that's not on the mark. The correct answer is "C."

5. How can a company absorb lower profits, declining market share, and a depressed stock price and still be considered world class?

   A. Because things in the external world occur which are beyond anyone's control. For example, the "tech wreck" of 2000, September 11, etc. Many excellent companies struggle through bad times and emerge even stronger than before.
   Correct
   This is the optimum answer.

   B. The world class title is only loosely applied to both good and mediocre companies.
   Incorrect
   That's not the case. The right answer is "A."

   C. Once a company receives that designation, it cannot be taken away.
   Incorrect.
   It can be taken away if the company is not performing at a level worthy of that title. The right answer is "A."

   D. They can continue to perform poorly until someone blows the whistle.
   Incorrect
   Whistle-blowers perform a vital function. But this may have nothing to do with a world-class organization. If they are not doing anything wrong, there's no reason to *blow the whistle*. The right answer is "A."

6. Why is it important for companies to give their employees something to believe in and care about?

A. People are isolated today and need a laudable cause.
   Incorrect.
   Although the sense of community is less than it used to be, this is not the best reason. "B" is the correct answer.

B. Because it makes people feel they are doing something significant and that makes them feel important.
   Correct.
   When people believe they are performing noteworthy work that translates into commitment.

C. People believe most organizations are self serving and this won't work.
   Incorrect.
   Many companies may be viewed that way. People do want to believe their company is different and want to support their choice to work there. "B" is the correct answer.

D. Because the pressures of work are more intense and stressful than ever.
   Incorrect.
   Although this is certainly the case, that's not the best answer. "B" is the correct answer.

7. Many managers would have no difficulty explaining what management is, but hedge when it comes to elaborating on leadership. Why is this so?

   A. For the last 100 years, the emphasis has been on management, and not on leadership.
      Correct
      Exactly. There have been majors in management, management workshops, management development, management books, management retreats, etc.

B. Management and leadership are essentially the same, so the small differences that do exist are tricky—at best—to explain.
Incorrect
Not at all! The correct answer is "A."

C. Leadership needs to exist at the top of an organization and management at all other levels. Leadership is for the leaders to explain.
Incorrect.
Leaders need to exist at all management levels. The correct answer is "A."

D. The concept of leadership is so cryptic it defies explanation.
Incorrect
Leadership can be explained. The correct answer is "A."

8. Managers who don't provide enough direction for their direct reports may later discover that…

A. Employees are happier with the lack of structure.
Incorrect.
The key words in the question are *enough direction*. This should tell you that it's simply insufficient. The correct answer is "D."

B. Collectively, their direct reports have risen to the occasion in spite of them.
Incorrect.
It's possible that a few people may actually do this. However, this is the exception and not the rule. The correct answer is "D."

C. Most people don't care one way or the other.
Incorrect.

People are generally not apathetic when it comes to performance issues that could affect their perceived security. The correct answer is "D."

D. Their people become frustrated and anxious about their job performance.
Correct.
People want to know what's expected of them. They also want a reference point by which to gauge their performance.

9. What is meant by managing the emotions of an organization?

A. This is the essence of effective leadership: responding to the predominant emotional needs that exist at any given time.
Correct.
That's right.

B. Offering an Employee Assistance Program for the rank-and-file.
Incorrect.
The correct answer is "A."

C. Listening and displaying genuine empathy to employees.
Incorrect.
No doubt this is critical, but not quite the right answer. The correct answer is "A."

D. Adults are children grown larger and a boss needs to treat them more as a parent would.
Incorrect.
Adults are not children grown larger. The correct answer is "A."

10. One of the rising trends in the country is for technical professionals to seek union representation. What do you believe is the underlying pivotal reason for this?

A. Strong arm tactics by coercive union representatives.
   Incorrect
   Some unions have a reputation for questionable practices in the past. This, however, is not behind this pattern. The correct answer is "C."

B. Lucrative union health plans and other fancy benefits.
   Incorrect
   They're not that fancy. The correct answer is "C."

C. The underlying lack of trust in top management.
   Correct
   There may be several reasons, but this is at the core.

D. Unions see white collar professionals as a new source of revenue to supplant their thinning ranks.
   Incorrect
   There may be some truth in this concerning union motivation, but that's not what this question is about. The correct answer is "C."

11. Why is integrity so critical to building trust within an organization?

    A. It's not. Integrity is a situational "thing."
       Incorrect.
       You may want to think this over again. The correct answer is "B."

    B. Without integrity, there is no possibility of trust. Without trust, there can be no worthy, long-lasting relationships.
       Correct.
       Good, we're on the same frequency.

    C. Integrity, by its very nature, plays a secondary role related to trust.

Incorrect.
It plays a primary role—always! The correct answer is "B."

   D. Virtue is back in style, so it's politically correct to say integrity is critical.
Incorrect.
Virtue is back in style because it is observed less and less. Let's hope it's here to stay. Integrity is a virtue and it's vital to our society because without it our institutions, relationships, and agreements fall apart. This has nothing to do with political correctness. The correct answer is "B."

12. Why is it important to show *authentic concern* for people?

   A. We live in a "feel good" age where managers are being taught en masse to *make nice to people.*
Incorrect
The correct answer is "C."

   B. Human Resource managers have made this an important appraisal characteristic that receives consistent scrutiny.
Incorrect
It may be part of an evaluation process, but that's not the overriding reason for doing it. The correct answer is "C."

   C. First off, authentic means it's real. People aren't being manipulated. Secondly, concern means you care. When you show that, people care about what they do.
Correct
Research always seems to back this up.

   D. People expect it and it meets that tepid expectation.
Incorrect
The correct answer is "C."

13. Many technical managers feel *like a fish out of water* when it comes to being visionary. Why do they feel this way?

    A. They missed, or dropped out of a visioning course in their undergraduate work.
    Incorrect.
    The correct answer is "D."

    B. It's not in their current job description.
    Incorrect.
    I'm sure that's so. The correct answer is "D."

    C. They believe visioning is analogous with being a psychic like Nostradamus.
    Incorrect.
    The correct answer is "D."

    D. They compare themselves with great visionaries in the media and apparently come up short.
    Correct.
    Not a fair comparison, but, nonetheless, the correct one. Visioning is a process that can be learned by practically anyone.

14. What is a Vision Statement?

    A. It's a code of practice ethics for ophthalmologists.
    Incorrect
    We don't see eye-to-eye on this. The correct answer is "C."

    B. It's a mission statement written in the future tense.
    Incorrect
    Some people might see it this way. Unfortunately, that's not appropriate. The correct answer is "C."

C. It's a compelling, powerfully worded, hoped-for state for an organization. A destination to be achieved in unison sometime in the future.
Correct
Yes, this is it.

D. A carefully worded document that nobody pays attention to.
Incorrect
This lamentably can happen, but it's not what a vision statement is. The correct answer is "C."

15. An example of aligning a Vision Statement in an organization would be…

A. Straightening the framed Vision Statement on the lobby wall.
Incorrect.
The correct answer is "C."

B. Having the top management team share their sentiment for it.
Incorrect.
Certainly, we want that. However, the correct answer is "C."

C. Supporting the Vision Statement through relevant training, coaching, and performance evaluation.
Correct.
This is part of aligning values and beliefs with capabilities and skills.

D. Making sure all margins are even on the final printed copy of the vision statement.
Incorrect.
The correct answer is "C."

16. In the final analysis, the bottom line for leaders is what?

A. Maintaining shareholder value.

Incorrect
That's what Wall Street believes. The correct answer is "B."

B. Achieving results.
Correct
This is the right answer.

C. Increasing profitability, or in the case of not-for-profit or non-profit organizations, cutting costs.
Incorrect
These are overall strategies. The correct answer is "B."

D. Creating "brand recognition" for products and services.
Incorrect
The correct answer is "B."

17. What was John Goddard's claim to fame?

A. He was the first to establish international theme parks.
Incorrect.
The correct answer is "C."

B. He was an unconventional religious leader.
Incorrect.
The correct answer is "C."

C. He achieved a remarkably difficult number of very esoteric goals.
Correct.
This is the right answer.

D. He was a renowned rocket scientist.
Incorrect.
That was Robert Goddard. The correct answer is "C."

18. An individual's level of motivation appears to have a lot to do with how they perceive their probability of success. When do you suppose their motivation to achieve is at the highest level?

    A. When they seek the "low hanging fruit."
       Incorrect.
       The correct answer is "D."

    B. When they see their chances at about ten percent.
       Incorrect.
       The correct answer is "D."

    C. When they are entrepreneurial and have the freedom to perform as they see fit.
       Incorrect.
       The correct answer is "D."

    D. People are optimally motivated to achieve when they consider their chances at approximately 50/50.
       Correct.
       This is the right answer.

19. The most important criteria in helping a manager snap back from possible derailment is…

    A. Their strong personal desire for change.
       Correct.
       Good! This is the right answer.

    B. A confidential, forthright talk with their immediate supervisor.
       Incorrect.
       Often helpful, but not the correct answer, which is "A."

    C. A carefully considered promotion.
       Incorrect.

Promoting someone in derailment makes no sense. The correct answer is "A."

D. A transfer to another part of the organization.
Incorrect.
This usually passes the problem along to someone else. The correct answer is "A."

20. What's the difference between a management layer and a management level?

   A. There are <u>only</u> three layers of management and there can be multiple levels.
   Incorrect.
   You've confused layers and levels. The correct answer is "C."

   B. A management layer is specifically associated with managers who are assigned in an "acting role."
   Incorrect.
   The correct answer is "C."

   C. The three levels of management pertain to officers, middle, and lower management. Multiple layers can exist within each level.
   Correct
   This is the right answer.

   D. Layers relate to pay grades and levels to stock options.
   Incorrect.
   The correct answer is "C."

21. Which type of job task that an individual might perform provides the most organizational visibility and why?

   A. Negotiable Tasks because the person's adeptness in presenting a position may be noticed.

Incorrect.
The correct answer is "B."

B. Project Tasks because they often have strategic value.
Correct.
Absolutely right.

C. Routine Tasks because when things go wrong, everyone is probably looking.
Incorrect.
The correct answer is "B."

D. Troubleshooting Tasks because it might instigate an emergency situation.
Incorrect.
The correct answer is "B."

22. The greatest weaknesses of technical professionals often lie within which skill set?

   A. Their Conceptual or Strategic Skills because they tend to be focused on the here-and-now.
   Incorrect
   The correct answer is "C."

   B. Their penmanship frequently is hard to decipher because their thoughts race faster than their hands can move.
   Incorrect
   The correct answer is "C."

   C. Their Interpersonal Skills because it's typically not their strength, nor have they had much training in it either.
   Correct
   This is right.

A. Their inclination to disregard current fashion or the importance of proper business attire.
Incorrect
The correct answer is "C."

23. Technical professionals customarily identify more with their field than with their organization. Why is this so?

    A. They have made an immense investment of time, money, and effort in learning their field.
    Correct.
    This is the right answer.

    B. They may be new to the organization and haven't quite adapted.
    Incorrect.
    The correct answer is "A."

    C. The propensity of companies to continuously cut staff.
    Incorrect.
    The correct answer is "A."

    D. Their company may have them working on mundane, boring projects.
    Incorrect.
    The correct answer is "A."

24. Technical professional thrive mostly on…

    A. Impulsive opportunities to do things differently.
    Incorrect.
    The correct answer is "D."

    B. Intuitive synthesis of apparently unrelated items.
    Incorrect
    The correct answer is "D."

C. Opportunities to do stand-up presentations in front of a group.
Incorrect
The correct answer is "D."

D. Challenge and achievement.
Correct
This is the right answer.

25. There are three progressively more meaningful levels of listening. What are they?

A. One-on-one, small group, and large crowds.
Incorrect.
The correct answer is "C."

B. Verbal, nonverbal, and intuitive.
Incorrect.
The correct answer is "C."

C. Hearing, comprehending, and understanding.
Correct.
This is right.

D. Acting, thinking, and feeling.
Incorrect.
The correct answer is "C."

26. Nonverbal communication represents a major part of our overall communications. What might be a typical example of non-verbal communications?

A. Gestures, or tone of voice, or facial expression.
Correct
This is right.

B. *Reading between the lines* with respect to what someone says.

Incorrect.
The correct answer is "A."

C. Gut-level reactions to a given situation.
Incorrect.
The correct answer is "A."

D. Past, present, or future tense of the message.
Incorrect.
The correct answer is "A."

27. Paraphrasing and reflection are two key responding skills that help you to…

A. Keep the conversation going.
Incorrect.
This is a following skill. The correct answer is "B."

B. Verify and clarify.
Correct
Good, this is right.

C. Identify where a project went off track.
Incorrect.
The correct answer is "B."

D. Maintain a calm attitude in a difficult situation.
Incorrect.
The correct answer is "B."

28. The two most prevalent reasons keeping technical managers from delegating are…

A. Job pressures and an unwillingness to invest more time guiding or counseling their people.
Incorrect.

The correct answer is "C."

B. Novice staff and limited administrative controls.
Incorrect.
The correct answer is "C."

C. Their lack of trust and fear of losing control.
Correct.
Can you see my smile in your minds-eye?

D. The scarcity of time and their own impatience.
Incorrect.
The correct answer is "C."

29. What is the principle of leverage as applied to leadership?

A. Heavy objects can be moved with ease when a fulcrum is set in the proper place.
Incorrect.
Not the right kind of leverage. The correct answer is "D."

B. Manipulative behaviors can move people to action, but there's a price the leader may pay.
Incorrect.
Considerable truth here. Nonetheless, the correct answer is "D."

C. Output has an inverse relationship to input.
Incorrect.
The correct answer is "D."

D. You are able to expand your influence and impact on others through effective delegation.
Correct
This is accurate.

30. An employee's initiative must be at the highest level when he or she acts and routinely reports. Why is this so?

    A. Their visibility in the organization mandates nothing less.
       Incorrect
       The correct answer is "B."

    B. They have control over both the timing and the content of what they do.
       Correct
       Exactly right.

    C. Very likely they're a high potential employee.
       Incorrect
       The correct answer is "B."

    D. It's established by a Memorandum of Understanding (MOU).
       Incorrect
       The correct answer is "B."

31. Why do even good changes cause people some level of personal stress?

    A. Only major good changes cause personal stress.
       Incorrect
       Not true. The correct answer is "B."

    B. It means doing things differently and that takes extra energy.
       Correct
       Yes, you're right.

    C. It's just another responsibility to add to the list of "To Do's."
       Incorrect
       The correct answer is "B."

    D. Good changes almost always have strict, short deadlines.

Incorrect

The correct answer is "B."

32. How was the standard gauge of most railroad tracks settled on?

    A. It was established when the transcontinental railroad was built across the United States in the 19th Century.
    Incorrect
    The correct answer is "D."

    B. It was a compromise worked out by the League of Nations after World War I.
    Incorrect
    The correct answer is "D."

    C. It's based on 1/10 the distance of the standard length of a railroad boxcar.
    Incorrect
    The correct answer is "D."

    D. It's probably based on the axle length of ancient Roman Chariots.
    Correct
    Nero would have been proud of you if he stopped fiddling.

33. When everything is considered, two of the most ubiquitous reasons for resisting change are…

    A. Impatience and personal disorganization.
    Incorrect
    The correct answer is "D."

    B. Not trusting the organization and not respecting the boss.
    Incorrect
    The correct answer is "D."

C. Not understanding the change, nor buying into it.
Incorrect
Not doubt this can be a big problem. But, the correct answer is "D."

D. Fear of the unknown and fear of failure.
Correct
You're absolutely right.

34. What types of internal organizational initiatives almost always require a high commitment to teamwork?

A. TQM, Business Process Re-Engineering, ISO 9000, etc.
Correct
You are right.

B. Reduction in force, or consolidating operations.
Incorrect
The correct answer is "A."

C. Improved Human Resources processes such as new performance appraisals, various interviewing formats, etc.
Incorrect
The correct answer is "A."

D. Implementing new executive compensation programs or defined pay grades.
Incorrect
The correct answer is "A."

35. What's the most basic difference that defines a group as compared to a team?

A. A group is a temporary unit and a team is far more permanent.
Incorrect.
Either can be temporary or permanent. The correct answer is "B."

B. People working in close proximity to each other are a group. Members of a team are committed to their goal and to one another.
Correct.
Yes, you're right.

C. Team's have leaders and groups don't.
Incorrect.
The correct answer is "B."

D. A group is made up of the people you supervise at work and a team is what you might observe in the sport's world.
Incorrect
The correct answer is "B."

36. The four specific phases of team development are…

A. Individual contributor, spectators or crowd, group work, and team work.
Incorrect
The correct answer is "D."

B. Getting acquainted, discussing goals, confirming guidelines, and fitting into a group.
Incorrect
The correct answer is "D."

C. Creating a vision, defining your mission, action planning, and implementing the plan.
Incorrect
The correct answer is "D."

D. Forming, Storming, Norming, and Performing.
Correct
Good.

LESSONS 1 - 12 POST-TEST
(Answers Beginning on Page 317)

Directions: Circle the letter of your preferred answer. When done, determine your score.

1. What is meant by managing the emotions of an organization?

   A. This is the essence of effective leadership: responding to the predominant emotional needs that exist at any given time.
   B. Offering an Employee Assistance Program for the rank-and-file.
   C. Listening and displaying genuine empathy to employees.
   D. Adults are children grown larger and a boss needs to treat them more as a parent would.

2. Which type of job task that an individual might perform provides the most organizational visibility and why?

   A. Negotiable Tasks because the person's adeptness in presenting a position may be noticed.
   B. Project Tasks because they often have strategic value.
   C. Routine Tasks because when things go wrong, everyone is probably looking.
   D. Troubleshooting Tasks because it might instigate an emergency situation.

3. Generation Xers tend to be somewhat lacking in their interpersonal skills when compared to other generations preceding them. Why is this so?

   A. Gen Xers spent more time interacting with technology in their youth than they did interacting with each other.
   B. Public education did not stress this as an important skill set.

C. Gen Xers are still in a learning curve regarding these skills. It's still too early to tell.
   D. Gen Xers are so good at mastering technology, it makes their interpersonal skills look weak by comparison. It just isn't so.

4. What is the principle of leverage as applied to leadership?

   A. Heavy objects can be moved with ease when a fulcrum is set in the proper place.
   B. Manipulative behaviors can move people to action, but there's a price the leader may pay.
   C. Output has an inverse relationship to input.
   D. You are able to expand your influence and impact on others through effective delegation.

5. How can a company absorb lower profits, declining market share, and a depressed stock price and still be considered world class?

   A. Because things in the external world occur which are beyond anyone's control. For example, the "tech wreck" of 2000, September 11, etc. Many excellent companies struggle through bad times and emerge even stronger than before.
   B. The world class title is only loosely applied to both good and mediocre companies.
   C. Once a company receives that designation, it cannot be taken away.
   D. They can continue to perform poorly until someone blows the whistle.

6. Generalized statements made about any generation usually pertain to about what percentage of that group?

   A. One standard deviation from the mean, or 68% of the people.
   B. About 80% of the people.
   C. The entire generation.

D. About 20% of the people.

7. What was John Goddard's claim to fame?

   A. He was the first to establish international theme parks.
   B. He was an unconventional religious leader.
   C. He achieved a remarkably difficult number of very esoteric goals.
   D. He was a renowned rocket scientist.

8. What's the most basic difference that defines a group as compared to a team?

   A. A group is a temporary unit and a team is far more permanent.
   B. People working in close proximity to each other are a group. Members of a team are committed to their goal and to one another.
   C. Team's have leaders and groups don't.
   D. A group is made up of the people you supervise at work and a team is what you might observe in the sport's world.

9. There are three progressively more meaningful levels of listening. What are they?

   A. One-on-one, small group, and large crowds.
   B. Verbal, nonverbal, and intuitive.
   C. Hearing, comprehending, and understanding.
   D. Acting, thinking, and feeling.

10. In the final analysis, the bottom line for leaders is what?

    A. Maintaining shareholder value.
    B. Achieving results.
    C. Increasing profitability, or in the case of not-for-profit or non-profit organizations, cutting costs.
    D. Creating "brand recognition" for products and services.

11. What do we mean by the term *world-class organization?*

    A. A high technology, trendy organization.
    B. A company that has its operations spread around the globe.
    C. An organization that sets the standard for others to follow.
    D. A company that generally makes the news.

12. Paraphrasing and reflection are two key responding skills that help you to…

    A. Keep the conversation going.
    B. Verify and clarify.
    C. Identify where a project went off track.
    D. Maintain a calm attitude in a difficult situation.

13. When everything is considered, two of the most ubiquitous reasons for resisting change are…

    A. Impatience and personal disorganization.
    B. Not trusting the organization and not respecting the boss.
    C. Not understanding the change, nor buying into it.
    D. Fear of the unknown and fear of failure.

14. Why is it important to show *authentic concern* for people?

    A. We live in a "feel good" age where managers are being taught en masse to *make nice to people.*
    B. Human Resource managers have made this an important appraisal characteristic that receives consistent scrutiny.
    C. First off, authentic means it's real. People aren't being manipulated. Secondly, concern means you care. When you show that, people care about what they do.
    D. People expect it and it meets that tepid expectation.

15. The two most prevalent reasons keeping technical managers from delegating are…

A. Job pressures and an unwillingness to invest more time guiding or counseling their people.
B. Novice staff and limited administrative controls.
C. Their lack of trust and fear of losing control.
D. The scarcity of time and their own impatience.

16. Many managers would have no difficulty explaining what management is, but hedge when it comes to elaborating on leadership. Why is this so?

    A. For the last 100 years, the emphasis has been on management, and not on leadership.
    B. Management and leadership are essentially the same, so the small differences that do exist are tricky—at best—to explain.
    C. Leadership needs to exist at the top of an organization and management at all other levels. Leadership is for the leaders to explain.
    D. The concept of leadership is so cryptic it defies explanation.

17. Gen Xers tend to be jaded and leery about trusting organizations with their financial security or career. Why?

    A. Most of them had stay-at-home moms who encouraged them to avoid big organizations.
    B. They distrust anyone over thirty years of age.
    C. They watched lots of TV portraying organizations as big and impersonal.
    D. They witnessed the hypocrisy of mass layoffs, lukewarm teamwork, and poor quality of life for their parents.

18. The four specific phases of team development are…

    A. Individual contributor, spectators or crowd, group work, and team work.

B. Getting acquainted, discussing goals, confirming guidelines, and fitting into a group.
C. Creating a vision, defining your mission, action planning, and implementing the plan.
D. Forming, Storming, Norming, and Performing.

19. One of the rising trends in the country is for technical professionals to seek union representation. What do you believe is the underlying pivotal reason for this?

    A. Strong arm tactics by coercive union representatives.
    B. Lucrative union health plans and other fancy benefits.
    C. The underlying lack of trust in top management.
    D. Unions see white collar professionals as a new source of revenue to supplant their thinning ranks.

20. Managers who don't provide enough direction for their direct reports may later discover that...

    A. Employees are happier with the lack of structure.
    B. Collectively, their direct reports have risen to the occasion in spite of them.
    C. Most people don't care one way or the other.
    D. Their people become frustrated and anxious about their job performance.

21. Why is integrity so critical to building trust within an organization?

    A. It's not. Integrity is a situational "thing."
    B. Without integrity, there is no possibility of trust. Without trust, there can be no worthy, long-lasting relationships.
    C. Integrity, by its very nature, plays a secondary role related to trust.
    D. Virtue is back in style, so it's politically correct to say integrity is critical.

22. Technical professional thrive <u>mostly</u> on…

    A. Impulsive opportunities to do things differently.
    B. Intuitive synthesis of apparently unrelated items.
    C. Opportunities to do stand-up presentations in front of a group.
    D. Challenge and achievement.

23. Why do even good changes cause people some level of personal stress?

    A. Only <u>major</u> good changes cause personal stress.
    B. It means doing things differently and that takes extra energy.
    C. It's just another responsibility to add to the list of "To Do's."
    D. Good changes almost always have strict, short deadlines.

24. The most important criteria in helping a manager snap back from possible derailment is…

    A. Their strong personal desire for change.
    B. A confidential, forthright talk with their immediate supervisor.
    C. A carefully considered promotion.
    D. A transfer to another part of the organization.

25. An individual's level of motivation appears to have a lot to do with how they perceive their probability of success. When do you suppose their motivation to achieve is at the highest level?

    A. When they seek the "low hanging fruit."
    B. When they see their chances at about ten percent.
    C. When they are entrepreneurial and have the freedom to perform as they see fit.
    D. People are optimally motivated to achieve when they consider their chances at approximately 50/50.

26. Many technical managers feel *like a fish out of water* when it comes to being visionary. Why do they feel this way?

   A. They missed, or dropped out of a visioning course in their undergraduate work.
   B. It's not in their current job description.
   C. They believe visioning is analogous with being a psychic like Nostradamus.
   D. They compare themselves with great visionaries in the media and apparently come up short.

27. What's the difference between a management layer and a management level?

   A. There are only three layers of management and there can be multiple levels.
   B. A management layer is specifically associated with managers who are assigned in an "acting role."
   C. The three levels of management pertain to officers, middle, and lower management. Multiple layers can exist within each level.
   D. Layers relate to pay grades and levels to stock options.

28. The greatest weaknesses of technical professionals often lie within which skill set?

   A. Their Conceptual or Strategic Skills because they tend to be focused on the here-and-now.
   B. Their penmanship frequently is hard to decipher because their thoughts race faster than their hands can move.
   C. Their Interpersonal Skills because it's typically not their strength, nor have they had much training in it either.
   D. Their inclination to disregard current fashion or the importance of proper business attire.

29. What types of internal organizational initiatives almost always require a high commitment to teamwork?

    A. TQM, Business Process Re-Engineering, ISO 9000, etc.
    B. Reduction in force, or consolidating operations.
    C. Improved Human Resources processes such as new performance appraisals, various interviewing formats, etc.
    D. Implementing new executive compensation programs or defined pay grades.

30. What is a Vision Statement?

    A. It's an ethics code of practice for ophthalmologists.
    B. It's a mission statement written in the future tense.
    C. It's a compelling, powerfully worded, hoped-for state for an organization. A destination to be achieved in unison sometime in the future.
    D. A carefully worded document that nobody pays attention to.

31. Why is it important for companies to give their employees something to believe in and care about?

    A. People are isolated today and need a laudable cause.
    B. Because it makes people feel they are doing something significant and that makes them feel important.
    C. People believe most organizations are self serving and this won't work.
    D. Because the pressures of work are more intense and stressful than ever.

32. An employee's initiative must be at the highest level when he or she acts and routinely reports. Why is this so?

    A. Their visibility in the organization mandates nothing less.

B. They have control over both the timing and the content of what they do.
C. Very likely they're a high potential employee.
D. It is established by a Memorandum of Understanding (MOU).

33. An example of aligning a Vision Statement in an organization would be...

    A. Straightening the framed Vision Statement on the lobby wall.
    B. Having the top management team share their sentiment for it.
    C. Supporting the Vision Statement through relevant training, coaching, and performance evaluation.
    D. Making sure all margins are even on the final printed copy of the vision statement.

34. Technical professionals customarily identify more with their field than with their organization. Why is this so?

    A. They have made an immense investment of time, money, and effort in learning their field.
    B. They may be new to the organization and haven't quite adapted.
    C. The propensity of companies to continuously cut staff.
    D. Their company may have them working on mundane, boring projects.

35. Nonverbal communication represents a major part of our overall communications. What might be a typical example of non-verbal communications?

    A. Gestures, or tone of voice, or facial expression.
    B. *Reading between the lines* with respect to what someone says.
    C. Gut-level reactions to a given situation.
    D. Past, present, or future tense of the message.

36. How was the standard gauge of most railroad tracks settled on?

   A. It was established when the transcontinental railroad was built across the United States in the 19th Century.
   B. It was a compromise worked out by the League of Nations after World War I.
   C. It's based on 1/10 the distance of the standard length of a railroad boxcar.
   D. It's probably based on the axle length of ancient Roman Chariots.

Now check your responses on page 317 and come up with a percentage of correct answers. Compare your post-test results with your pre-test results. How did you do?

LESSONS 1 - 12 POST-TEST ANSWERS AND ORIGINAL REFERENCE

Question	Correct Answer	See Original Explanation[3]	Page Number(s)
#1	A	#9	271
#2	B	#21	274-275
#3	A	#1	269
#4	D	#29	277
#5	A	#5	270
#6	B	#2	269
#7	C	#17	273
#8	B	#35	278
#9	C	#25	276
#10	B	#16	273
#11	C	#4	270
#12	B	#27	276
#13	D	#33	278
#14	C	#12	272
#15	C	#28	276
#16	A	#7	271
#17	D	#3	269
#18	D	#36	279
#19	C	#10	271-272
#20	D	#8	271
#21	B	#11	272
#22	D	#24	275-276

---

[3] See these original explanations for the question numbers on the page listed to the right.

#23	B	#31	277
#24	A	#19	274
#25	D	#18	274
#26	D	#13	272-273
#27	C	#20	274
#28	C	#22	275
#29	A	#34	278
#30	C	#14	273
#31	B	#6	270
#32	B	#30	277
#33	C	#15	273
#34	A	#23	275
#35	A	#26	276
#36	D	#32	277-278

LINKS

LESSON 1 LINKS

https://www.amazon.com/generation-x/s?page=1&rh=i%3A
aps%2Ck%3Ageneration%20x
Amazon.com
1-16 of over 20,000 results for "Generation X" Click Try in your search results to watch thousands of movies and TV shows at no additional cost with an Amazon Prime membership. Zero Hour for Gen X: How the Last Adult Generation Can Save America from Millennials.

https://en.wikipedia.org/wiki/Generation_X
Wikipedia
Generation X or Gen X is the demographic cohort following the baby boomers and preceding the Millennials. There are no precise dates for when Generation X starts or ends. Demographers and researchers typically use birth years ranging from the early-to-mid 1960s to the early...

http://www.jenx67.com/who-is-generation-x
Personal Blog
Generation X was born during the greatest anti-child phase in modern American history. Our childhoods were underscored by the following: Legalized Abortion (Roe vs. Wade)...

https://www.thebalancecareers.com/common-characteristics-of-generation-x-professionals-2164682
The Balance Careers
Generation X, called the "middle child" of generations, includes Americans born between 1965 and 1980. This generation is expected to contribute to the workforce in numbers totaling 65.8 million by 2018.

https://www.cnbc.com/2018/04/11/generation-x--not-millennials--is-changing-the-nature-of-work.html
CNBC
That finding is backed up by research by Nielsen, which revealed that Gen X is the most connected generation. Nielsen found that Gen Xers use social media 40 minutes more each week than millennials.

http://www.pewresearch.org/fact-tank/2014/06/05/generation-x-americas-neglected-middle-child/
Pew Research
Generation X has a gripe with pulse takers, zeitgeist keepers and population counters. We keep squeezing them out of the frame. This overlooked generation currently ranges in age from 34 to 49, which may be one reason they're so often missing from stories about demographic, social and political...

LESSON 2 LINKS

https://www.fastcompany.com/
Fast Company
Fast Company is the consummate Gen Xer magazine. They chronicle leading edge companies which are setting the standards for the new millennium.

https://www.wsj.com/
The Wall Street Journal
The Wall Street Journal on-line offers a review of the top business stories of the day. Very helpful for keeping up with what the largest

companies are doing and their impact in their specific industries. This site, however, does have a $59 annual charge for in-depth content. But you can still access free areas.

http://www.msnbc.com/news/default.asp?cp1=1
MSNBC
A large site that brings together key news sources from NBC and MSNBC, stories from Newsweek and other publications like The Wall Street Journal. A lot of background information fills out the gaps in coverage that might be available elsewhere. Includes an interesting business site that's worth your while.

http://www.newstrawler.com/nt/nt_home.html
NewsTrawler
NewsTrawler is a search engine that draws from hundreds of news sources from around the world. You're able to search the archives of numerous journals on a variety of topics, including business.

LESSON 3 LINKS

http://www.ccl.org/index.shtml
The Center For Creative Leadership
The Center For Creative Leadership is one of the premier leadership development organizations worldwide, as rated by Business Week. They offer a number of public and in-house programs in leadership effectiveness. Furthermore, they do extensive, on-going research and publishing on the topic of leadership and other related issues.

http://www.hbs.edu/
Harvard Business School
Harvard Business School's web site. Harvard is number two in leadership development worldwide. Their programs encompass a broad range of needs from MBA and Doctoral Programs, to Executive Education, research, and publishing.

http://www.amanet.org/index.htm
American Management Association
The web site for the American Management Association (AMA). AMA offers hundreds of courses and seminars in management. Their programs are offered in major cities across the country and on-line. They also publish numerous books on relevant, contemporary management topics.

LESSON 4 LINKS

http://www.advancedeq.com/index.html
Center For Advanced Emotional Intelligence
The Center for Advanced Emotional Intelligence is the first firm in the world dedicated to converting the science of emotional intelligence (EI) into pragmatic, results-oriented programs for leadership development. EI provides a comprehensive and structured framework for affecting changes in rapidly changing, complex technological environments.

http://www.greenleaf.org/index.php
Greenleaf Center For Servant Leadership
The Greenleaf Center was founded in 1964 to help people understand the principles and practices of servant leadership; to nurture colleagues and institutions by providing a focal point and opportunities to share thoughts and ideas on servant leadership; to produce and publish new resources; and to connect servant-leaders in a network of learning.

Their catalogue has valuable books, videos, audio tapes, and conferences listings on contemporrary servant-leadership issues.

http://www.leadership-trust.org/index.html
The Leadership Trust
A non-profit association established to build and organize leaders and promote leadership as a profession. Through the trust, leadership as a profession receives attention, training, support, guidance, and social oversight through a professional body of leaders dedicated to the quality and ethics of leadership and its practice.

LESSON 5 LINKS

http://www.plausiblefutures.com/
Plausible Futures Newsletter
Interesting on-line newsletter that also has links to numerous other sites that specialize in various fields, such as technology, aviation, politics, economics, etc.

http://www.techreview.com/index.asp
MIT Enterprise Technology Review
Broad-based reviews on emerging technologies and their impact on society and the world. Extremely comprehensive and informative.

https://www.newscientist.com/
New Scientist.com
This web site bills itself as the world's number one science and technology news service. Includes archives of a multitude of scientific articles of interest, opinions, links, jobs and career opportunities, etc.

LESSON 6 LINKS

http://www.toastmasters.org/
Toastmasters International
A worldwide, non-profit organization dedicated to helping professionals improve their communication skills, particularly their public speaking. Toastmasters helps members lose their fear of public speaking, become better listeners, conduct effective meetings, and generally learn techniques that vastly improves their speaking skills.

http://www.nctp.com/
National Center For Technology Planning
The National Center for Technology Planning (NCTP) is a clearinghouse for the exchange of many types of information related to technology planning. This information may be: school technology plans available for downloading via a computer network; technology

planning aids (checklists, brochures, sample planning forms, etc.); and/or electronic monographs on timely, selected topics. The NCTP was created for those who: need help, seek fresh ideas, or seek solutions to problems encountered with planning.

Although this site is geared primarily for educators, there are many good ideas here, useful techniques, and numerous resources.

https://www.udemy.com/goal-setting/
Udemy
This course will teach you how to achieve more in less time. By learning how to use SMART Goals you will gain a concise, structured method to help keep you motivated and on track.

LESSON 7 LINKS

https://www.effective-mind-control.com/
Effective Mind Control
An interesting on-line site which discusses different aspects of self-improvement, from goal-setting, self-awareness, hidden emotions, happiness, to a large variety of topics related to the mind and mind control.

http://www.mensa.org/
Mensa International
Mensa "provides a forum for intellectual exchange among members. Its activities include the exchange of ideas by lectures, discussions, journals, special-interest groups, and local, regional, national, and international gatherings; the investigations of members' opinions and attitudes; and assistance to researchers, inside and outside Mensa, in projects dealing with intelligence or Mensa."

http://www.transformation.org/
Institute for Transformation
Located in Kirkland, Washington, the Institute for Transformation represents a unique concept in inner growth and behavioral change.

They are an education and research center delivering multimedia products and services via Internet, print, radio, audio and classroom experience. They are dedicated to helping people maximize their highest potential—personally, professionally, individually and in groups. Their fundamental purpose is to help people access and utilize their highest potential, by observing the ways in which certain behavioral traits determine personal success.

LESSON 8 LINKS

https://www.skillsyouneed.com/interpersonal-skills.html
Skills You Need
A website which offers multiple sources of information on timely topics regarding interpersonal skills, presentation skills, writing skills, etc., and also offers downloads of ebooks on a variety of related subjects.

https://www.theladders.com/
Ladders
Ladders has gained a dedicated following by becoming a formidable clearing house of $100K jobs, offering resumé templates, job hunting services, and all sorts of interesting articles on business, personality, interviewing, and career building advice.

https://www.dice.com/
Dice
Dice is top dog for STEM jobs, with a focus on technology, security clearance, financial services, energy, and healthcare. While the site lets you search for openings like Indeed and Glassdoor, their career-building toolkit is quite impressive.

Dice's "career explorer" helps tech and engineering professionals find their footing, with insights into their market value, projected salaries, and possible career paths. In addition, the site offers hundreds of blog posts, studies, and forums focused on helping you get hired in these fast-growing fields.

LESSON 9 LINKS

http://www.amanet.org/selfstudy/00994.htm
American Management Association Self-Study Course
Self-study courses in management, leadership, Human Resources, communication, etc., are readily available on this site. These programs for managers equip you with the necessary hands-on tools you'll need to inspire employee cooperation, conduct meetings, facilitate interviews...sell products and services...enlist the support of top management...or implement business plans.

http://www.asme.org/education/index.html
American Society of Mechanical Engineers
ASME provides programs to support pre-college education, formal engineering education, and the career and professional development of engineers and other professionals. The ASME Continuing Education Institute provides training opportunities for practicing engineers and other technical professionals.

Short Courses — Live public programs
In-Company Programs — Live corporate programs
Global Training — Courses in your country, in your language
Technology Seminars — Bioprocess, MEMS, Nanotechnology, and Biotechnology
Distance Learning — Online learning, videos, and CD-ROMs

http://epdweb.engr.wisc.edu/courses_at_your_site/courses/pem2.html
University of Wisconsin, Madison
Leadership and Management
Introduction: Rapid changes in technology along with employee retirements and external economic pressures are driving a need for more technical leaders. But you'll have to be more than just tech-savvy

to succeed in these roles—you'll also have to be people-savvy. Get ready to tackle a leading role in your organization or improve the way you're approaching your current management role with a course from UW-Madison. Learn how to manage projects and technical teams, adopt new standards of asset management, communicate with your key stakeholders, and establish yourself as a thought leader in your organization. Choose from short courses, the Technical Leadership Certificate, or our online degree programs to strengthen your skills.

LESSON 10 LINKS

http://www.ecs.csus.edu/
Sacramento State University
Introduction: We strive to be a valued community of scholars in which students are engaged in diverse learning experiences with faculty who are devoted to student success and technical achievement. Through contemporary curricula, engaging pedagogy, scholarship and applied research, we produce career-ready graduates prepared for a lifetime of professional achievement and intellectual growth. We value student success, academic excellence, scholarship, innovation, a balance of theory and practice, diversity, opportunity, community engagement, integrity, and accountability.

https://www.engineeringforchange.org/news/10-best-sites-for-free-online-education/
Engineering For Change
The cost of a university education is becoming staggering—it has more than doubled in the last two decades in the United States. But, fortunately, so is the number of high-quality courses available for free online. Ivy league and other respected institutions are offering full programs for certification and hundreds of courses in dozens of fields.

Those courses include specializations in engineering, programming, math, physics and other sciences. There are also courses in design, business management and marketing that could interest entrepreneurs and jumpstart a small business endeavor.

The new online education boom means that anyone in the world with an internet connection can give themselves world-class training without leaving the comfort of your home.

LESSON 11 LINKS

http://www.emeraldinsight.com/jocm.htm
Journal of Organizational Change Management
"The Journal of Organizational Change Management seeks to help build more promising futures for the societies and organizations of tomorrow by analyzing new approaches and research theories."

About this journal:
The world today is changing faster than ever before. Technological developments, financial constraints, expanding markets, restructuring and mergers, new philosophies and government legislation are all putting pressure on organizations to change and stay dynamic. Yet the process of change is far from easy, and implementing it successfully makes considerable demands on the managers involved. This journal is unique in its ability to set the management and organizational change and development agenda, by analyzing new approaches and research theories.

http://www.bpubs.com/info/about.htm
Business Publications Search Index
Mission Statement: BPubs.com is a directory based Internet search engine that strives to cover the topic of Business Publications. By eliminating the noise of "homepages, index pages, and other extraneous web site components", our users are able to extract what they truly searching for—content. Our target audience of corporate and business users will become repeat visitors because we save them time finding the information they need.

https://learn.org/articles/Organizational_Transformation_and_Leadership_Masters_Degree_Program_FAQs.html
Learn.com
Excellent resource for searching through a vast array of degreed and certificated programs at a multitude of colleges and universities nationwide. The particular page noted centers on Courses in a master's degree program in organizational transformation and leadership (or a similarly titled program) focus on the latest research and best practices for planning and managing organizational changes. Topics cover a number of issues, such as communication, group dynamics, productivity improvement and diversity in the workplace.

LESSON 12 LINKS

http://www.pcfl.com/
Pacific Center For Leadership: Team Building
At today's pace of change, effective leaders and teams are essential to propel an organization into an exciting future of exceptional results. Corporations need leaders who are creative, and who lead change, take risks, coach, and inspire those around them. Exceptional results depend on outstanding team performance: clear communication, commitment, creative solutions, and personal accountability.

Since 1987, the Pacific Center for Leadership has enhanced organizational performance through team and leadership development. They have successfully coached, trained, and assisted executives, managers, and corporate teams throughout North America and in Europe to achieve outstanding business and personal results.

http://www.ventureteambuilding.co.uk/team-building-activities/
Venture Team Building
The site contains more than sixty fun and free **team building activities** that can improve teamwork, develop trust, and enhance problem solving skills. The best part is, the majority of these team

challenges can be delivered anywhere, by anyone and with limited or no equipment.

All you have to do is click on the link of one of the team building activities and you will be taken to an information page containing: challenge description, equipment requirements, and suggested learning outcomes.

If you need some help on how to teach a team building session then make sure you check out their workshop delivery section featuring helpful articles and video tutorials.

https://www.rivertrail.com/package/teambuilding-it-team-advent/
River and Trail Outfitters
Introduction: Team building programs are tailored to meet both the needs and goals of individual groups. A typical land-based team building program consists of a progression of activities that aim to bring groups to greater cohesion. The time spent on each level of the progression varies by the amount of time available and how well the group already knows one another. All such programs begin with Icebreakers, to get the group warmed up. Games follow, giving the group the opportunity to engage in more energetic activities or in closer proximity to one another. Challenges and Initiatives are the time when groups really have a chance to push their limits, and engage in activities that allow them to reach their goals such as teamwork, improved communication and demonstration of leadership.

GENERATION X READING RECOMMENDATIONS

Beaudoin Tom and Harvey Cox. Virtual Faith: The Irreverent Spiritual Quest of Generation X. Jossey-Bass Publishers, San Francisco, CA. 1998.

Brokaw, Tom. The Greatest Generation. Vintage Digital, London. 2010.

Brokaw, Tom. The Greatest Generation Speaks: Letters and Reflections. Random House Trade Paperbacks, NY. 2005.

Celek, Tim Dieter Zander. Inside The Soul of a New Generation. Zondervan Publishing House, Grand Rapids, MI. 1996.

Coupland, Douglas. Generation X: Tales For An Accelerated Culture. St Martin's Press, New York, NY. 1991.

Lobdell, Scott. X-Men: The Origin of Generation X. Phalanx Covenant, 2001.

Long, Jimmy. Generating Hope: A Strategy For Reaching The Postmodern Generation. InterVarsity Press, Downers Grove, IL. 1997.

Raines, Claire. Beyond Generation X: A Practical Guide For Managers. Crisp Publication. 1997.

Thau, Richard D. (Introduction), Jay S. Heflin (Introduction). Generations Apart: Xers Vs. Boomers Vs. The Elderly (Contemporary Issues). Prometheus Books, Amherst, NY. 1997.

Tulgan, Bruce. Managing Generation X: How To Bring Out The Best in Young Talent. W.W. Norton & Company, New York, NY. 2000.

Tulgan, Bruce. The Manager's Pocket Guide To Generation X. HRD Press, Amherst, MA. 1997.

CLASSIC LEADERSHIP READING RECOMMENDATIONS

Blanchard, Kenneth and Spencer Johnson. The One Minute Manager. William Morrow and Company, Inc., NY. 1981

Block, Peter. The Empowered Manager. Jossey-Bass Inc., Pub., San Francisco, CA. 1987.

Bossidy, Lawrence and Ram Charan (with Charles Burck). Execution. Crown Business, New York City, NY. 2002.

Collins, Jim. Good To Great: Why Some Companies Make The Leap...and Others Don't. HarperCollins Publishers, New York City, NY. 2001.

Covey, Stephen. The Seven Habits of Highly Effective People. Simon & Schuster, NY. 1989.

Davis, Brian L., Carol J. Skube et al. The Successful Manager's Handbook. Personnel Decisions, Inc., Minneapolis, MN. 1992.

Deming, W. Edwards. Out of The Crisis. MIT, Cambridge, MA. 1982.

Depree, Max. Leadership Is An Art. Bantam Doubleday Dell Publishing Group, NY. 1989.

Drucker, Peter. The Effective Executive. Harper & Row, Publishers, Inc., NY. 1967.

Ferguson, Henry. Tomorrow's Global Executive. Dow-Jones-Irwin, Homewood, IL. 1988.

Fritz, Roger. Think Like a Manager. (3rd Edition). National Press Publications, Shawnee Mission, KS. 2001.

Gladwell, Malcolm. The Tipping Point. Little Brown & Company, New York City, NY. 2002.

Gladwell, Malcolm. Blink. Little Brown & Company, New York City, NY. 2005.

Gladwell, Malcolm. Outliers. Little Brown & Company, New York City, NY. 2008.

Hersey, Paul, Kenneth H. Blanchard. Management of Organizational Behavior. Prentice-Hall, Inc., Englewood Cliffs, NJ. 1977.

Hersey, Paul. The Situational Leader. Warner Books, Inc., NY. 1984.

Kissler, Gary D. The Change Riders. Addison-Wesley Publishing Company, Reading, MA. 1991.

Likert, Rensis. The Human Organization. McGraw-Hill Publishing Company, NY. 1967.

McCall, Morgan W. High Flyers. Harvard Business School Press, Boston, MA., 1998.

Patterson, Kerry et al. Crucial Conversations. McGraw-Hill, New York City, NY. 2002.

Peters, Tom. <u>Thriving on Chaos</u>. Harper & Row, Publishers, NY. 1987.

Schein, Edgar H. <u>Organizational Culture and Leadership</u>. Jossey-Bass Inc., Publishers. San Francisco, CA. 1985.

Senge, Peter M. <u>The Fifth Discipline</u>. Bantam Doubleday Dell Publishing Group, NY. 1990.

INDEX

A

Active Listening, Lesson 9, Chapter 2
Apple Computer, Lesson 2, Chapter 3
Andreeson, Marc, Lesson 5, Chapter 1
Antoinette, Marie, Lesson 7, Chapter 2
AOL, Lesson 5, Chapter 1
AON Consulting, Lesson 9, Chapter 1
Armstrong, Neil, Lesson 5, Chapter 2
Arthur Anderson, Lesson 4, Chapter 3
AT&T Long Lines Division, Lesson 9, Chapter 1
AT&T, Lesson 3, Chapter 2
Avon, Lesson 11, Chapter 2

B

Barksdale, Jim, Lesson 5, Chapter 1
Bateson, Gregory and Robert Dilts, Lesson 5, Chapter 4
Behaviors, classic negative, Lesson 4, Chapter 2
Bennis, Warren, Lesson 4, Chapter 1, 2, 5, Lesson 5, Chapter 1, Lesson 6, Chapter 1, Lesson 7, Chapters 1, 3, 5
Bono, Lesson 6, Chapter 1
Buhler, Patricia M., Lesson 8, Chapter 4
Bush, George W., Lesson 3, Chapter 3

C

Carter, Jimmy, Lesson 3, Chapter 4, Lesson 10, Chapter 1
Chambers, John, Lesson 12, Chapter 1
Change Model, Lesson 11, Chapter 3
Cisco Systems, Lesson 12, Chapter 1
Churchill, Winston, Lesson 3, Chapter 3
Collins, Jim, Lesson 5, Chapter 3, Lesson 8, Chapter 3
Communication, Six Keys of, Lesson 2, Chapter 4
CNN, Lesson 1, Chapter 2
Constraints, Lesson 6, Chapter 4

D

Derailing Factors, Lesson 7, Chapter 2
Disneyland, Lesson 12, Chapter 1
Disneyland Operations, Lesson 5, Chapter 3
Disney, Walt, Lesson 2, Chapter 3, Lesson 5, Chapter 2
Donne, John, Lesson 12, Chapters 1, 2
Dual career paths, Lesson 1, Chapter 4

E

Einstein, Albert, Lesson 8, Chapter 3

Electric Boat Company, Lesson 9, Chapter 1
Enron, Lesson 2, Chapter 2, Lesson 3, Chapter 3, Lesson 4, Chapter 2

F

Five Functions of Management, Lesson 3, Chapter 2
Firestone, Lesson 4, Chapter 3
Five M's, Lesson 3, Chapter 2
Ford, Henry, Lesson 5, Chapter 2
Fortune Magazine, Lesson 2, Chapter 4

G

Gates, Bill, Lesson 5, Chapter 2
German Blitzkrieg, Lesson 3, Chapter 3
"Goals on Steroids," Lesson 6, Chapter 3
Goddard, John, Lesson 6, Chapter 2
Golden Rule of Delegation, Lesson 10, Chapter 3
Giuliani, Rudy, Lesson 4, Chapter 4, Lesson 9, Chapter 1
Grove, Andy, Lesson 4, Chapter 4

H

Hewlett-Packard, Lesson 4, Chapter 4, Lesson 8, Chapter 1
Hidden Agendas, Lesson 12, Chapter 4
Hoover, Herbert, Lesson 3, Chapter 4
Horari, Oren, Lesson 8, Chapter 2
Hughes, Howard, Lesson 5, Chapter 2

I

IBM, Lesson 11, Chapters 1, 2
Ibuka, Masaru, Lesson 5, Chapter 4
I-Messages, Lesson 9, Chapter 3
Institutionalization, Lesson 11, Chapter 3

J

Jobs, Steve, Lesson 2, Chapter 3

Jung, Andrea, Lesson 11, Chapter 2

K

Kennedy, Marilyn Moats, Lesson 8, Chapter 1
Kennedy, President John, Lesson 5, Chapter 2
Kimberly-Clark, Lesson 5, Chapter 3
K-Mart, Lesson 4, Chapter 3
Kinlaw, Dennis, Lesson 8, Chapter 4

L

Latchkey kids, Lesson 1, Chapter 2
Leadership Bank Account, Lesson 3, Chapter 4
Lee, General Robert E., Lesson 3, Chapter 1
Lexus, Lesson 7, Chapter 3
Level Five Leadership, Lesson 5, Chapter 3
Level of Effort, Lesson 6, Chapter 3
Likert, Rensis, Lesson 7, Chapter 4
Linking Pin Concept, Lesson 7, Chapter 4

M

Machiavelli, Lesson 11, Chapter 1
Maslow, Abraham, Lesson 12, Chapter 2
Maximum Allowable Performance, Lesson 6, Chapter 4
MBNA, Lesson 2, Chapters 1, 4
McGuire, Jerry, Lesson 1, Chapter 3
Minimum Standard of Performance (MSP), Lesson 6, Chapter 4
MTV, Lesson 1, Chapter 2

N

NASA, Lesson 5, Chapter 2
Netscape, Lesson 5, Chapter 1
Negotiable Tasks, Lesson 7, Chapter 4

O

Obstacles to Team Development, Lesson 12, Chapter 4
Organizational Culture, Lesson 3, Chapter 3
Outward Bound (See Ropes)

P

Paraphrasing and Reflection, Lesson 9, Chapter 2
Parsons, Dana, Lesson 5, Chapter 3
Perfectionists, Lesson 8, Chapter 3
Peters, Tom and Bob Waterman, Lesson 9, Chapter 4
Phases of Team Development, Lesson 12, Chapter 2
Point of Implementation, Lesson 11, Chapter 3
Positive Reinforcement, Lesson 9, Chapter 4
Proctor & Gamble, Lesson 5, Chapter 3
Project Tasks, Lesson 7, Chapter 4

R

Rankin, Dr. Paul, Lesson 9, Chapter 2
Reflection (See Paraphrasing and Reflection)
Reichheld, Frederick, Lesson 9, Chapter 1
Relevancy/Value Crisis, Lesson 11, Chapter 3
Restraints, Lesson 6, Chapter 4
Roman Empire, Lesson 11, Chapter 2
Roosevelt, Eleanor, Lesson 7, Chapter 1
Ropes (or Outward Bound), Lesson 12, Chapter 3
Rosenbaum, Bernard L., Lesson 8, Chapter 2
Rosenthal, Robert, Lesson 4, Chapter 4
Rousseau, Jean Jacques, Lesson 7, Chapter 2
Routine Tasks, Lesson 7, Chapter 4
Rumsfeld, Donald, Lesson 4, Chapter 4, Lesson 9, Chapter 1

S

Sabbaticals, Lesson 1, Chapter 4
Scott Paper, Lesson 5, Chapter 3
Sears, Lesson 2, Chapter 2
Signing Bonuses, Lesson 1, Chapter 3
Skills Necessary at Various Management Levels, Lesson 7, Chapter 2
S.M.A.R.T. Goals, Lesson 6, Chapter 3
Smith, Darwin E., Lesson 5, Chapter 3
Smith, Fred, Lesson 5, Chapter 2
Smith, General Gustavus, Lesson 3, Chapter 1
Sony, Lesson 5, Chapter 4
Sun Microsystems, Lesson 5, Chapter 1

T

3M, Lesson 5, Chapter 4
Task Grid, Lesson 7, Chapter 4
Toastmasters International, Lesson 6, Chapter 4
Tolle, Eckhart, Lesson 7, Chapter 3
Troubleshooting Tasks, Lesson 7, Chapter 4
Truman, Harry, Lesson 4, Chapter 4, Lesson 9, Chapter 1
Trump, Donald, Lesson 4, Chapter 4
Tyson Foods, Lesson 4, Chapter 3

U

U.S. Malcolm Baldrige National Award, Lesson 12, Chapter 1

V

Valley of Despair, Lesson 11, Chapter 3
Valuejet, Lesson 4, Chapter 3
Vision Statements, Lesson 5, Chapters 1, 2, 3, 4, 5

W

Walker Information, Lesson 9, Chapter 1

WalMart, Lesson 2, Chapter 2
Walton, Sam, Lesson 5, Chapter 2
Wilson, Woodrow, Lesson 3, Chapter 4

Y

You-Messages (See I-Messages)

Z

Zawinski, Jamie, Lesson 5, Chapter 1

www.ingramcontent.com/pod-product-compliance
Lightning Source LLC
Chambersburg PA
CBHW021348210526
45463CB00001B/28